200
KITCHENS

200

KITCHENS

confessions of a nomad cook

GAWAIN BARKER

bushbrother

For my teachers – Terry and Victor

CONTENTS

Up there with Love and Death

Golden light was hitting the clouds over the reef; behind us sulphur-crested cockatoos squawked in the rustling palms. Dusk was not far off, and Don, my good friend and fishing-guide to this bit of paradise, passed me a well-earned cup of tea. Our icebox was full of freshly caught fish and the fire was going nicely. What more could we want? A couple of nice ladies to share this with said Don. Just then the sound of a vehicle came down the track to the beach and stopped. We smiled at this serendipity.

Then three figures came out onto the sand and my guts hollowed right out. They were not nice ladies at all. With ponytails, ripped black jeans, jail tattoos and scruffy beards, the three men exuded criminal menace as they swaggered towards us.

Don had brought me to this wonderfully remote place, turning off from hours of unsealed road onto kilometres of sandy track. It was one of those lost beaches that you find in the Tropical North of Australia

– pristine and deserted, full of great fishing and sixty kilometres from the nearest house or police station. Don groaned quietly as the trio came up.

"Hello boys – you're in our spot," said one fella who looked like a gypsy pirate. "But that's alright. We like to share."

A tingle of shock went through me as I saw the sheath knife attached to his belt. With growing dread, I wondered what else was in their vehicle. A shotgun? Rope and shovels? Feeling like two lambs meeting some kebab cooks, Don and I uneasily let the scurvy intruders join us. What else could we do?

The fattest wild colonial boy had plastic bags with the essentials of outlaw life; bottles of rum, tins of corned beef and peaches in syrup. Dropping them onto the sand he sat down on our cool box. Gypsy Pirate and his nuggety mate, who looked like a tattooed Smurf, sat down too and rolled up cigarettes. Around us a beautiful sunset was starting. Big Belly dug out a bottle of rum and after big swigs the boys turned their attention to Don and I.

"Where you sprogs sprung from?" Gypsy Pirate rasped. "I see you got rods but no fish!"

"Yeh what are you good for?" laughed Big Belly, raising his hand as if to cuff me around my head. It was the kind of thing a big brother might do jokingly, but this was no joke. If Don and I remained passive then there was no telling what these bullies might do.

I jumped up and looked into their bags of food.

"Dearie me – this stuff is rubbish." I wagged my finger at Big Belly. "C'mon – get up. Shift your arse."

He looked outraged but he stood, and I bustled in close making him step back. From the cool box I dug out the big packet of fish fillets.

"Oh – you got some fish," said Big Belly.

"Yeah of course we did," I shot back. "There's Dart, Black Bream, Trevally – even a little Barramundi. And you impatient bastards just couldn't wait to start running us down."

Gypsy Pirate's eyes narrowed to slits.

"So!" I loudly slapped my hand down on the fish. "You want a proper feed or what? I'll make you bastards dinner."

The Bad, the Bad and the Ugly stared at me in bewilderment. Big Belly grudgingly said, "Ahh maybe," but his stomach betrayed him with a loud gurgle that made Nuggety Smurf giggle like a baby psycho.

"Alright then," I said, looking them all seriously in the eye – loading the moment with real significance. I was pleased to see their confusion grow.

While Don got the box of cooking things from the car, I built up the fire and got some rocks to support a wok. The hard boys sat there drinking, silently passing around the rum and staring at me with cold eyes.

It was bad luck these meat-heads had chosen our beach. This was the early nineteen-eighties and the

North of Australia was still a wild place. Small gangs of feral hoodlums, some on the run from the police or rivals, would hole up at beach camps or by rainforest creeks. Bad stuff happened around them – car thefts, break-ins, rapes and worse. Gunfire and screams got swallowed up by the vastness of the country.

Don returned, and from my cooking box I got the things I needed. As I began cutting the fish into strips, Big Belly wrinkled his nose.

"Whatcha doing? You cook the fillets whole," he commanded.

"Nah. I'm making goujons," I said.

"Gou-johns!? What the hell is that?" the dirty three hooted in derision.

In a steel bowl I made a mix of my own hot spice-rub with flour, and began tossing the fish strips through it. As I did, I gestured to Gypsy Pirate to give me a hit of rum. He snarled like a rubbish-tip dog in defence of its bone. Wordlessly I kept beckoning for the bottle.

"Give him a drink will ya," said Big Belly. "He's making a feed for us ain't he?"

Gypsy Pirate grudgingly handed me the bottle. I wiped the top, took a big swig and passed it back.

"Cheers mate," I grunted.

I put the spiced fish on a plate, washed the bowl out with seawater, cracked eggs and whisked them in the bowl. I got Don to drizzle oil in as I beat the eggs. Nuggety Smurf's mouth was open in concentration as I whisked and whisked. When the mix was nice and thick, I seasoned it with salt and pepper and thinned it with a little lemon juice.

"What's that?" said Big Belly.

"It's mayo," I said. "No way!" said Big Belly. "You get mayo in a jar!"

I held out the whisk and he took it and tasted. "Ha! That's bloody great. It's like mayo but really good!"

"You sure are lucky bastards meeting me then," I said.

Maybe it was the great sunset or that first taste of real mayonnaise, but Big Belly cackled through broken teeth and Nuggety Smurf grinned and squirmed in the sand like a kid. Gypsy Pirate didn't do happy and became suddenly interested in a flock of Torres Strait pigeons flying far out over the metallic blue sea.

The wok got hot and I fried the fish. When the first lot was done, I began heaping plates. Big Belly, his nose and eyes wide at the food, jumped up and helped me. There was a meditative hush as the two of us handed around the food. Nuggety Smurf and Don said thank you and Gypsy Pirate made a strange soft sound in his throat, his eyes intent on his plate.

"Tuck in boys!" I said and they began eating, dipping the goujons into the mayonnaise. I cooked off all the fish while I ate and soon beards and fingers became shiny with mayo and oil. Sighs and grunts of pleasure could be heard over the champing of jaws.

Yep – five guys were sitting on a beautiful beach in the middle of nowhere eating a great dinner of fresh fish.

When the last goujon had been scarfed we all sat back, happily burping and sighing. Big Belly cracked a new bottle of rum and offered it to me. The look in his eyes was both grateful and apologetic.

"Ahh sorry mate – we were just mucking around before," he said. "You blokes are alright. But man I gotta tell you – that's one of the best feeds I've ever had!"

The sunset was killing it now and Gypsy Pirate's frown had softened heaps. Nuggety Smurf couldn't contain himself. "Maaaate! That was magic mate! Bloody magic!"

Earth Ovens and Escargot

Food is magic. It sits up there with love and death as one of life's absolutes. Even that crew of hard bastards on Don's beach could appreciate food's primeval power. Its allure cuts through the boundaries of age, race, language, culture and gender. I began to understand all this at an early age, due to my parents, and also because of where I grew up.

In the late nineteen-sixties, when I was two, my family immigrated to Fiji, a group of tropical islands in the South Pacific. At that time, Fiji was one of the last outposts of the British Empire, but the Fijians, being a tough and gregarious people, felt in no way subjugated by this colonialism. Pale young district officers might bustle around making rules, but the locals would just smile and go fishing like they'd always done.

This amicable indifference to the Englishman's ways also extended to their cuisine, and this was no surprise as there were no tempting culinary delights to ponder. The colonial canteens and hotel dining rooms mainly served over-cooked and under-flavoured British Imperial stodge.

This was a major source of irritation to my Mum and Dad as they really enjoyed eating good food. To them, dining out at a restaurant was like entertainment or art. This serious appreciation was a result of them both growing up in England during the Second World War, when food was scarce.

That unfortunate experience, and the traditional English cooking that preceded it, had been hard on their nascent palates. But they managed to escape, and through their globe-trotting careers in journalism and advertising, had gratefully inhaled a whole world of food from Europe to America; from Asia to the Pacific.

My parents would talk in the most interesting way about restaurants and certain dishes, and about certain dishes from certain restaurants. This gave me the feeling that food was exotic and mysterious; that it could take you somewhere. My Mum was a good cook, full of epicurean curiosity, and tucked away amongst her many recipe books I found a stash of restaurant menus from faraway places. I would pore over them like they were treasure maps.

Then one year a restaurant opened in the capital city Suva where we lived, and my world would never be the same. Everything about food, cooking and dining that my parents had alluded to now became real.

Scotts Restaurant was the marvellous creation of

Peter, a switched-on East Ender from London. He'd travelled all over the world and possessed that crucial restaurateur mix of good taste and street-smarts. He had arrived in Fiji and decided it was ripe for a grand restaurant. He most certainly created one.

He bought an old guesthouse, a huge run-down colonial edifice built with beautiful forest timbers, and renovated the hell out of it. Then he decorated it in the most incredible way. It was an over-the-top cornucopia of amazing things; like a Hollywood take on Victorian England, but gone troppo.

Real and fake antique furniture filled the rooms and vibrant carpets covered the polished wooden floors. Massive crystal vases bursting with fresh flowers and palms growing in ceramic pots brought lush nature indoors. Mantle pieces had lace doilies set with retro knick-knacks, objects like scrimshawed whale's teeth, old engraving tools and gleaming ocean shells. With cut glass chandeliers hovering overhead and Persian kilims underfoot I wandered Scotts in wonder. Used artillery shells of polished brass sprouted long red and green ginger blooms, and somehow lost amongst it all were two grand pianos.

For a kid growing up on the basic stimulus of library books and local radio – this was like a movie come to fabulous life.

The immense building was just made for me to explore. There was a cute little nook in a bay window where two could enjoy a romantic cocktail. Next to it a stuffed river bird paused against the wall. Behind long curtains lay a private dining room, done out in duck-egg blue, that seated sixteen. Tucked away in a big back room was a cocktail bar done up in in browns and reds; its timber counter ringed by stools and leather booths. The main bar was semi-circular, impressively big and filled with strange bottles, huge amounts of glassware and many mirrors. I could stand there and see myself seven or eight times.

The dining room had polished timber floors and seated sixty. The tables were set with crisp white linen, gleaming silver cutlery and miniature glass vases, each containing a single white gardenia or scarlet hibiscus flower. Candelabras on every table provided immediate light, and overhead the glittering spray of chandeliers slowly dimmed as the night went on. In one corner was a snow-white Steinway grand piano. I got to know this room well.

The food was classical French, with a few Italian and Russian favourites thrown in, and every dish was prepared and served in the traditional way. My parents were well pleased and began contentedly educating my brother and I in the intricacies of a-la-carte fine dining. Rarely did a week go by without a dinner at Scotts, and it was there that I first felt like an adult doing adult things.

Opening the big heavy menu was a thrill. So many

choices and so much mystery. My parents patiently interpreted and explained each dish, and I could order anything. I tried everything eventually and I liked it all. Some dishes were set on fire at the table flambé style and my brother and I sure liked ordering them.

As I happily worked my way through the menu, I learnt how to winkle escargots out of their shells. With a little practice I could eat one side of a whole fish, peel off all the bones, and then resume eating. I found out the best way to eat caviar – with little chewing, just slowly squashing the salty bubbles with my tongue. I learnt to sit up straight and tuck in a napkin. I learnt to eat soup without slurping. I learnt how to eat with gusto but with grace.

Ably guided by the expertise of my parents, I also learnt about drinking alcohol. I discovered champagne and marvelled at the infinite streams of tiny bubbles in the blonde coloured wine. I also discovered how good it made me feel. Red wine, to my surprise, had to 'breathe' and I swear that I saw the newly opened bottle minutely expanding and contracting in the candlelight.

To my ten-year-old eyes Scotts Restaurant was a place of infinite majesty, like a temple or a church. I studied hard, learnt my scripture and by the age of twelve I was a seasoned bon vivant, used to ordering and eating Zabaglione and Coquille St Jacques. I'd even take a glass of dry sherry before dinner and then sip a port afterwards.

Rudy, the Chef at Scotts, was a big friendly man, and to my great excitement he'd let me come into the kitchen, stand in a corner and watch. I was mesmerised by what I saw, smelt and heard.

The kitchen was a hot, bright and busy place and all the stainless-steel and steam made it look like the inside of an incredible machine whose moving parts were people. Everyone looked very focused, but casually moved at speed in a strange dance. Totally fascinated by the sizzle and flare and flashing knives, I instinctively knew that this was a transformative place.

Here, solids, liquids, and, indeed human beings, were undergoing metamorphosis. I understood that in this torrid humming room, oral alchemy was routine; the incredible habitual. Most intriguing was the matter-of-fact way that everybody in the kitchen just got on with making the magic. It all looked very cool to me.

Rudy was also a wonderful pianist and sometimes, still in his white chef's uniform, he would play the white Steinway in the dining room to the applause of the diners. This was truly god-like behaviour and it made my mind gently simmer with inspirational thoughts.

But even as my parents supervised my epicurean education I was being schooled in an entirely different world of food and eating - the world of tropical Fiji.

In that era, the sixties and seventies, most people had vegetable gardens and fruit trees. Chili bushes and herbs grew along fence-lines and big old mango trees shaded backyards. Bananas and paw paws flourished next to outdoor toilets and sheds, and staples like bele, daruka, cassava and taro sprouted in every patch of wet or unused ground. It was a lush place and you'd be hard pressed not getting something to eat.

My friends at school were Fijian . . . and Indian, Rotuman, British, Tongan, Papuan, Chinese, Maori, New Zealanders, Scottish and Australian.

Like most kids, when we weren't playing games or getting into trouble, we were looking for something to eat. Fruit grew everywhere and we ate whatever was in season. Walking the long way home from school, our gang would often hide our school bags in the bushes and ascend a mango or guava tree. Like a mob of cheeky birds, we'd perch in the high branches and spend the afternoon eating fruit, bullshitting and hurling the pips and skins at unsuspecting passers-by.

Or we might take a detour to a breadfruit tree loaded with ripe specimens. What few cents we had would be given to the fastest runner. He'd then sprint to the closest store for a half of block of butter, and maybe cadge some salt from a nearby relative.

While our man did this, we'd make a fire and bake the breadfruits whole; charring their leathery skins. When the condiments arrived, we'd tuck in full-speed.

During the mango season, hordes of determined kids, little barefoot locusts in torn t-shirts, would climb up mango trees or hurl sticks to dislodge the fruit. Some trees were next to homes and sticks shattered windows and kids peered down into houses. Irate homeowners would run out yelling and give chase, trying to wack us kids with brooms and sticks. We thought that was great fun.

The place where you could get a feed and not get hassled was the sea. Being a whole group of islands, Fiji is a fishing paradise and from an early age Fijians take to the ocean with fishing lines, spears, homemade spear guns, traps and even their bare hands.

I rapidly learnt how to fish and clean my catch because everybody was keen to show you. Kids, mums, dads, grannies, and it seemed, even toddlers, all had a line or spear in the water. The kilometres-long seawall in town always had people fishing off it, and on the bay, there was always the movement of boats, outriggers, and canoes – all bent on catching a good feed.

Night fishing was always special. Joining a mob of excited kids, chaperoned by their uncles or big brothers, I would scamper down a sandy track to the ocean. Everyone would spread out so as not to cross lines or catch a hook in the face. There would be yells and splashes as a lucky angler got a bite and kerosene lanterns and torches would congregate on the spot where the fish was being landed. Back at the high tide line someone would be playing a guitar and there would be warm bottles of Fiji Bitter or home brew from which I just might be allowed a swig.

There was one real delicacy that would come out at night – Coconut Crabs. Also known as robber crabs, or in scientific lingo as Birgus Latro, these crustaceans are big. Weighing up to four kilos they have black shells with hairy spines and a crayfish-like tail. They live in burrows close to the sea and eat coconuts, using a pair of big scary claws to get into the nut. If you've ever opened a coconut without a machete then you'll know that this is some feat. The crab's size means that there's a fair bit of meat in them and this flesh tastes like the coconuts they eat. It's a bit subtle, but definitely there. Naturally everybody wanted to catch and eat them.

This wasn't so easy as Coconut Crabs run very fast, scuttling down their numerous burrows in a flash. They are also nocturnal, favouring the new moon when it's pitch-black. With kerosene lanterns and torches throwing shadows every which way, it's difficult to see them. We'd run and twist and dive like rugby players after an invisible ball. Kids hooting and yelling, "There! Crab there! It's gone there! Where?! There!" Collisions were inevitable and feet got whacked with sticks.

Sometimes the big crabs would spin around and counter-attack, and everybody would scatter, trying to escape their toe-crushing claws.

When one was finally captured, there'd be a big

hoo-ha and the large crab would be tied up very carefully. Kids knew just what a prize it was; something that adults would be very appreciative of. Just the sort of thing to make up for some later transgression.

Fijians are totally fearless in the ocean, and men and women loved to swim along a reef for a few hours with a spear and a pair of swimming goggles, looking for dinner. One school holiday I joined up with some local guys spear-fishing out on the reef. I'd swum nearly a kilometre out to them and after their initial surprise and delight at finding a little *kaivalagi* kid in mask and flippers amongst them, I was invited to tag along.

As we glided over the reef, one man stopped and dived down to a large coral head. With firm kicks of my fins I followed. He began prodding in the coral with his spear and as I swam up everything happened really fast.

He whipped a good-sized octopus out from the coral with his spear and stuck his head right into it! The octopod's tentacles slithered tight around his neck and head and it was a most peculiar sight – a man with an octopus for a head. Black ink erupted and the man's feet danced on the reef as he tried to stay vertical. For long seconds they fought. Tentacles flicked out of the inky cloud; then went limp. The man wrenched the octopus off his face and darted to the surface with his prize.

Up top we gulped air. Tendrils of ink stuck to his face and chest. Tentacle-sucker marks pockmarked his neck and shoulders, some of them bleeding.

"Oh yeah – kuita! I love to eat this one!" he laughed happily. Treading water, I asked why he'd stuck his face right into the beast, something I would have crapped myself doing.

"That's how you kill them," he explained. "The brains are up in the middle. You just bite and bite until you get it."

On another occasion, swimming along an outer island reef with a group of fishermen – dinner bit back. We'd come in an open, outboard-engine boat to the reef and anchored. The only sight of land was a hazy smudge on the horizon. I joined a fisherman as he investigated a dinner-plate sized hole in the coral. Something was lurking in there and we both surfaced for air.

"Eel," he said. "Big eel in there." We submerged again and he moved his spear slowly towards the hole. As he flexed his fingers and got his grip right, the great head of a moray eel flashed out and then back into the hole. It was unbelievably quick but I saw very pointy teeth snap down onto the man's hand and he instantly wrenched it away. There was a sudden flurry of blood, a dull underwater shout of shock and we both quickly surfaced. Blood squirted from the fisherman's hand and he spread his fingers to see the damage. The monster eel had totally removed one of his fingers! The man shouted again, cursing the eel, and then laughed madly.

Heads bobbed up around us, alerted by his yells, and there were loud cries of disbelief and sympathy.

Everyone swam to the boat and the guys clambered in and had a look. With much mirth the grinning injured guy got cuffed around the head for being so stupid. Not wanting to bleed all over the boat he held his hand over the side. Blood splashed into the sea. Finally, someone tore up a t-shirt and bandaged up the wound.

I didn't want to get in the way, and remained in the water, hanging off the boat's side and just watching the proceedings. Then an old dude noticed me.

"Hey *lialia*!" he shouted at me. "Get in! Get in the boat!"

Everyone spun around and I was grabbed bodily by arms, hair, whatever and yanked into the boat. I sat up, pissed off at this manhandling and the old guy gestured at the sea around the boat. The big dorsal fins of a couple of sharks were cruising in, attracted by the blood. The expression on my face made the whole boat-full of men yell with laughter.

An easier way to get fish, and nearly everything else, was at the sprawling old markets near the Suva waterfront. On one side was the main wharf so there were lots of seafood, and on the other side was the main bus depot so there was lots of fruit and veg. The whole place had the smell and din that tropical markets have. I loved hanging out there.

Hundreds of stalls sold a huge array of produce. Bananas – long Cavendish, sweet little ladyfingers and plump plantains for cooking – and all kinds of greens from lettuce to spinach to bok choy. Lentils, rice and multi-coloured bags of freshly ground spices filled wicker baskets. There were bunches of sugar cane, giant bush lemons and glistening limes. Fat spiky strings of green and red chilies hung like jewellery and freaky-eyed goats butted the sides of their bamboo cages.

On big pandanus mats there were pile after pile of mandarins and five-corner fruit, luscious soursops and spiky jackfruit. In rows of steel and plastic buckets of water live shellfish blew bubbles. Flocks of chickens hog-tied with strips of vine clucked in protest, and everywhere for sale were recycled liquor bottles filled with coconut oil. They gleamed like melted bronze and were often tightly stoppered with compressed leaf-fibre plugs. There were also well-frequented stalls that sold weighed-out brown-paper bags of different sizes, each full of *yaqona* powder, or kava – the traditional and legal narcotic that Fijians drank.

Near the ice works, whole Skipjack and Albacore tuna, gleaming like metallic blue torpedoes, rested on blocks of ice. There were twenty kinds of fish and five kinds of prawn, and stacks of live mud crabs; claws and legs lashed with strips of bark. In ice tubs lay schools of tiger-striped Mackerels and dark silver Walu, their eyes gone dull in the market glare.

The sidewalks here had slick patches of melting ice, fish scales and slime. It was easy to slip over and I would tread slowly in the crush of shoppers.

Throughout the market everyone yelled happily, touting their goods. Most stallholders had a personal stake in the produce – they'd grown it or caught it, or it came from their village and they were sure proud of it. People knowledgably discussed the merits of fruit from this area compared with that area. They knew where the best prawns were coming from and who was growing and grinding the top-shelf *yaqona*. Fijians possess a real enthusiasm for food, knowing that it is one of the most central and enjoyable things in life.

Next to the market were many brightly painted, wheeled stalls that sold things that every kid wanted. Needed! You could buy fireworks, slingshots, spinning-tops and marbles – ceramic ones were called Scotties. There were Phantom skull-rings, 007 belt-buckles and jawbreaker chewing gum. Fans of martial arts could purchase nun chukkas, shuriken throwing stars and posters of Bruce Lee. There were sunglasses just like the ones that Bruce wore, and packs of cards, playing dice and carrom boards. I haunted those stalls.

There were many items for grown-ups too. The fashion-conscious could browse through palm-frond hats, silk saris and brightly patterned cotton *sulus* and *mumus*. For cosmetic and grooming needs there were sheets of stick-on bindis, jars of kohl, packets of henna, big wooden combs for frizzy hair and small plastic ones for straight hair. There were incense sticks and cones, and glittering little religious statuettes for Hindus and

Christians. Smokers purchased coils of bush tobacco; black as liquorice, or bought packs of Consulate or Pall Mall cigarettes. Single cigarettes were two cents apiece.

Best of all were the lolly and snack vendors. I would blow what was left of my pocket-money on an incredible selection of sweet and savory treats. Things like pickled green mango skins and the salted dried plums known as Chinese lollies. There were two and five cent brown paper bags filled with peanuts or 'bean' – the name for salted roasted peas. Deep-fryers pumped out bhajis, taro chips, pakoras and amazingly sticky Indian sweets. I'd gorge myself on these treats, but I always left space for a curry and roti.

Ahhh yeah – those two words always make me feel hungry. Curry and roti had been brought to Fiji by indentured Indian workers in the 19th century and now everybody ate it.

The rotis were made daily, using butter, atta and sharps flour – but with no yeast or rising agent. Rolled out and press-cooked on a hot plate, the unleavened discs blistered and puffed up. Onto the roti would go a serve of curry (goat, potato and pea was my favourite) and then it was all rolled up like a wrap.

Sitting in the sun on the Suva seawall eating one of those parcels of joy is a memory my tummy will never forget.

Food in Fiji could be magical and I saw people calling to the fish and then honouring them when they were caught. When I de-husked a coconut, I could see the face of an eel on it — the very creature from whence the first coconut originated. Festivals and ceremonies often had special food, and there were clan customs concerning the collecting, preparation and cooking of certain foods. Sometimes food was eaten for reasons that didn't include hunger.

Maria was my nanny and lived with us for many years. She was also a traditional healer. At one place she had her own cottage and on most evenings a few people would respectfully appear at her door for a consultation and one of her special preparations.

One day after school I went into the kitchen and saw a pot on the stove with something unidentifiable, but meaty, simmering away in it. I asked Maria what it was. Sheep's heart she said. Not for you. Now even more curious, I had to be chased away with whacks on the bum from a sasa (coconut leaf stem) broom.

On another occasion I was having dinner with my schoolmate Lali and his family. There was lots of food and when Lali's mum came out with yet another dish, excited murmurs in Hindi went around the table.

"Bring it over here Ma," said Lali's Dad and he spooned a good serve of this new food, steaming meat dumplings in a fragrant sauce, onto my already full plate. Embarrassed by the attention, I shot Lali a look.

With a grin, he winked back at me.

"So," boomed Lali's Dad at me. "Are you ready for your hockey match tomorrow?"

I nodded. Our school was playing another school and I was a defender on our team.

"You better eat up good," continued Lali's Dad. "Get lots of power and energy into you. Lali tells me you're the smallest man on the team. Seems like you'll need an extra something."

The whole table laughed.

"Well this food is sure to do the trick," I said respectfully. Everyone laughed louder and Lali's Dad nodded at the dumplings. "Go on son – tuck in."

I began to eat and found that the meatballs were very chewy and salty. I ate one and then another while Lali and his family watched happily. I finally finished and Lali's Dad slapped me on the back.

"Ah ha! You have the energy now. I wouldn't bet on that opposing team at all. I'd say you're going to be the proverbial bull in the china shop tomorrow!"

The whole table roared.

At the match the next day I was utterly fearless. Faced with two-metre-tall Fijian guys with solid wood hockey sticks, I felt tough. Hell, even as a defender, I felt the possibility scoring a goal.

The whistle went and I played my best hockey match ever, running and swerving like a mad beast. I didn't score any goals but managed to stop one from going in. Throughout the match I felt no intimidation from the stampeding attackers because I was pretty certain that none of them had eaten four bull testicles the night before — like I had.

With the bounty of the land and sea all around, and not much refrigeration, most people ate fresh daily. With such great ingredients there wasn't much need or appetite for complex sauces and preserved seasonings. The best Fijian food had a simple but precise fusion of flavours.

Palusami is a classic dish utilising coconut milk, known as *lolo*. This is made from fresh grated coconut and a little water, repeatedly squeezed to produce the rich milk. The crumbly coconut meal is discarded after a couple of squeezings. The coconut milk, infused with a fine dice of onion, chili and tomato, is used to poach or bake *rourou,* or taro leaves. Baked in an oven, Palusami is something divine, a smoky, creamy, jellied delight, unexpectedly rich and totally addictive.

For some real oral zingo Fijians liked to eat *kokoda* — their take on fish ceviche. Very fresh white fish like Trevally, Mahi Mahi or Snapper is cubed and marinated in lemon juice, lime juice and diced chili. The citric acid 'cooks' the fish for forty-five minutes while some *lolo* is made. Add a fine dice of capsicum and red onion to it, then mix with the drained fish and eat cold.

This truly sublime combination of exotic luxury and industrial grade protein is Pacific perfection.

Then there's the traditional Fijian earth oven or *lovo*. It's the same as a Maori *hangi* or a Torres Strait *kup mari* and it's great.

A pit is dug, a big fire made next to it, and into the fire are placed igneous rocks (they don't crumble or explode). The rocks, when white-hot, are used to line the bottom and sometimes the sides of the pit. Parcels of food wrapped up in banana leaves, palm fronds and burlap sacks go onto the rocks. More banana leaves, wet burlap sacks and a layer of earth make a lid over the food, keeping the steaming heat in.

After three or four hours of cooking the *lovo* is opened and out of the pit come whole pigs, chickens and fish, yam, taro, and that yummy *palusami*. Meat just falls off the bone and everything is imbued with a beautiful smoky flavour.

One time I attended a *lovo* luncheon on a farm and the lads were a bit late putting the food in. Older folk were grumbling and kids were snoring by the time it was ready. Some of the guys had drunk beer while they were waiting and were getting foolish in the hot sun.

Fijian guys can be pretty macho as they have a warrior tradition going back many hundreds of years. They play rugby union at kindergarten and as soldiers have served with front-line distinction in the Second World War and as members of the the British SAS.

Well, as the steaming food parcels were opened, and the food carefully cut up, a drinker riled up one of his beer-buddies and a brawl erupted by the *lovo* pit. The sober men began breaking up the fight but there were a few scamps who wouldn't stop.

A big guy, fed up with the nonsense, grabs the leg of a whole cooked pig and starts donging the fighters on the head with it. The pig's leg is big; there's a bone in it and whoever he hits goes down stunned and greasy-haired. Everyone shouts out with laughter every time this happens.

The last few guys fighting stop to see what the hilarity is all about and dong! – another one goes down. The fighters now stop and burst into delighted laughter; the peacemaker with the pig's leg laughing the loudest.

Growing up in Fiji gave me two distinct views on food, cooking and eating. I understood European fine dining with its complex tastes, different courses and wines, linen and cutlery.

I'd also learnt the Fijian way — that food could lush but simple. That it was magical, visceral and hands on. I'd climbed trees for it; seen it swimming, running and biting back. I'd even seen it used to dong someone on the head. All this knowledge was to serve me well when I got into cooking professionally.

The Restaurant at the End of the World

In the early nineteen eighties I moved to a mountain-top village in the remote tropical north of Australia. I was nineteen, long-haired and lived under a blue tarpaulin. By day I bush-walked and swam in jungle water-holes with other young naked hippies; by night I drank, smoked and tripped with the colourful locals. Around my bush camp giant spiders ate the little birds and immense pythons ate the larger ones. At night weird creatures screamed in the vast rainforest which glowed and sparkled with luminous fungi and fireflies.

Even wilder was the yearly wet season. Monsoon troughs and cyclones could drop half a metre of rain or more in a day or two. The road up the mountain range, dangerous at the best of times, would get cut for a day or more due to multiple landslides and fallen trees.

These biblical deluges made the electricity fail and phone lines go dead for days at a time. Sometimes major floods on the coast would cut off all access to the nearest town — the port of Cairns. Milk, bread and fresh food would run out as the flooding could last a week.

I liked this lush feral wildness and decided to stay for a while in the little village. On a bougainvillea covered 1920s-era building on the main street was the only licensed restaurant in town. Its sign featured a big tree frog. Walking past it one day, I saw three people sitting inside cleaning dining-chairs. It was the wet season and the restaurant was closed, but I went in to see if I could get a job for when they re-opened.

Inside I met the owners. Dressed in shorts, all sun-tanned, trim and fit; they looked like musicians or yachties. The two guys were shirtless, moustachioed, their hair a bit long, and the woman wore a bikini top. I expressed my desire for work and in reply was invited to sit down and help them clean chairs. I immediately surmised that this was a test to see if I really was a worker. I grabbed a cleaning rag and got into it. A few hours later I was given a cold beer and a job. I was going to work with one of these guys in the kitchen.

Terry, who was the Chef, was a Londoner and his partners, his wife Lillian and her brother Rain, were Dutch. They were a pretty hip bunch, coming of age in London and Amsterdam during the sixties, and they'd travelled and lived in places like Afghanistan, India, Bali & New Zealand in the seventies. They liked, make that loved, good food and drink. With this nous, and lots of hard graft, they made Frogs Restaurant into something rather special. It was a beacon of fine dining in a far-flung and often roughneck land.

Far North Queensland back in those days was basically known for the Great Barrier Reef, with its snorkelling, marlin-fishing and seafood, and also for growing big commercial crops of sugarcane, tobacco and marijuana. The long highway from down south was hell-rugged and flights into Cairns infrequent. It was like the end of the world, but beautiful.

Terry lent me the money to buy uniforms, I cut my hair, donned a new pair of boots, and started my first kitchen job. There was just the two of us and Terry began instructing me on the preparation of the food on the menu – 'the prep', and the cooking and serving up of each dish – 'the service'. It was impressed upon me the utmost importance of having all the prep done before service started, and so began a race against time that lasted decades.

The kitchen was small and on one bench was the 'cold larder' section. In this little space I made salads, cold sauces, vinaigrettes and cold entrees. I grasped processes like blanching and emulsifying, and learnt to scrutinize, smell, and taste ingredients for quality and freshness. I was taught how to make pâtés, terrines and crab bisque – then the desserts. I was enthralled and just about ran into work each day.

Terry taught me to respect the ingredients, to not bruise, shatter or dehydrate these delicate pieces in the culinary puzzle. Discovering just how ingredients came together to make a dish was supremely satisfying. There was a means to an end, and following each step with precision would result in something that worked – and tasted great too. I already liked eating chocolate mousse but making it turned out to be just as good.

I was as green as a bean, making mistakes, but with time these errors became the exception and not the rule. Terry told me, "I'll show you how. If you balls it up – I'll happily show it to you again. Second time you make the same mistake I'll get irritated. If you make the same mistake for a third time – you're fired." This warning worked – I've never been fired.

Working cold larder was enjoyably arty but there was dirty nasty work too. Cleaning kilo after kilo of prawns; quickly removing their shells and snotty guts while not getting stabbed by their pointy rostrums. Shucking oysters, not fingers. Cracking open Moreton Bay Bugs (slipper lobsters) and not gashing my palms open on their tough sharp-edged carapaces.

Fiddliest of all were the chunky Mud crabs. The legs were cleaned of meat using a teaspoon handle; a meat mallet cracked open the claws. The big test was the body – full of compartments loaded with juicy meat. These nooks were separated by the thinnest shell that easily broke into small sharp shards. It took some time getting all the meat out; my legs fidgeting as I willed my hands to be precise.

I also served as the kitchen hand, washing pots and pans, feeding the dishwasher with plates and cutlery and sweeping and mopping the floors. This taught me to work clean.

At service I was told to read all the order dockets – not just the ones for cold larder. When I first worked at Frogs, the dockets were hand-written. Most kitchens now have docket machines that print the orders and the noise these machines make when it's busy can haunt your dreams.

The dockets usually represented a single table's order with the people sitting at the table known as the 'covers.' When front of house – Rain and Lillian – took the food out they impaled the corresponding docket on a metal spike and I, hopefully, never had to refer to it again.

I was drilled in the necessity of rotating stock in the cold room – moving the oldest food to the front. This is essential, otherwise awful entropy takes over. Food grows funky green Afros, jars noxiously bubble, and spoiling fruit and veg release dribbles of rank liquid. A cold room is set at four degrees but things still go off – just more discreetly. Later on, down the cooking track, I'd always sniff the cold room when job-hunting. If something smelt bad in there at four degrees, then it had to be really stinking. Like the place.

Under Terry's tutelage I learned the principle of time and motion – of using every minute and second to its utmost. I never walked across the kitchen empty-handed. I thought out my prep first and made the least number of trips to the cold room as possible. Soon I was doing three prep jobs at the same time – roasting nuts in the oven, cooking prawns and slicing cucumbers. Was I cool or what?

Then I got to go where the flames burnt blue – doing the pan dishes on the gas rings. Unlike the cool inert world of cold larder – things got hot and changed quickly! A meal could start to burn very swiftly indeed. The pans demanded my full attention and grabbed at my every brain cell. But I knew I couldn't stand there watching each meal until it was ready.

I tussled mightily with this quandary. Without the confidence to turn my back on cooking meals to do something else – I was stuffed. I might as well hang up my new white jacket right now.

With Terry's quiet encouragement I plugged away at this seemingly intractable problem. It took me a little while, but I got it. With a lot of trust in myself, and with my short-term memory in top gear, I felt a new way of thinking, feeling even, blossom in my head. Time became malleable. I was absolutely in the here and now – but not trapped by it. Each minute now beautifully expanded and filled with space. The present moment became a comfortably fluid point of reference for half a dozen courses of action. This was some kind of wizardry alright! From then on, I was hooked.

Working pans made physical demands on me as well. I got quite dizzy if I didn't drink enough fluids and flames performed thermal epilation on my forearms if I let them. Heat soaked into pan handles and metal utensils and they would scorch my hands. A folded-up tea-towel became essential while working pans. It had to be bone-dry as any moisture conducts heat instantly from metal to hand. I found out real fast about that.

As the months passed by, I made less and less mistakes and got quicker and quicker, moving between the cold larder and pans with ease. Then I came into work one morning and Terry gave me the news. I was going to work on grill!

The grill was hot and difficult, and also the alpha spot in the kitchen. Here the dockets arrived and were put in a head-height rack to be read. Most meals were plated up by the grill and put on the 'pass' – a counter next to the grill where the front-of-house would collect the food. There was a shiny silver call-bell to summon them. Kitchens and dining rooms are noisy so I learned to give the bell a swift double tap in case a loud noise drowned out the first ding. It's very bad form however, to repeatedly sound the bell. Good waiting staff have sharp ears and don't need your demented dinging to remind them how busy it is.

The grill and pass were the nexus of control and I revelled in it. I would 'call away' a table, telling the whole kitchen (just Terry actually) to put all that table's meals up on the pass. It was also a big thrill to cook the high-end protein, the eye-filet steaks and ocean-caught fish. Bit by bit I got the feel of medium-rare compared to rare. I mastered the knack of serving up seafood that finished cooking as it got to the table. I worked grill during the early part of service, but as I got better Terry and I swapped sections totally. When I got flustered, Terry told me to take a moment to re-read the orders and the way forward would become apparent. He was right. Amongst all those words on all those dockets there was always the best course of action.

After ten months Terry put me to the ultimate test. One evening before service he said he was going home. It was a Tuesday without any bookings but I was immediately worried for his business. Terry stood firm. Goodnight, and remember to check that the gas is off when you leave.

Butterflies started doing judo in my tummy. What if I forget how to make something? Is the prep all done? Is there enough? Oh God what if . . .

Then like a big shot of vodka, pride warmed me. I'm the man tonight. This kitchen is my responsibility. I went and re-checked the cold room again. It and I were cool. I think cooked for five tables of two that night and blissfully floated home after several celebratory beers with Rain.

I was very lucky to have this responsibility thrust upon me at such a young age. Terry put his trust in me, leaving his kitchen, and his reputation, in my hands. With that kind of faith in me – there was no way I was going to let him down.

The food at Frogs was a mix of global classics. The sweetest local prawns and the creamiest avocados from just up the road made for a devastatingly simple entree. To find European favourites like Tournedos Rossini and Oysters Kilpatrick on a menu in the middle of the jungle just blew people away. There were lamb skewers that came with a gloriously dark and treacle-thick Indonesian peanut sauce. Terry loved India and made great curries. The fish curry, in a golden sauce flecked with the green of coriander and mint, was scrumptious, and the cardamon and blueberry lamb curry bubbled with rich flavours.

The Coral Sea and the Gulf of Carpentaria provided a cornucopia of amazing seafood. Barramundi, Mud crab, Mackerel, Snapper, Red Emperor, calamari, Moreton Bay Bugs, prawns and more, overflowed into that little kitchen. I grilled many fillets of crisp-skinned but soft-centered Barramundi, serving them with a melting disc of Pernod butter. I pan-fried oceans of Prawns and Bugs, caramelising them to perfection in garlic and butter. Frogs' own spaghetti marinara was famous - the creamy reduction loaded up with all kinds of marine morsels. A great special was a twenty-five-centimetre-long leader prawn grilled on a sugarcane skewer. The beautiful seafood was abundant and cheap and I reckon I'll never see the like of it again.

A lot of our fruit and veg came from the nearby Atherton Tableland. On red dirt farms with rainforest peaks in the distance, European settlers had farmed the Tablelands for over seventy years. There was tropical produce; lychees, bananas, mangoes, pineapples, and also veggies from the 'Old Country' – tomatoes, capsicums, eggplant, zucchini, potatoes and herbs. The Tablelands has such rich topsoil that a local marlin fishing-boat skipper said, "If you stuck your dick in that soil – it would grow another six inches."

I loved going into the kitchen each day. I was enthralled by the constellations of details and processes I was learning. Daily, hourly, minute by minute – I was wonderfully challenged by the fact that every single action required a perfect result. I chopped, not crushed, fresh herbs with my knife. I shaved, not sliced, red onion for a salad. Each steak alighted upon the plate with a sublimely caramelised crust. Every prawn dished up, had a rapidly shrinking translucence at its core. The real task of every task was doing it just right.

I became seriously absorbed in this sensual science. I inhaled the verdant scent of crispy steamed green vegetables. I marvelled at how the funky stink of prawn-paste cooked right out, and then provided a subtle underlying tone to a sauce. I sniffed in the boozy fumes of a deglazing pan. I savoured the rich gelatinous jelly given up by simmering fish heads. I made soup that was liquescent bliss, with all its ingredients united in glossy full-bodied flavour. Water went from milky to clear as I washed Basmati rice, and when cooked into fragrant fluffy clouds, each nutty grain tumbled freely. I was in a world of magic.

Terry and I were avid readers and also thirsty for good new music and we swapped books and albums and discussed them during prep sessions. Some days we played games of chess in the kitchen. No-one stood around puzzling moves, but when one of us called out, "Check!" during service, it was hard not to run over to the board. It felt like I was working with a cool big brother.

Every kitchen has its mini-crises and moments of madness but Terry remained super-cool, unflappable and perpetually cheerful. He had a resolute positivity and this attitude was something else I endeavoured to master. I didn't know it then but I would work for Terry at four other restaurants he would own.

To be above the Coral Sea, surrounded by a World Heritage Area full of the most incredible flora and fauna was amazing. But to also sit in a cool vintage timber building, eating really good food and drinking wine and cocktails, made Frogs a unique experience.

There was always somebody from somewhere eating at Frogs. With cattle ranches, dairies, mines, fishing trawlers and large-scale agriculture all around, most North Queenslanders were pretty much salt of the earth people. Families, business partners and workers came from all over to celebrate birthdays, anniversaries or business deals. Or just to have a decent restaurant feed. At times some tough characters ate at Frogs.

One evening, Rain asked a customer at a table of cattle farmers how he'd like his steak done. "Mate, just take off the horns and wipe its arse," was the reply.

Many international travellers graced the shiny wooden tables at Frogs too. One night a dozen men in crisp white Royal Navy uniforms stood and boomed out a toast to 'Dizzy Lizzy'. On another night, members of seminal American band The Grateful Dead sat for hours, enjoying themselves eating steaks and seafood; drinking South Australian white wine and Kentucky bourbon.

The marlin-boat skipper often brought his hard-drinking clients in after a day's fishing out on the big blue and they'd heartily go through bottles of spirits. Erudite botanists, marine biologists and wildlife gurus gathered to eat well and talk shop. There were musicians, artists and rich hippies following the golden sunshine and electric blue Ulysses butterflies. Shorts and sandal-clad CEOs and their spouses unknowingly sat next to local outlaw entrepreneurs; the dope growers and smugglers kicking back and living large after a successful season.

It was like a scene from a movie at Frogs. From time to time a mix of guests would end up out on the back-veranda partying on after close, their laughter and storytelling competing with the chorus of frogs that gave the restaurant its name.

On one of those nights I sat at a candle-lit table loaded with bottles, glasses and ashtrays. Around me a dozen people in various stages of intoxication made merry. Terry and Lillian were explaining to a sun-tanned American couple how to find an especially beautiful beach up the coast. Rain, who lived in a flat behind the restaurant, was now shirtless and making cocktails at the bar, charming the hell out of two French women. I was on my fourth beer and wondering what the cocktails Rain was making tasted like.

The exotic scent of the big trumpet-shaped Datura flowers in the garden floated in. The only light came from the restaurant; outside it was dark, the trees and bushes blocking out the few lights still on in town. We were in our own little midnight world.

With all the great food, drink and company it was hard to believe that there was so much wilderness around us – the trackless rainforest, the dry empty gemstone and mineral country out west, and the great reef-crossed expanse of ocean just down the mountain.

A sudden thundering fell upon the veranda's tin roof, drowning out conversation. It was raining hard, again, and people turned to look at the candle-lit sheets of water pouring off the roof's edge. A green-thumbed local passed around the fruits of his labours and it was a good smoke.

Sitting on that veranda I felt just great. I loved my job and after a year I'd proved equal to the task. I had a boss who not only encouraged and trusted me, but was also a friend. If this was the life of the cooking professional – then I was sold. Little did I know how lucky I was.

Magic and Industry

It's early and the first entrees of the night have gone out. No new orders have come in but there's a fair few bookings. In this pre-rush lull let's leave my story up on the docket rack for a few minutes and dig into what's at the very core, the very guts of this whole cooking caper. Like anything of real substance and creativity it looks effortless from the outside but is rather more complicated on the inside. You see, there's a paradox at work; a battle going on, and anyone who is serious about cooking commercially must fight this battle each and every shift they work.

Way back in the beginning we all shared a single demographic – the perpetually hungry. Our lifestyle choices were all the same – find food – and the rise and fall of supply dictated where we lived and for how long. When not engaged in finding food we made things to help fill our empty bellies – traps, hunting weapons and grinding stones. Outside of these tools there was no mechanism, financial or otherwise, between us and our chow. No supermarket queues, no restaurant bookings, no indecision about what to eat tonight. You just went and got whatever was there. That's the theory anyhow, because if you and your tribe were unlucky then you'd all die of starvation. In the quest for survival every tribe needed a few very special people who always found the food. The Lucky Hunter is the original mythical figure to embody the magic of food.

These ancient superheroes were celebrated for bringing home the bacon. On the walls of deep caves, beautiful painted, and in ritual dances often wearing the skins of a long-ago dinner, our grateful ancestors paid homage to the Lucky Hunter. And also asked the gods for more luck.

Then at some point in our prehistory, a truly earth-shattering event occurred and we humans really proved ourselves to be superior to the birds and beasts. Someone cooked a feed.

Like us, animals practice monogamy, polygamy, and bisexuality. They feel friendship, pride and shame; they use tools, build and decorate homes and live and work in cities. They get drunk, dress-up, show-off, accumulate assets and get stomach ulcers from stress. Animals do just about everything humans do – but we are the only cooking animal.

It was most likely a bush fire or a lava flow that sparked this miraculous discovery. Imagine the ecstasy of the first hominids eating cooked food! What a stone-age epiphany – the taste difference between the raw and the cooked. One of the best things in life just got better.

The sensory experience of cooked food is pretty nice. The most tantalizing smells are produced, but the true magic is the amazing heightening of taste. At about 160°C food becomes loaded with flavour from the caramelizing of sugars and fats that roasting and frying produces. The sweetness of oven-roasted garlic is an example of this delectable phenomenon.

Cooking food is so evocative of the shelter of camp and the safety of home that I believe it has encoded and defined civilization. Onions cooking in butter might say more about who we are than Leonardo da Vinci ever could. Fortunes and fashion come and go, empires rise and fall – but a well-baked loaf of bread is timeless.

With the advent of cooked food, a new magical hero appeared – the Good Cook. Just as the Lucky Hunter always found the food to cook there would be always someone who could cook it good. Traditionally this was Mum.

From the very beginning she fed us from her own body, and from infant to teenager and on into cherished memory, most people's experience is of Mum as the provider of all that cooked food. Dad's quest as Lucky Hunter securing the money to buy the food didn't stack up against Mum actually making dinner.

The wonderful sense of security and the gut-felt

experience she consistently provided was fully backed up by the fact that she'd made us inside her and then served us to the world. We were all buns in the oven once.

If food is magic then the cooks are the magicians. The practise of magic requires ritual, will-power and imagination. Cooks first master the rituals – the recipes and techniques; then apply their will power – the ability to make everything just right again and again. Now their imaginations can work – creating new techniques and recipes.

The cook, like a doctor or shaman, puts stuff into people's bodies. It's no surprise that the first cookbooks hardly distinguished between the medicinal and the culinary. Recipes were often remedies. This connection is shown in the word 'restaurant'. It originally described a thing, not a place. A restaurant is a restorative broth or bouillon, something rich and nourishing for those who were too ill or exhausted to eat solid food.

As society evolved the Good Cook was no longer the preserve of a lucky tribe – they became the valuable servant of the powerful and rich; an essential member of royal entourages. Cooked food was the first luxury item, and brought forth for your guests it was a solid sign of wealth. Rocking a paunch used to mean power; corpulence meant success. Not anymore.

Food is essential so it's the original industry. After an extra successful day, the tribe sat back with full bellies and considered the rare sight of uneaten food. Wondering if they could keep it for a time when food was scarce or when the Lucky Hunter was sick, they experimented with its preservation. Vegetable tubers were turned into starch paste. Meat was hung, dried and smoked. Seeds and grains were ground into flour.

This was a life changing revolution – the nomads now had time. Preserving food amplified its intrinsic power to keep you alive for a few days, into the power to keep you alive for weeks if not months. Freed from the endless quest for instant food our ancestors had time to cultivate crops and develop hardier strains. By herding and then penning, they gradually domesticated animals, and now experimented with cross breeding to get better yields of meat, eggs and milk. They invented cheese. In chiselled cave silos full of grain and in dusty cattle yards the industry of food was born.

The nomadic tribes stopped moving and began to settle down in permanent camps, and behind thorn fences and rock walls a new kind of power began to evolve. When food became something more than pure fuel, it was hoarded, counted and then traded. Now systems of valuing and accounting came into being. Food had become money.

Animals, seeds and grain were probably the first forms of cash. Other valuable things – cloth, perfume, gemstones, spices and dyes – resulted when people had enough food, and therefor enough time, to find, process and produce this cool new stuff. Then tiny, durable and easy to transport symbols of all this stored food and new goods began to be used. Pieces of gold, silver and copper were fashioned into quickly addable and divisible units that made it easy to travel and trade.

These traveling traders needed to eat and they found their vittles at wayside inns and village markets. From these beginnings the cooking industry grew. Today it is huge and from humble one-burner street stalls to haute cuisine palaces there is choice for everyone.

The fundamental thing these eateries all share is the bottom line. Passion, imagination and creativity are wonderful, but every commercial kitchen needs a good system of percentages that create a profit. Rising wages, rent, food and energy costs make this goal ever harder. Owners and Head Chefs must shave closer to the bone seeking to maximize their staff output and minimize their costs. This is industry.

And this is the crux of the matter – the conflict between magic and industry. Any 'magical' cook makes food at home they would love any customer of theirs to eat. It's a wish of real giving, using the best ingredients and taking unlimited time to share their passion. Unfortunately, in commercial kitchens where deadlines and making a buck are paramount, compromises are made and the sense of perfection is invariably postponed.

The 'Magicians' feel this schism and often suffer

the conviction that no-one understands the choices they daily make . . . except for the other crazies in kitchens.

This battle royale between industry and magic throws up extremes of perception. Foodie-ism and cooking shows are great for conjuring up the magic, but they also create unreal expectations about the actual industry. Customers want high-end perfection – but on a budget. Apprentices want to do all the groovy plate presentation – but without the mess and slog. Chefs are pressured to be innovative when maybe just being good is enough.

This clash, taken to its logical extreme, produces fast-food chains who represent a flawless, but utterly base, fusion of magic and industry. Laboratory-perfected thrills concocted from fat, salt and sugar are seamlessly melded to a profits-before-all system of ingredients, preparation and service.

And that's OK, because the magic of food is so sublime it's indescribable. Just like sex and music, it's absolutely personal and no one else's opinion matters. Deep down, beyond peer pressure or cultural influence, you know exactly what hits your spot. I can dig that food has got to fulfil that very personal craving but it doesn't mean it's got to be crass, unhealthy or boring. I bet people who eat bad fast food have sex the same way every time and never ever change their radio station.

The Old School

After three years at Frogs Restaurant I wanted to see if I could hold my own cooking in a big city. With Terry's blessing and encouragement, I moved to the southern Australian metropolis of Melbourne and got a job at a restaurant called Ringos. Smack dab in the CBD and right next to the theatre and cinema precinct, it was always busy. Big, bright and open plan, with skylights and an atrium on two levels, Ringos had over two hundred and fifty seats. There was a sizable bar that was popular with office workers who came for lunch, and in the evening the restaurant kicked on when crowds arrived for pre or post-show dinner and drinks.

Ringos was my first experience of a good-sized traditional kitchen; a template for many of the kitchens I later worked in, and so bears some examination. It was also where I first encountered the old school of the cooking brigade.

The legendary chef Escoffier, after time in the army, developed a kitchen system of sections and ranks. At Ringos this hierarchy soldiered on. The kitchen crew wore pressed white jackets, ironed houndstooth pants, properly folded neckerchiefs and tall chef's hats known as toques. These uniformed troops were the brigade.

The kitchen was purpose built. I'd never seen so many white tiles in my life. Big stainless-steel benches filled multiple sections and work areas. Ringos' kitchen featured the classic 'line' - a bank or island of mainly gas-powered cooking machines. It was a combination of flat-top grill plates, ring-top ranges, ovens, steamers, double deep-fryers and salamanders. Salamanders? No ma'am, these aren't big aquatic lizards, but super gas-powered overhead versions of the griller in a domestic stove.

I started out on the pans, working the ten-burner ring-top range. Often there were more than ten pan dishes ordered at a time but I had to share the gas rings with chefs sealing fish and meat in pans for the ovens. Two burners were also taken up with pots of hot water used to rapidly heat up serves of blanched vegetables and precooked pasta. I quickly learnt be very clever about my use of the gas rings and the different sized pans.

It was hot-metal mayhem with dozens of spoons, ladles and tongs in close proximity to the blue flames. With lots of cooks and chefs moving things around, I treated *every* utensil as though it might be red hot.

Running parallel to the line were stainless-steel benches – actually the tops of reach-in fridges. I would load my reach-in before service with the food I'd need. There was a set place for everything and eventually I could open the reach-in door and without looking, grab what I needed. Even closer to hand were cold inserts in the bench top, filled with much used ingredients and garnishes.

In between the line and the reach-ins was the manic space where the crew worked. At first, I couldn't believe how much food was being cooked. Two, often three hundred covers each weekday lunch and later in the week the same amount of covers for dinner. Fridays and Saturdays were cooking marathons going to six or seven hundred covers.

Getting the hang of the pans, I was watched by Lyle, one of the Sous-chefs. He was small and tough, older than most of the crew, and a veteran of cruise-ships and big hotels. His deceptively droopy eyelids concealed an all-seeing gaze. Any mistake – a portion a tad too large or a slightly messy plate presentation – would attract his attention. This merciless eye of Lyle had me making unforced errors. When I told him that he was making me nervous he gave me an evil grin.

"Oh dear. Well you'll get over it, but you won't have developed any bad habits in *my* kitchen."

Lyle was also a stickler for hygiene and if my fingernails weren't clean – he'd make me go clean them. Sometimes as I was leaving Lyle would call me back and point out a tiny uncleaned corner of my reach-in. In my street clothes I'd get hot soapy water and finish the job.

I was slightly consoled to see that he cast his eagle eye over others too – it just seemed to land on me more.

The other Sous-chef, Chris, was a tearaway; often charming, always foul-mouthed, and very fast. Flying by the seat of his pants, running on the buzz in his head, he boasted of being perpetually hung-over and ever ready to rock and roll. Zipping around the kitchen swearing and laughing, he wasn't that interested in monitoring me. As long as I put my meals up on time, he was happy.

Ringos ran a day and night shift and aside from an hour overlap when the shifts changed, Lyle and Chris never worked with each other. They each ran a shift, swapping days and nights each fortnight. They cooked and prepped as needed and also co-ordinated service. They both kept abreast of the raw produce and stock, ordering more as needed. Very importantly they had to make sure that everything for service was correct, fresh and ready to go.

Lyle would check with each section throughout his shift for quality and quantity – he didn't want any surprises on his watch. He could instantly tell the Head Chef what amounts of food were in the kitchen and what the state of prep was.

Chris wasn't so evangelical and was somewhat oblivious to what his shift got up to. It was basically our responsibility to be on the ball, but he'd get as bitchy as hell if things weren't right. Rushing through his prep-lists and produce orders, Chris would often leave before the shift ended, nicking off to a wild night ahead.

Every section had a Chef de Partie. A Chef de what? Yes, they often do, but partie means section, so this chef runs their own little patch. In very traditional kitchens they have groovy names. The confusingly titled Chef Saucier runs the grills and the Chef Poissonier takes care of the fish and seafood. In the realm of soups and vegetables the Chef Entremetier rules and the Chef Garde-Manger lords it over the cold-larder. In a full brigade there's a different Chef for soup, ice cream, pastry, salads, deep-frying and confectionery.

On Fridays and Saturdays, I had an apprentice to help me, but on most shifts the pan section consisted of just me. Lyle also expected a full prep list for the next shift, and a list of anything that needed ordering. I had become a Chef de Partie.

At first, it was a crew of new faces each day, with different white-jacketed bodies in a weaving, bobbing scrum around the cooking machines. Every fortnight my roster swapped between day and night shifts and it took some weeks before I got to meet and work with everybody in the kitchen. There were fifteen of us all up, including three, sometimes four, apprentices.

One of the line cooks, a heavily moustached fella called Izzy, was very happy to be working at Ringos. A rocket strike had killed most of his immediate family during the war between Iran and Iraq and he'd escaped his homeland, deserting from the army. One day he pulled off his boot to show me where he'd lost several of toes to frostbite while fleeing through the mountains of Pakistan. I liked Izzy, but not his habit of pinching me.

"Oh, so you are awake!" he'd roar happily. After many pleas to desist and warnings of retaliation I finally punched him forcefully on the arm which made him bellow with laughter. But he stopped with the pinching and I felt like I'd passed some kind of test with him.

A grill cook, Boz, was a world-weary trouper with nicotine-stained fingers. He had many years of cooking under his belt and a limp to show for it. He didn't say much but he groaned a lot. If his heart wasn't in it, his scarred-up hands certainly were and he moved like an automaton during service. I had the impression he could cook with his eyes closed and this made me feel a strange mix of pity and envy towards him.

I gradually met the other chefs and cooks, Gary, Tom, Mitch, Scotty, the four apprentices and all the kitchen hands. There were also twenty-six people who worked on various shifts front of house. It felt like an army to me.

I got fairly quick on the pans and I began to help out the apprentice on the fryers and steamers. Lyle noticed, shook his head, and indicated I should help the other chefs and not molly-coddle the apprentice.

So, I got to work popping pans of meat and fish into the ovens. They were a row of three heat-radiant monsters with red-hot maws and I felt their dragon's breath every time I swung open the heavy doors. At service they got filled up with food . . . and sometimes danger.

During a particularly hectic pre-theatre service, I saw Mitch nearly melt his face off. Stupidly, he put a steel boat of demi-glace into the oven, balancing it on the very top oven rack. To compound things, below the brimming gravy boat was a baking tray, re-used too many times for finishing serves of rib filet. It now had a centimetre of hot fat sizzling in it.

A few minutes later Mitch squatted down, leaned into the oven to get a main that had been called away, and knocked the gravy boat over. Demi-glace hit the oil in the tray below and exploded. Mitch squawked and fell back on his bum. A cloud of smoke blew out of the oven, revealing flames, and the line cooks hooted and cheered. Mitch sprang to his knees, reached into the burning oven and rescued the main.

Blindly grabbing a plate from the overhead warmer, he quickly plated and garnished the meal. With the fire still going in the oven, he called out to Chris who was running the pass.

"Chef! Chef! Table ten's main up!"

Mitch's face ran with exploded gravy; it blistered badly later, but he was tremendously pleased to have saved the meal. It meant *he didn't have to cook it again.*

It was much cooler in cold larder. Away from the heat behind a half wall, and serving from its own pass, this section made the cold entrees, cold mains, salads, sweet sauces and savory dressings. All the hot and cold desserts – things like tarts, flans and mousses were also made at this well set-up station. There was even a pastry section in its own small room with a cool marble-topped bench for maintaining the integrity of the pastry while it was made. Yep, it sure looked nice and mellow in the cold larder section.

For three days a week the only woman on the crew ran cold larder, overseeing two teenage second-year apprentices. Mary was in her sixties and tiny, so we were all paranoid of bumping into her. She was of no little stature though, having been the Head Chef and owner of a celebrated Chinese restaurant. She drove a two-door sports car and the boys loved her for that too.

Mary was supposed to be retired, but she just couldn't stay out of the kitchen. Sharp-eyed, she bustled around in immaculate whites, making amazing Chinese specials while happily cajoling and chastising her young charges. Mary was very cool but I never got to work with her. It seemed I was always needed on the line.

Ringos, after nearly a year of operation, was starting to hit its straps. It got busier by the month. The food was good; the prices reasonable and waiting times minimal, even when we were packed. The mix of styles on our menu also attracted downtown diners.

This mix included four pastas, many salad mains, two styles of lamb and three kinds of top-shelf steak. There was seafood – prawns, oysters, crab and calamari, and also daily specials of fresh Southern Ocean fish I'd never seen, or cooked, before. They had the most colourful names – Orange Roughy, Pink Ling and Blue Eye Trevalla – and tasted great. Ringos was next to Chinatown and we shared the vibe; with Mary's input there were juicy pork dumplings, crispy Spring Rolls and deep-fried noodle wrapped prawns.

Cold larder made many different flavours of ice-cream, gelato and sorbet each week, and a dedicated deep-fryer crackled throughout service with the dozens of serves of beer-battered tempura vegetables and seafood that we sold. We kept a core of around fifty popular dishes and every three months the rest of the menu changed to reflect the season. There were nearly a hundred items on the menu – a lot to prep and cook. The person responsible for this was the Chef de Cuisine or Head Chef.

Our Head Chef, Michael, was a rather smooth character. He wore a neatly groomed beard, a gold bracelet, blue jeans and highly polished western-style boots. His white chef's jacket, embroidered with his name, never got a mark on it as he was far too busy to prep and cook. Ringo's had a sister restaurant, equally as big, with two function rooms and Michael was responsible for it too. He was always driving across town, sourcing produce and running both places.

Michael had to deal with lots of pressure because like with any Head Chef – the buck stopped with him. Being the kitchen's wellspring of creativity, charged with making interesting and possibly innovative menus to engage our target audience with, was only half the battle. Coming up with the smart package of money-making formulas and percentages that are the perfect marriage of magic and industry was the real nub of the matter.

This is the nut that every Head Chef must crack. Their pure artistic vision will invariably be skewed by mundane factors. Things like accurate costings so that a profit on each dish is actually made. Like choosing the right quantity of menu items as too many can lead to wastage and slows the speed of preparation and service. And especially making the optimum use of the space, equipment and staff skills available. This cold reality is unavoidable. Cooking menu items that a kitchen can't cope with is like trying to dice carrots with a peeler.

Michael also had to deal with the kitchen crew – the hours, duties and abilities of each of us. When it went sour with someone, he had to be judge, jury and executioner too. Fortunately, Michael had the classic good Head Chef approach.

He'd casually stop by to see how you were and then he'd hit you with a question about 'the incident' last night. All smiles, he'd subtly grill you. In the privacy of his office 'the incident' would be brought up with the Sous-chef in charge of the offending shift – usually Chris. Michael would make his displeasure known and Chris would then go to the Chef de Partie of the section where the offence occurred and kick his arse. Then the Chef de Partie would find the person who made the error and kick their arse. This was the hierarchy at work and Michael got to have everyone's arse kicked, but not ostensibly, by him.

On Friday and Saturday nights, and on weekend lunches, Michael would run the pass at Ringos, cracking filthy jokes to keep us smiling. But first making sure that Mary wasn't on. He'd sweat from the heat lamps above the pass. These telescoping lights kept the meals hot and also spotlighted any Jackson Pollock style plating-up techniques. Michael was a good leader, and like Terry at Frogs, he always set a positive tone in the kitchen.

I kept doing OK on pans and eventually Michael and Lyle decided I should work grill. Gulp. I felt nervous because the grill at Ringos was giant; a flat top range to knock the stuffing out of you. It had metres of gas jets under it and the radiant heat was intense. It was kept on full but a line of gas jets was turned down on one side so that sauces, soups and pans of food could stay hot there, but not cook to glue or dust.

The Chef de Partie of the grill was Gary, who was

highly focused but not real friendly. He didn't have time to talk or smile or put up with pretenders in his section, and though he never shouted or swore, everyone was wary of him. I got a bit of stick at first, mainly do-it-this-way-not-that-way stuff, and I quickly did it his way.

What was difficult about Gary though was that he gave me instructions out of the corner of his mouth in a low monotone that sounded like buzzing. This was done without looking at me and he'd get irritated when I didn't respond. I didn't even know he was talking to me! I soon learned to listen to every noise he made. Behind his back he was known as The Fly.

On the grill I cooked steaks, lamb and veal, game and seafood sausages – amongst other things. With so much sizzle going on, I got coated in a sheen of fat. My pores clogged and my eyelashes stuck together. Long hours in a kitchen made me smell of food but working grill made me stink of it. Pets love an unwashed grill cook. Dogs follow them home; cats lick them with real passion.

It could get very filthy working on the grill and throughout service I had to repeatedly scrape and wipe it down. I took great care to avoid getting this grill tar and carbon rubble on the cooking food or my jacket.

Cleaning the grill back to lovely shininess was an unwelcome job at the end of a long shift. Ringos used grill-cleaning chemicals, which though quick, were also highly corrosive. Hurrying to finish up one night, I unknowingly flipped a blob of caustic pink juice over my shoulder and onto my back. Pain sank into me like an assassin's stiletto and I frantically spun around looking for the source of this torment. Then realising what I'd done I raced to the sink, ripped off my jacket and flushed the burning spot with water. I got a nasty blister out of that hasty error, and a little smile out of Lyle. He knew I wasn't going to do that again.

Each service I fed the grill with kilo after kilo of meat from the reach-in fridges under my section's bench. The cuts and portions of meat had been 'cleaned' – all the fat, sinew and sometimes bone had been trimmed off. Other meat had been pre-processed into serves; tubs of game sausages, trays of grease-proof paper separating lamb koftas and weighed-out serves of chicken strips.

A few manic steps away from the line was the chilly heart of the kitchen – the walk-in cold room. In here was more prepped food– back-up for the reach-ins on the line. The amount of traffic in and out of the cold room was phenomenal. It was used sixteen plus hours a day, seven days a week and a groove had been worn into its floor.

Grill was a white-hot cyclone, but with The Fly or Boz, sometimes Lyle, by my side, I managed to prevail over some rampaging services. The Fly seemed pleased with me, but without actual words or real eye-contact it was hard to tell. Lyle however, checked every second or third meal I put up, and always got me to go through all my prep with him just prior to service.

Actually, I began to detect a softening in Lyle's attitude towards me. Now and then, after a particularly hectic rush, I'd get a tiny nod of approval. I'd hung in for six months and it was looking like I was a keeper so Lyle began to let me off grill prep some mornings so he could show me how to make bulk items of prep.

At the back part of the kitchen was a secondary line of machines for prep, and sometimes service. One was the mighty Bratt pan – two meters long with deep sides and a heavy lid. Lyle showed me how use it to cook large amounts of food – like a hundred and forty litres of brown stock or eighty kilos of pie filling.

One of the first-year apprentices, Cambo, had an instant opinion about everything. When he insisted that the Bratt-pan was big enough to lay down in, everyone shook their heads and said, "Nahhh. Lay down in it? No way – it's too small."

Of course, a discussion developed. A poker-faced Izzy was even willing to wager money and Cambo finally had to lay down in the big machine to prove his point. Quick as a flash the big lid was brought down and secured. Loud heartless laughter drowned out Cambo's muffled thumps and cries. A wag called out, "We're going to turn it on now!" More laughter. Over in cold larder Mary shook her head sadly.

Izzy's screams of delighted laughter now brought

Michael into the kitchen and someone made him aware of a curious banging noise the Bratt pan had developed. He went to investigate and everyone managed to drift away but still be in viewing range. The lid was thrown back to reveal the red-faced apprentice. As Cambo sheepishly clambered out, Michael tried hard to look angry before ordering him to clean it.

Ringos' arsenal of heavy-duty gear also included industrial grade stick blenders. Weapon sized, nearly a metre long, with tough blades that spun at six thousand five hundred rpm, they were the perfect thing for blending hundred litre pots of soup and sauce.

Cambo thought it was fun to threaten another apprentice with the stick blender while it was buzzing. Leering like a bad guy in a movie, he was oblivious to the havoc it could wreak. Although there is a circular guard around the radius of the blades it is still very possible for a finger or nose to get shredded.

Mary saw this and shouted at Cambo not to be a bloody idiot. Chris, running the shift, just laughed. The next day Lyle heard about this foolishness and gave Cambo fifty lashes of the wet noodle – a short sharp talking to. He sulked for the rest of the day – something that he did well.

Truth was, Cambo was never going to be a chef. He whined about how hard the jobs he was assigned to do were. He actively avoided work by taking many toilet-breaks and sick days and he skulked around the kitchen wasting time between tasks. Things repeatedly slipped through his fingers too. One day he dropped a twenty-litre tub of salad dressing in the back cold room. In a flash he limped back into the kitchen, told another apprentice he was hurt, and went home. The huge slick of dressing was left for others to clean up. The next day his limp had gone. The longer he worked at Ringos the less everyone liked him. He began to feel persecuted and he wasn't wrong.

One shift, Chris dragged Cambo into his own personal nightmare, his Room 101 from Orwell's 1984. We were selling hundreds of bowls of yabby soup each week and these little freshwater crayfish arrived alive in big polystyrene boxes, their insectoid bodies stunned and unmoving from the chill of the refrigerated truck. Pots of water would be put on to boil in readiness for a rapid killing immersion. But as the chill wore off the yabbies would start to rattle and scuffle in the boxes. This noise would send a giddy thrill of terror through Cambo. He absolutely refused to go near them. The very sight of them scared him too and he'd always find some excuse to leave the kitchen as we up-ended the boxes into the pots. Dead or alive – he hated yabbies.

On this particular day the yabbies turned up late during service and the delivery guy put them in the cold room. After service I went into the cold room and saw that one box of cunning crustaceans had engineered a mass break-out. Emerging from their comatose state, they had flipped their lid and now dozens of them were crawling around. The box was incorrectly left next to trays of food and the escapees were in amongst it all. yabbies rattled on shelves; tried to burrow into lasagne. yabbies squirmed on lemons and hid in bags of bread.

As I started grabbing them, Chris appeared in the cold room, saw the rumpus taking place and with a nasty smirk told me to stop. He had someone else in mind for the job. He nipped back to the kitchen and returned with Cambo. Seeing the runaway yabbies, the poor apprentice nearly fainted, but Chris was stony-hearted and made him find and put each yabby back in the box. Cambo wouldn't talk to him for weeks.

The brigade system traditions and senior/junior dynamics are open to abuse, but for a chef to hassle an apprentice for anything else outside of the quest for speed or quality is just power mongering.

Sometimes apprentices lash out. In a staff room in London I saw a chef, apparently sleeping amongst the grubby trainers on the staffroom floor. As I took a closer look, an apprentice appeared from the change room in his street clothes. His shift had just begun and I brusquely inquired what was going on. The apprentice showed me the freshly grazed knuckles of his right hand and I quickly stepped back. The hardass apprentice stalked out the door never to return.

Aside from Cambo the other problem child in the kitchen was Chris. He was a real Jack the Lad, always with something for sale. One week it was a diamond, the next week home-bake heroin from Tasmania, the week after that – cases of really cheap olive oil. We got on OK and I went out for drinks a few times with him, joining a hard-raging crew of chefs and waiters from Ringos and other restaurants. These boys were all certified party monsters and although I usually went drink-for-drink with them, I declined offers of lines of white powder. I didn't like those sorts of chemical effects and hangovers.

Chris was hyper in the kitchen, even when it was quiet, and I guessed he was getting loaded at work too. He'd get snide and stroppy with front of house when it was busy and then fawn insincerely over them later. His shifts had too much laughter and horseplay and front of house would complain about the noise being made.

Chris wasn't one for checking his prep either and one night he began to run out of Hollandaise sauce. He darted over to cold larder and surreptitiously swiped some mayonnaise. Back at his station he whipped it into the last of the Hollandaise.

The Fly observed all this and called him out on the suspect move. Chris, with a combination of shrug, scowl and grin, topped several fish mains with the fake sauce, banged them up on the pass and gave the bell a savage ding-ding. The Fly buzzed angrily

Of course, Lyle got to hear about this home-brew cooking and Chris went for a meeting with Michael, reappearing from it red-faced and tight lipped. Behind their backs he started giving Lyle and The Fly the stink eye.

I now saw that in an understated way, Lyle was the hands-on boss in the kitchen. He was an archetypal Sous-chef who, like a sergeant-major, kept the kitchen in line and maintained the morale of the shift. He was both a cheerleader and an enforcer, a good cop/bad cop rolled into one. He dealt with slackness, sickies and outbreaks of madness and mutiny . . . the stuff that doesn't get taught at cooking school.

Sous-chefs can understudy the Head Chef and move up to the top position one day. If the other Sous-chef is also a contender then a healthy competition can develop. This shouldn't include threats of violence.

Some years after Ringos I shared Sous-chef responsibilities with a drunk, whose prep was half-arsed and her food sometimes crappy. When I voiced these concerns, her nostrils flared alarmingly. She told me to step outside – now! The chef was big, previously a bikini mud-wrestler in tough pubs, and there was no way I was going out back to be knee-speared or helicopter thrown. So, I went out of the kitchen . . . into the dining room.

Out there, shaking with rage, she informed me in a low snarl that I was an uppity little smart-arse who needed a good slapping. Nodding numbly, I wondered if she'd dare try a scissor lock on me in the dining room. She also said that the kitchen wasn't big enough us both. She was right – the next day she got fired.

At Ringos, there was nothing for Lyle to worry about though. He was a gun chef, and Chris, with his wild after-work lifestyle, was hanging in there by his apron strings. It was no contest really, but I sensed that a showdown was coming – sooner than later.

I'd used a microwave oven at Frogs for heating timbales of cooked Basmati rice. In Ringos there were several. Referred to as the 'mike', which is also the verb for microwaving, as in 'mike that mash', they were helpful during prep. I could melt or soften butter and defrost urgently needed things. Limes and lemons got mike-warmed prior to squeezing so as to increase the yield of juice. During service we heated up portions of carbs or serves of soup in them.

I witnessed a few non-food applications for mikes too. Forgotten coffees given new life, various damp but *clean* items of work apparel dried fast, front of house melting wax out of glass and ceramic candle holders. I even saw Chris, with a cheeky grin, drying some fresh cannabis in one. Storing money in the mike, though, is not a good idea.

Back in the days before polymer bank notes, a night-shift chef at Frogs, who had fiscal responsibilities, left his safe key at home. He cunningly hid the day's takings under the plate in the microwave; he'd ring first thing in the morning to explain where to find them. At knock-off time, a waitress got a slice of pie and decided to have it hot. She used the mike and sixty seconds later eight hundred plus dollars had turned to ash.

I always learnt from my work-mates' mistakes. Kitchens usually have, tucked under a bench-top or in a corner, a twenty-litre drum of oil with a tap on its side. One busy service Izzy started wailing in anguish, "Look the floor! My God the floor!" We looked down and saw a tide of oil creeping in. Izzy, hastily filling a squirty bottle, hadn't fully turned the tap off. At any second someone was going to go oil-surfing skull-first into the corner of a steel bench. With huge amounts of moaning and grumbling – huge amounts – we stopped for a few precious minutes and cleaned up the dangerous slick.

Prep and service always produced monumental amounts of dirty things from the kitchen and dining room. This culinary collateral was dealt with in the 'wet area'. Here, a hardy soul known as the dish pig leaned into deep stainless-steel sinks, utilising a lever-action high-pressure tap hanging from a flexible hose. Next to him (it's usually a him) a hefty commercial dish washer hissed away, its operating temperature of 80°C killing microbes as well as cleaning. Every few hours the dish pig would do a sweep of the bins and lug out 75 litre bags of kitchen trash.

Dish pigging is a tough job, and a good dish pig is a mighty link in the kitchen chain – a VIP indeed.

Ringos boasted one of these in the person of Meli, a well-built Pacific Islander, who worked six days a week.

He would also smash out basic prep, topping and tailing beans, peeling twenty kilo bags of potatoes and onions, and straining stocks. Like any other kitchen professional, Meli totally understood the principles of time and motion, performing all of these tasks for maximum chronological advantage.

As well as being a rubbish humping sink jockey and prep wizard, Meli was our porter too. This meant he brought in the kitchen supplies and put them away in the various store-rooms, freezers and cold rooms. His portering duties were made a fraction easier as the freezers and the cold room for raw food were all situated right by the back door where the deliveries arrived. The cold room here was twice the size of the one in the kitchen and held all the unprocessed produce, back-up alcohol for the bar and many, many desserts.

Down the back next to this cold room was a maze of sorts – comprising an office, three store-rooms, a staff-room, toilets and several corridors to service them. The windowless staff-room had a full-length mirror for front of house to check out how scruffy and hung-over they looked. The furniture comprised a battered table and a slew of mismatched chairs, including half-broken specimens from the dining room.

Most kitchens have some sort of back-area maze like this and over the years I saw many strange, sad, and occasionally beautiful things in these sub rosa places. A chef crying in rage and banging his head on a wall. Three groovy waiters, in perfect sync, busting out disco moves. A steaming-hot cook, jacket off, rubbing freezer snow on his chest. Cross-legged on the floor with a beatific smile – a waitress meditating. And, shouting for help – a kitchen-hand, stuck head-first behind a freezer

while trying to retrieve a dropped prawn.

A Melbourne autumn kicked in. The trees shed their leaves and chilly winds blew them down the city canyons. I bought winter clothes for the very first time, groovy jackets and boots that I styled around in.

At Ringos there was a new menu for the season and it had an Australian Bush Tucker theme. I made a rich nutty soup from Witchetty Grubs (the fat larvae of the cossid moth) and individual Kangaroo Wellingtons – using Slippery Jack mushrooms in the duxelles filling. Other dishes included Emu steaks with a Pepper Berry crust and Barramundi cooked in paperbark and Lemon Myrtle. The cold larder made desserts like Davidson Plum ice cream and Wattleseed panna cotta.

This was all pretty hip for the time and proved to be a hit with the customers. Michael's menu garnered some good reviews and management showered him, and by extension us, with praise.

Being part of a happening team was pretty cool

but the smouldering negative energy between Lyle and Chris now threatened to set the kitchen on fire.

The crew formed into two sides. Some of the boys liked Chris, as he didn't ride shotgun over them like straight old-school Lyle did. A couple of them, Boz and Scotty, along with some rascal waiters, were part of Chris's party gang. At the end of an evening shift this righteous crew would assemble, flipping a pre-rolled joint into the air and laughing loudly in anticipation of their night's adventures in excess.

In the other corner were those who either liked Lyle or disliked Chris for his cowboy style. Cambo, still mentally scarred by the yabbies, was on this team and he would run to Lyle with any perceived slight or error. Mary and The Fly were definitely in the pro-Lyle camp and they resolutely ignored Chris. This made him blink rapidly and turned his face red. Izzy looked bewildered, but was savvy enough to keep quiet. Like me, he kept his head down; not joining in the digs and giggles made at Auntie Lyle's expense and pretending not to hear Cambo's accusatory whispers and The Fly's outraged buzzing.

Ringos was my first real taste of the politics that can occur in kitchens, usually big ones, and I clearly saw what a waste of valuable psychic energy it all was.

In siding with their respective champions, the kitchen crew at Ringos were coming dangerously close to derailing the once smooth operation of the kitchen.

Communication between the chefs, cooks and waiters on the opposing sides began to suffer and little mistakes became points to be scornfully scored.

A rude and anatomically improbable drawing of Lyle appeared on the white board. One of Scotty's chef's knives vanished; according to him – stolen. Chris grew cockier but Lyle remained as inscrutable as ever. The usual kitchen chatter became shrill at times then quickly faded into foreboding silence. It felt like we were all walking on eggshells. I kept expecting Michael to step in, but Lyle was keen to swing the axe on his own.

One afternoon a newly arrived Lyle asked Chris into the small office at the back. The kitchen was full with chefs arriving and finishing up. Within a minute, the sound of Chris yelling drew everyone's attention. He stomped back into the kitchen, crimson-faced and swearing. He had just been fired, effective immediately.

Curious front-of-house staff peered through the pass. Izzy and the apprentices stood opened-mouthed as dismissed Chris vented his rage. Boz and Scotty stared sullenly, their knives poised over their chopping boards. In cold larder Mary clapped her hands in glee, yelling something out in Chinese, possibly rude and insulting. I was prepping for grill, and from behind me I could hear The Fly buzzing triumphantly.

Chris grabbed his street clothes and stormed out. I looked around to the office at the back of the kitchen.

There against the tiled back wall was the small crisp figure of Lyle, his chef's toque neat on his head; his hands behind his back. He saw me, winked, and then gestured for me to keep working. What a killer.

Months later I found out that Chris had received multiple warnings, twice by letter, about his slack work practices. He could have been fired quietly, upstairs in Michael's office, but Lyle wanted a public execution, something to go down in Ringos' lore. It was a clear warning to any other slack-arses in the kitchen that there was only one way to do things – the right way.

Ringos was my first big commercial kitchen, with a brigade and its politics. I was fortunate in having Lyle on my case in the beginning. He consolidated and built on everything I'd learnt from Terry. There had been many lessons but one of the most important ones I worked out for myself.

It started one morning after an unusually quiet day before. We had almost zero prep to do and Lyle appeared in his civvies and told me to change back into my street clothes. We then hopped into his car and drove out to a major food wholesaler.

Out of his chef's whites Lyle looked strange; kind of nondescript and his aura of cold command was totally absent. He joked with me and told me a bit about his wife and kids just like a normal guy would. He was happy not to be the Sous-chef for an hour or two.

Our destination was a giant warehouse complete with refrigerated and frozen food sections. Lyle was on a mission to check them out as possible suppliers for the restaurant.

Inside I goggled at all the food. There were great towers of tomato paste in jumbo-sized four-litre tins. Twenty-litre drums of oil filled a whole warehouse bay. Cooking wine was in twenty-litre casks and in the chiller rooms - twenty-five kilo blocks of butter reached to the roof.

Fully kitted up like Antarctic explorers, in boots and hooded freezer jackets, Lyle and I checked out the giant walk-in freezers. Inside was food to feed armies. Drums of ice cream and cases of french-fries were stacked up to the rafters. Flocks of turkeys and chickens roosted on frosty shelves. Box after box of pastry, pies, cheesecakes and pre-cut vegetables lined the frozen aisles.

Shedding our polar gear, we made another epic journey through two mega-sized meat-chiller rooms that were full of thousands of vacuum-sealed clear plastic packets. In cuts, dices and minces was every sort of meat imaginable. Sausages packed by the hundreds, lamb racks fifty to a case; maybe even rumps of emu and camel for our Bush Tucker menu.

Then I saw pallets stacked with cases of pre-cut T-bone and rump steaks – strapped down and ready to be fork-lifted into refrigerated delivery trucks. I was amazed. This was provisions in gargantuan portions; an abundance of food that was staggering. Then it hit me.

Food on this large scale held a real danger for cooking professionals. While repeatedly ordering, then processing food, putting it into multiple containers and then endlessly duplicating preparation, cooking and serving processes, I could see I easily risked a kind of subjective numbness. Instead of being wonderfully sensual, all this food could easily become just product. Superbly flavoursome ingredients like delicate shiitake mushrooms, ruby red kangaroo fillets, coddled duck eggs or freshly grated nutmeg would just coldly register as parts in a chase for profits; mere items in a prep-list of tasks to scramble through in a shift.

The machine crushes the artist when the cook turns hack or ham. Industry beats magic when a once enthusiastic and interested crew become the culinary equivalent of a tired covers-band churning out soulless pap. This was the rub – how could I work with food in industrial quantities and yet not become inured to its sublime magic. This was a battle I fought, and usually won, in the years to come.

Bottom End Grunt

It's a Tuesday night at Ringos and it's going to be quiet. The big crowds don't really hit us until the later part of the week and it's been rainy and cold the last few days. Tonight's forecast is no different, so it's time to get ahead with the prep. There's just three of us on – Lyle, Meli the kitchen hand and myself. Mitch is on holiday, so I'm doing some of his shifts, working without days off and I'm now on day eleven. I'm feeling pretty knackered but I know I'll be fine. The apprentice is off sick and Lyle has decided not to get anyone else in.

He's going to clean and marinate beef, lamb and chicken and then get onto making some sauces. Meli is filling buckets with peeled onions and will soon process bags of garlic. Then he'll find some cleaning job to do. I'm going to cook for whatever customers come in and turn a few kilos of root vegetables in between. We might do fifty covers tonight at best.

Come 7 pm and Lyle goes out to the back cold room looking for some more sirloin to clean. Then the docket machine clatters - a table for eight. I'll need help to dish their mains up. I start on their entrees and the docket machine goes again. Cool - a table for six and a table of four. Then the docket machine chatters again and again and a waiter appears at the pass. "Chef, it's filling up! I don't know where they're coming from but they're pouring in."

Lyle returns, sees the orders on the rack and we smile, pleased that the night is turning out a little busier than expected. He puts his prep away and grabs his duplicate dockets from the printer at cold larder. I'm doing the grill and seafood, he's doing the pans and cold larder, and we'll share the hot and cold entrees.

I scan through my dockets looking for the same items. Twelve Orange Roughy have been ordered across five tables. I get them out, season and butter them ready for sealing. I grab out serves of steak and lamb and put them near the grill to warm up. Lyle and I go hard on the entrees for six tables. Dumplings go into steamers, prawns wrapped in twirls of seasoned noodles hiss and bubble in the fryer's hot oil. Mayonnaises, dressings and vinaigrettes squirt from squeezy bottles.

The docket machine chatters. I ignore it, intent on the first wave of entrees. They hit the pass and ding-ding! – the bell gets a good double tap. Now I tear off the new orders; rack them and read them. Another four tables, one with nine covers. As I'm reading, the docket machine rattles again. It's busy now!

I become a super-slick robot turning on a dime, wasting not an iota of movement, in and out of the reach-ins and instead of getting individual serves of rice, potatoes and vegetables I grab the tubs out. It's time for bulk food and I rush it into the appropriate areas ready for cooking. Lyle counts the pasta mains and there's a lot. He calls for Meli to get another pot of hot water on for dunking the pre-cooked pasta. I grab pots, wack them on the grill plate, and quickly fill them with multiple serves of the most popular sauces.

More entrees get plated up and sent on their way. The docket machine rattles away and I take precious seconds in putting up a good handful of dockets and reading them. Yowsah – there are over seventy meals now and it's going to be a log jam with so many at the same time. A few people will have a wait but if we can get the entrees out fast it won't be so bad.

The new orders run through my mind even as I work on entrees, putting dumplings and prawns onto plates. Lyle finishes his entrees – carefully composed veggie stacks, slices of duck terrine, a few bowls of papaya gazpacho and up they all go. Ding-ding!

Two harassed looking waiters appear at the pass, grab the entrees and tell us that there's at least eight tables yet to order, dozens of people at the bar and more customers coming in! Lyle and I exchange glances. This is hardcore. We are snowed under with what's already been ordered and it's still ramping up.

Every single minute for the next two hours or so is going to be crammed to capacity. And then some. We will not have the time to think or consider. We'll be in a pure existential space where instinct and training, habit and ritual are all.

The orders keep coming and Lyle and I whirl and spin between the reach-ins and the line. Doing a dozen different things every minute, we cook food en masse – three, five, nine serves at a time. I'm putting a tray of sealed fish into the oven without even reading the orders – I know they're going to be eaten. The salad leaves for entrees are all gone now and Meli runs fresh boxes from the back cold room and rapidly washes and spins them dry.

A vinaigrette runs out and Lyle somehow collects the ingredients and makes more. He stops in mid-whisk and scoots over to toss each of the eight pan dishes he's got going. He gets Meli onto the line with us, shows him how to dunk and drain serves of pasta. Meli is fast and neat and I blurt out praise. He grins uneasily.

A minute later, Meli knocks three bowls of pasta off the edge of the stove to smash on the floor. Freezing in shock, he gives me a horrified look. I boot-scoot the pasta and crockery shards under the stove. Meli looks like he's about to run back to the safety of the wet area so I put on a silly posh accent – "Three new spaghetti for Signore Lyle please Signore Meli."

He smiles with relief and does the pastas again.

I'm cooking thirty plus mains at a time now, the salamanders flaring and crackling and the grill sizzling, while simultaneously setting up plates for hot entrees and small tables of mains. Plates rattle out of stacks. Boots squeak on tiles. There's no talk – just occasional bursts of raw information. "Table nine is ready!" "Table twenty's Roughy up!" Or terse requests and enquiries. "Meli – fettuccine for three please." "Table three mains? Ready?"

We're putting up three or four tables at a time but orders are still curling out of the machine. My heart sinks when a waiter comes back in with three steaks I've just sent out.

"You got the sauces wrong," I get told. I find the order on the spike and – damn, I have too. I cast a guilty look Lyle's way but even though he heard he doesn't look up. I take the steaks, noting how each one is cooked, wash the sauce off them in the hand sink and place them back on the grill. I garnish three new plates, turn the steaks over and after I put the accompaniments on each plate, I add the steaks and apply the correct sauces. Ding-ding!

They're away. I look over at Lyle and he raises his eyebrows – are the re-done meals good? I flash a thumbs up and get a nod in return.

We press on in manic tight rhythms and the docket machine clatters long enough for me to know a really big table has ordered. I tear it off and there's nineteen covers on it. I rapidly calculate what I'll have to grab out of the reach-ins. Bloody hell - I'm going to run out of some food. The normal Tuesday night prep is being gobbled up. I need to start counting everything ordered from now on so I can warn front-of-house.

I get Meli doing all the vegetables now. Like with the pasta he's a quick learn, dolloping different kinds of mash onto plates, blanching asparagus and beans. He's a mensch – saving our arses big time. I flick a look at the clock and it's a shock to see it's after nine o'clock. This wave has been breaking over us for nearly two hours!

The prep containers begin to empty. I run out of garnishes, lamb and dumplings, and quickly inform front of house. Lyle also says that we can only do two of the desserts tonight – the ones that require minimal effort. The duty manager totally understands; they are being rocked out the front too. Luckily, few desserts are being ordered.

Eventually we get all the meals on the big table assembled and dispatched. The pace slackens and then dies right off. Lyle riffles through the dockets and pulls an impressed face. Two hundred and seventeen covers. That's a record for a Tuesday night. Aside from running out of a couple of dishes, and one easily placated steak and sauce mix-up, everything has gone pretty well.

We take a break, have some cold drinks and Lyle half jokes that he wants Meli as a chef when it's busy.

GAWAIN BARKER

Meli half jokes that Lyle has to buy him a few beers.

Then we see the immense pile of dirty pots and plates in the wet area. Lyle sighs. He wants to get home to his family, but after Meli's sterling effort there's no way he's not going to help. Leaving me to clean up the kitchen, Lyle removes his toque and neckerchief, dons the big plastic dish pig apron and snaps on some rubber gloves. It takes another two hours of work before he gets to go home.

A service that busy would normally require three chefs, two apprentices and a kitchen hand as good as Meli. Being understaffed under pressure is a real test of a cooking professional's mettle. When a crew keep their calm and help each other, the impossible becomes do-able and the insurmountable conquered. This is Bottom End Grunt.

Bottom End Grunt is not the sound of flatulence, and it's not a term referring to some poor schlepper at the lowest level of the kitchen food chain either. It's mostly a wonderful thing, a compliment for those who possess stamina, both physical and mental, and who also exhibit grace under pressure. But before the Grunt can kick in, there's a whole skill-set that good cooking professionals must already have.

Firstly, every chef, cook and apprentice needs a good short-term memory. Learning a lot of stuff over a

82

long period of time is good, but you must be able to remember a lot more stuff for a short period of time. A good operator can keep track of thirty meals at a time, like an air-traffic controller fixated on multiple airplane paths. As soon as a plane's landed – it's forgotten about. Just like a table of orders going out the kitchen door.

A good memory is not the only fundamental. You must also mentally organise and sequence a huge array of actions at great speed. You must work out in what order you are going to perform all the actions necessary to get each one of the thirty meals finished. Trickier still, is that this mental organising must be fluid, as there is no absolute set order and timing in cooking the meals. You must operate with constantly changing priorities, and coordinate with others to dish up all the meals on a table at the same time. You have to choose when to start processes or when to slow them down – and then be able to change these decisions minute by minute.

Then these thought-out and constantly mutating courses of action must also be physically performed at great speed. Your sense of time and motion is in top gear; your hand-eye co-ordination becomes paramount and the correct judgement of spatial/time relationships is crucial.

Over time, this ability to move and think fast, continuously evaluating a huge range of changing details and instantly coming up with the best solutions, becomes the next core skill of the cooking pro.

So far so good, but this stream of intellectual and physical tasks, though performed simultaneously, are often quite unrelated to each other. While you are doing *this,* you are actually thinking about *that.* You have to be thinking about the next sequence of things you're going to do while you do the things you've already thought about. You have to split your mind into many different streams of thought. It's controlled dislocation of a high order and produces stress levels that can mess people up, causing serious problems like insomnia and drug addiction.

If you can master all of these things and stay cool, you'll get to a strange but calm place. Even though your mind is fragmented with many trains of thought, and even as you move as fast as an athlete, you will find yourself thinking about a song you heard today. Or you'll notice there's a small piece of paint peeling up there on the kitchen roof. How the hell you find time to think about this kind of stuff is some kind of Zen mystery to me.

But what truly separates the masters from the grasshoppers is to stop thinking about the song or the peeling paint up there. Instead take that extra, almost supernatural awareness, and redirect it with love at the food and at your workmates. This is no hippy trippy bullshit. This is hard-earned knowledge from a sharp-edged world of stainless steel and fire. This isn't next level – this is THE level.

So, with that sorted out, imagine you've worked eleven days straight and those days have all been twelve or fourteen hours long. You're weary and frazzled and on that quiet night when the team is already one person down – you get slammed. You make great food and you don't burn or cut yourself, or spill or break anything. Then someone like Meli, under the same pressure as yourself, makes an honest mistake. They expect you to cuss and shout but instead you make them smile. And like Lyle, even when your day is done, you still chip in for another two hours to help a team-mate. This is Bottom End Grunt.

Spending long hours in a hot and stressful room demands not just one's culinary skills. The best crews forgive the cock-ups and spin-outs, as long as they are rare, and from this mutual support an iron-clad ethos is forged – we are all in this frickin' madhouse together.

Now the crazy whirl of hectic services and under-the-gun prep sessions can be harmoniously overcome. The non-stop adversity breeds real camaraderie and a collective pride rears its golden head. This group morale is the natural place for Bottom End Grunt to flourish.

But what can really affect a cook's physical and mental abilities, and test their Bottom End Grunt, are the hours. Fifty to seventy hours a week is often the norm and I've done many weeks of ninety to hundred plus hours. There are several reasons for this insanity.

The oldest one is the traditional militant style of kitchen with the brigades and titled positions. Gruelling hours create the talent to advance through the ranks, and this competitive system means constantly proving your toughness and commitment by doing the hard yards.

A real big reason for doing mad hours is that cooks and chefs are chasing the magic that they know is there. That's the passion we hear so much about. They'll come in early and stay late; take on extra shifts and days. They obsess over the food and the reputation of where they work.

Then there are some mean employers who wring every last bit of work out of anyone on a salary, under-staffing shifts whenever they can. Any objections are greeted with procrastinatory bullshit or threats of the sack.

Or sometimes it's hard to get on short notice crew who can do the job. At a resort in the Northern Territory of Australia I was already doing ten-hour shifts when the breakfast cook did a runner. I put my hand up for the breakfast shift, the 5.30 am start adding another five hours to my day. I'd surface in the dark at 5.00 am and be at work within thirty minutes. I got my half hour break after lunch but by 8.30 in the evening, right in the middle of service, I'd feel a bit rugged.

After twelve hard hours in the kitchen this level of tiredness is comparable to having a few drinks in you.

Every hour after that gets you more drunk. I've worked many twelve, fifteen and even eighteen-hour days – often straight through. Law dictates half-hour breaks taken every four hours, so these long shifts are illegal, but very common in the industry. Then there was the twenty-eight-hour day.

It was a catering job for a luxury European car company; a picnic-hamper style lunch for 1200 people. The event was at a vineyard forty kilometres out of town. The day before the lunch I started at 7.30 am in the catering kitchen and by late afternoon I was part of the first shift out at the vineyard – assembling eight food items to go into each one of 1200 hampers. We worked through the night and took a half-hour break at dawn. It really took some effort to get back up on our feet again.

At 9 am the next wave of chefs turned up. Around 10 am helicopters bringing VIP guests began arriving, touching down on a helipad among the grape vines. We worked another hour and a half and by then we were played out. The boss thanked us and told us to vamoose. I got a lift back with a colleague who dropped me off in the city at about 1 p.m. I stood there numbly in the hot sunlight like a chunk of weathered stone, ears buzzing, eyes gritty. I got a cab home and slept for 10 solid hours.

Years later I told a young chef about that long day and he was shocked.

"Twenty-eight hours?!" he freaked "Did you owe someone money? Was it a drug dealer?"

He was even more shocked when I told him that I did it because the other chefs did. It was a dare, a bit of a lark. It's how the old school roll.

Working seventy hours in a five-day week is hard work but many chefs don't work five-day weeks. Some owner-chefs don't take days off. I've worked twenty plus days in a row many times and on one occasion thirty-one days in a row. On my day off I was totally at a loss as to what to do with myself. This was at the remote Northern Territory resort so I had nowhere to go and no one to see. I slept in, which was nice, had a slow breakfast and went for a swim. I watched a movie, went for a walk and, damn it, if I didn't pop into the kitchen to see how the crew were doing!

All this work should guarantee a good night's rest but the hours of being in a maximum state of alertness can wreak havoc with sleeping. It might take several hours after work to calm down enough to crash out. But when your mind won't turn off it's a waking nightmare. Praying for sleep to come, you sneak a peek at your watch. It's 2.30 am! You start in three hours and need to be sharp for a fifteen-hour day. This is truly mind-warping stuff.

Many need help in the form of alcohol and drugs to switch off, and getting loaded with your co-workers is very common and in some kitchens – expected.

At my very worst (or was it my very best) I had a Monday to Friday job comprising 7 am til 7 pm shifts.

Many Tuesday, Wednesday and Thursday nights I'd go out dancing in clubs and necking tabs of E with the crew, coming home around 2 am. I'd lay in bed buzzing like a forgotten vibrator for a few hours, fooling myself that I was getting some sleep. Then I'd jump up and leave for work at 5 .30 am. On Friday nights I'd really let my hair down - partying past dawn. Thank God for weekends off to actually sleep.

Sometimes sleep doesn't provide rest and a chef, finally home and asleep in bed, can be plating up meals in their dreams, fretting over table numbers and side-orders. Or they sit bolt upright in the wee small hours trying to remember if they rang through the seafood order or turned off the gas.

The repetition of long prep jobs can also disturb your dreams. At one kitchen, along with another chef, I had to completely bone out a hundred and twenty fresh chickens twice a week. As the time went by, the same movements were repeated again and again. We worked quickly, and also very carefully, as the boning knives were razor sharp. This tension between speed and care must have put the zap on my subconscious while I slept.

One night I woke in a cold sweat, most unnerved by the vivid imagery of my dream. In it, I was neatly boning out my left hand – slitting my fingers and thumb open to pull off the flesh in one perfect piece.

Another big part of Bottom End Grunt is dealing with physical pain. A cut or a burn usually isn't enough to send you home, but every time you knock the injury it hurts. Heat from the grills and ovens also make it hurt. Pain becomes an unwelcome offsider on your shift. Working long consecutive days means your hands heal slowly and you go to sleep in pain and wake up in pain. It takes Bottom End Grunt to peel kilos of prawns or juice bags of lemons when your hands are like this. It's also a great incentive not to cut or burn yourself.

Bottom End Grunt reaches its apogee when chefs hurt themselves badly enough to get medical treatment and then are back at their station the next shift. Or within the next hour.

I was walking down the street returning from my break when I saw the Head Chef running towards me, his face as white as his jacket. He was clutching his left forearm, the blood spurting from it pulsing in time with his heart-beat. He saw me and yelled for me to run with him to the doctor's surgery just up the road.

Soon Chef was getting the deep gash in his arm stitched up. He'd sliced through a vein and muscle, helping front of house trim up some bamboo for a band-stand decoration. With lots of bookings I felt dread at losing him. But when all stitched up, he took a short break and then, like a legend, worked the busy service with me.

A major component of the Bottom End Grunt is keeping one's cool. Instead of punching a hole in the wall or slamming down a pot at their own stupid mistake, the calm cook fixes the problem and gets on with it. Instead of giving someone a chewing-out and putting them down like the lazy peck of poo that they are, the true purveyor of Grunt takes it in their stride. They understand a universal truth; getting angry does not help anyone – it only makes a hard scene worse.

This cool contains patience, and more precisely, the spirit in which this patience is practiced. We're talking about fortitude not sufferance, grit cut through with humility. It's the patience of calm dispassion but underpinned with real heart and soul.

A surly, slow or stressed-out team mate can ruin your shift if you allow them to. Instead of concentrating on the food you'll be getting distracted by the whys and hows of their displeasure or ineptitude. Be patient with the bloody fool. If it doesn't calm them, no matter – it will calm you. This patience is the vital lubricant in creating slick co-operation in the kitchen.

Patience is a balm for stress and, surprisingly enough – boredom. While doing the same thing for hours – say making hundreds of crepes – keeping one's mind occupied becomes a challenge. Kitchen crew deal with the boredom in different ways.

Chatting is popular. Mostly I don't, but some crew talk and talk and talk. Some kitchens don't allow idle talk at all, which isn't such a bad thing. Good crews prep in a companionable silence, occasionally broken by pertinent food, kitchen or menu observations, or by brief recommendations of new books, movies or music. The verbal noise level of a kitchen crew is often a good indication as to how good they really are.

In the best kitchens Bottom End Grunt, though unwritten on your resume, is expected. The laissez-faire of good kitchen crews comes from many shifts of not just physical and mental effort, but also real emotional support. Everyone becomes an expert in respect.

This steely resilience however, has a dark side. It's a weird machismo, or is it masochism, that cooks and chefs of both sexes practice. The natural pride in one's skills and abilities becomes morbidly competitive and your sense of duty to the team turns neurotic. The unwritten code of honour that is Bottom End Grunt becomes dangerously twisted.

The self-esteem that compels cooks and chefs to work long hours will also make them put up with the pain of injuries while working. They won't stop when hurt and often have an irrational fear of taking a sick-day, even if they really do need it. It's as though their kitchen and crew will not function properly or cope if they are absent. It's a psychosis and it's very common.

Then beyond the pathetic deficiencies of their feeble bodies are those moments when a cook reads an order wrong or screws up a meal. This mistake may not elicit an angry or scornful response from their mates on the line, but the cook will feel like it should have. Busy services with their super-charged blend of adrenaline highs and stressed-out lows have bonded the cook with their workmates. They'd rather get crucified or skinned alive than let the team down.

These cooks now develop a real phobia of failure, both personally and in a team context. It grows into a nagging fear of not keeping up mentally and physically. They obsessively strive to always match everyone else's pace and commitment. If their colleagues can do it then they must do it too.

And guess what? This driven cook's workmates feel the exact same way and, unconsciously or not, they all egg each other on to deeper and darker levels of the Grunt.

Sick, hurt, tired and stressed – they sail ever on into the maelstrom together. It's no surprise then, that many chefs and cooks suffer from depression – feeling guilt and anger for being mentally and physically weak, while also being poisoned by the fear of letting the team down.

Bottom End Grunt gone bad is a soul crusher. Hard-earned reputations devolve into high-pressure burdens. Workloads and expectations get ever higher as bodies and minds grow ever wearier. This self-inflicted worry and stress has driven unknown youngsters and famous veterans alike – to take their own lives.

And there is always the danger of the hard-earned communal confidence of Bottom End Grunt degenerating into mob egoism. Feeling pride is great but you want moxie without arrogance; guts unglorified. When a team falls into hubris and then disappears up its own collective arse, then it becomes much easier to worry about being part of the gang than about what you are actually doing. Bad habits become ingrained and new ideas are dismissed out of hand. Counterproductive 'us versus them' scenarios are played out, and cold room bullies lay down the law.

When the Bottom End Grunt is good then that's where you want to be. In many cooking agency jobs, I've turned up wondering what the hell to expect. Walking in for the first time with my antenna attuned, I'm hoping for the best. If you're living in the town or city where the job is, then it's not too hard to do one shift and not go back if it's horrendous. The agency won't be happy, but because you don't do this often, they'll understand and get you another job. If you commit to a remote job with air-fares paid and accommodation arranged then it's way more problematic to do a runner.

The first season I worked at the Northern Territory resort was on a four-month contract. It took a plane flight, an overnight stay in Darwin and a four-hour bus ride to get there. As the coach sped through the red landscape, I steeled myself for the possibility of a dysfunctional Head Chef and feral crew, probably hard drinkers who didn't mind a punch-on.

On arrival I put my bags in my cabin and went over to the kitchen to introduce myself. I paused at the screen door and looked in. It was a large kitchen and I could see just two chefs and a kitchen hand prepping busily and without chatter. Then the kitchen hand who looked like a boxer (he'd been a boxer) said something. They all burst into laughter – then silence returned.

I went in and the place looked tidy; the floors and benches spick and span. Nobody appeared to look up from their work but I knew they were checking me out. I saw the Head Chef in an office nook and went over. He was a small, wiry dude with old school tattoos on his forearms. I introduced myself and he shook my hand firmly. His brown eyes were alert and he kept smiling and raising his eyebrows in apparent delight as I told him about myself.

In soft, almost apologetic tones, he confirmed that I had agreed to do long shifts and work extra days when needed. He then explained the set-up and I was surprised to hear there were only four chefs employed at the resort's one hundred and sixty seat a-la-carte restaurant. I surmised that they must be well organised – and also work bloody hard.

At this point one of the chefs came in and his uniform was spotless. Chef introduced him, and he too was soft-spoken with a real smile and handshake. Then the ex-boxer rocked in and laid a huge arm around Chef's shoulder, boomed a cheery hello and grinned at me like the big lug I soon found out he was. The three men stood there smiling at me in welcome and I began to relax.

I was getting the vibe now. I'd come a long way, and was going to be doing some serious hours, but I'd seen enough to pick this crew. I'd scored. It was going to be alright, because I could tell, even without working an hour with them, that these lads had Bottom End Grunt.

A Million Miles from Anywhere

It was just after seven on a beautiful balmy night and through the insect–screened windows of the kitchen came the distinctive sound of a Boo-Book owl hunting for its dinner. Down on Orchid Beach it was high tide and I could hear the waves crashing on the sand.

I'm doing the dinner service at a small resort on a remote tropical island. The fish mains I'm about to plate up had been caught with my own hands that morning. Every day I designed a new menu for the guests. I was Lucky Hunter and Good Cook rolled into one. I had the best job in the world.

I was cruising along, happy as can be, when Jane my waitress walked through the little kitchen with some finished entree plates. "Table one's mains away," she said, going around the corner to the wash-up area.

There was just two of us working, as the resort accommodation was capped at thirty guests and tonight it was wasn't even half-full.

As I dished up a couple of nice serves of seared Golden Trevally, I heard Jane squeak in shock. She came back into the kitchen giggling nervously.

"Ah Chef, there's a little problem out here."

"Yep no worries. Here's table four's mains," I said. Jane picked up the plates with a huge grin of anticipation on her face.

"What?" I inquired, grinning back. "What?"

"Go and see," she smirked, and went out into the dining room. I took a peek in the oven at some mains that were coming to fruition and then went out to the wash-up area to investigate. I saw the problem straight away.

Sitting upright in the rubbish bin, eating scraps hand to mouth, was a lizard. A very big lizard. Known as a Goanna, this thing was nearly two metres in length and had ten-centimetre-long claws that could rip my face off. As a bonus bowel-loosener the Goanna's bite is poisonous and any wound it inflicted wouldn't stop bleeding.

I now saw a hole had been pushed through the insect screen on the open back door. This kind of break and enter had never happened before and I stood there feeling very nonplussed. Most unconcerned, the saurian munched away while giving me the old lizard eye.

Jane came back, stood behind me and peered over my shoulder. "So – what's the standard kitchen procedure for this?" she said.

We laughed nervously but I had to do something. This beast couldn't be left to roam unchecked around the kitchen, but I had tables of food on the go. I stepped forward and whacked the lizard on the nose with my tea towel, thinking it might turn tail and leave. There was a screechy hiss and I leapt backwards as an outspread claw whipped past my face. Whoaah – I nearly lost my nose! The lizard flicked its forked tongue at me and then peered down into the bin looking for more food. Jane and I weren't laughing now.

"Ri-ght," I said through clenched teeth, "I've got to dish up table eight."

"Yep," Jane agreed.

We hurried back into the kitchen and quickly got table eight's food out to them. Now I had to come up with a plan to see Godzilla off.

Jane watched as I grabbed a big pot, stuck it in the kitchen sink and started filling it with water.

"Close the door to the dining room," I said. Jane did and began oooo-ing as she saw what I was going to do. When the pot was half full, I took it out the back. Jane flitted behind me.

"Watch out," I warned her. "It might run at you."

Jane's oooohhhh-ing got louder as I went up to the Goanna, who began eyeing the pot with interest. Up as close as I dared – I emptied the water onto it. There was an explosion of rubbish, lizard and bin and Jane and I dashed back into the kitchen. We heard the loud skittering of claws on the floor, a big tearing sound and then silence.

We snuck back to the wash-up area and peeked around the corner. The bin lay on its side and rubbish was scattered everywhere. The lizard was gone; the fly-screen door quivering with the whole bottom half now torn out.

"OK. I'm going do tables six and one now," I said.

Jane smiled kindly. "I'll get you a nice drinky while you dish up."

After eighteen months working at Ringos I felt the beauty and wildness of North Queensland exerting its magnetic pull on me. Everyone was sorry to see me go and Lyle even looked a little sad.

I returned to Frogs Restaurant and after a busy year there with Terry, I scored a job as Sous-chef at the exclusive Hinchinbrook Island Resort. Here I began an adventure where things like giant marauding lizards became routine.

Goannas wandered around unmolested because they were protected. Hinchinbrook Island is a national park of forty thousand square hectares. Rugged rain-forest mountains push out granite rock formations into the sea, and with remote beaches, mangrove swamps and bays teeming with big crocodiles and dugongs, the island is a vision of primordial grandeur.

Cut off from the mainland for 100,000 years, the whole island had remained, outside of the resort and a bit of logging, pristine and primeval. It had a Jurassic-era atmosphere and everything, from the trees to the lizards to the insects, was out-sized. It really was The Land That Time Forgot.

The mainland was forty-five minutes away by fast boat, but it seemed a lot further. At dawn the jagged green mountains were engulfed in mist, the valleys and swamps lost in thick white cloud and you could feel the insignificance of time. Aside from the few hectares of single-story resort buildings, and a shed and water-tank on one beach, there were no other man-made structures on the island. No roads, no fishing shacks, no jetties. King Kong would have been right at home there. Living on Hinchinbrook felt like being a million miles from anywhere.

The resort had only twelve staff – with three of us cooking. I worked on my own, as did the Head Chef Steve. At first, we both helped the apprentice Mikey on his shifts but he got real good real fast and was soon doing breakfasts and lunches solo.

The resort, on the very tip of Cape Richards, was twenty-kilometres from the mainland. Food supplies came on an old barge once a week and I got canny planning my menus. Menu items on the last two days before replenishment would be ones that contained the fresh ingredients with the most longevity.

When the weather turned bad, with rough seas, or approaching cyclones, the barge couldn't make its run. We'd top up the fresh food, bread and dairy by utilizing the high-powered boats that brought the guests to the island. Their twin two hundred and fifty horsepower motors busted through the high seas, and boxes of fruit and veggies and crates of milk arrived dripping with sea spray.

The Head Chef Steve had been on the island for some years and he had the suppliers and produce lines down pat. With guidance from him I rapidly worked out how to order for my menus. A monster diesel generator tucked away behind a small hill provided the resort's electricity, but there wasn't much refrigeration space. Precision was needed with the amount of stock ordered, but sometimes last-minute bookings would swell guest numbers. It was a constant juggle but I managed not to drop any balls.

This remoteness taught me to be frugal. I learned to love every onion and drop of oil. Celery bunch ends and carrot tops were gratefully fed to the stock pot. It was a joy to fill a chest freezer to the brim and make use of every last kilojoule of electricity.

When there was food-waste, we'd take it to our living garbage disposal unit. It was illegal to feed the animals, but lurking by the jetty was George, an affable Queensland Grouper of colossal size, and we made an exception for him. He must have weighed two hundred kilos. His giant mouth would open like a door and with one swallow he'd suck our offerings down his gullet. I swear he'd wink at me as he consumed his meal.

The resort had no phones or TVs in the rooms, no games or organized activities. That suited the guests as they fell into two basic categories. The first wanted to sleep, swim, sun-bathe, eat, drink and do whatever it was they did in their cabins. This was not always what you thought. One quiet chap on his own had lots of expensive women's lingerie hanging up to dry in his cabin.

The second type of guest wasted not one second of their stay laying around or dressing up. Equipped with hiking boots, cameras, and all manner of bush-walking paraphernalia they headed off after breakfast, eager to see as many species of creature as they could. And were they in the right place!

Animals crawled, jumped, climbed, flew and swam everywhere. One day it was whales off the Cape, the pod swimming along in a protective ring of spouts around a frolicking calf. The next day, a five-meter-long Amethystine python snoozing in the sun near the kitchen. Wallabies hopped along Orchid Beach while fishing eagles circled overhead. Down at the boat jetty on dusk, dolphins leapt postcard perfect against the pink and orange sky. At night incredible pieces of jewellery fell dazed onto the candle-lit restaurant tables – then crawled away as beetles. It sure felt like the animals ran the joint.

Most of the them were quite unafraid of humans and ignored us, but some could be a bit tricky – like the Goannas. During the day they would attempt to slip into the kitchen or wash-up area looking for food. These cunning creatures moved incrementally, like a reptilian tide coming in. Long periods of innocent silence would be occasionally broken by the rasp of claws and slither of long tails.

One afternoon Steve nipped back to his cabin for a minute. In the oven a couple of roasts were cooking away. When Steve returned, he roared with anger. A Goanna was running out of the kitchen with a leg of beef in its mouth! Attracted by the lovely smell, the cheeky lizard had prised open the hot oven door and hooked out a nice takeaway. Poor Steve had to wipe up all the spilled fat and work out a substitute.

The Goannas could get mean during their egg-hatching season. One morning after my dawn swim, I wandered in for my breakfast/lunch shift. Strolling towards the kitchen I saw something move under the steps of the entrance.

Like many tropical buildings, the kitchen was built above the ground, and from the shadows beneath something slowly emerged. Ah – a big sleepy looking Goanna. It had probably just woken up.

Then it leapt up on its hind legs and ran at me. My guts did a triple back flip; my hair stood on end. This was the xenomorph from Alien! The Goanna's head was at chest height and its extended front legs, tipped with those razor-sharp claws, slashed through the air at eye level. As well as sprinting towards me, it was hissing like a burst steam pipe. I spun around and bolted, with my bum and legs cringing at the expected rip of claws, and though the staff deck was a hundred and fifty meters away – I reckon I got there in ten seconds. I flew up the stairs, fearfully looked back, and was extremely relieved to see that the sandy track back to the resort was empty.

I cautiously crept back. Under the stairs, hissing, and giving me a 'I'm-gonna-kill-your-human-arse' stare was the Goanna. I guessed it was a female that had laid her eggs there. We closed the door (from the inside) and put Day-Glo green tape up around it. The staff and guests were told to give the area a wide berth and fortunately no-one got slashed open or suffered heart failure. Eventually the bubby lizards arrived and we could re-open the door.

The cold-blooded lizards loved laying in the sun like the guests. Most afternoons the deserted two-floor staff accommodation deck hosted Goannas drowsing on the sunlit ground-floor passageways. Returning staff would roust them by stamping on the wooden deck and the startled lizards would vamoose, leaping metres to the ground or dashing down the back stairs.

One day, Donnie the barman and I returned from our breakfast/lunch shift. The usual mob of scaly layabouts was on the staff deck catching rays, but at the open door of Mikey the apprentice's room was a large Goanna looking interested in going in. Donnie and I wordlessly had the same idea. We grabbed a big piece of plywood and using it as a protective barrier, inched in towards the unsuspecting lizard. In a final rush we corralled it into Mikey's room and closed the door. Yes, we had just broken all kinds of laws regarding animals in national parks, but we hadn't hurt the Goanna and we knew it wouldn't be there long. Sure enough Mikey rocked up and we hid where we could watch the show.

The lad opened his door and went in. Donnie and I looked at each other with open mouthed glee. There was a shocked yell and the Goanna ran out and down the steps at top speed. A flushed and wide-eyed Mikey appeared at the doorway to be greeted by our cheers of delight. High on adrenaline, he happily swore at us before joining in the laughter. He wasn't angry because he recognized the mighty prank we had pulled. Besides, if the shoe had been on the other foot, he sure as hell would have done it to us.

The lizards mainly kept to themselves, but the rats were bastards. They were actually native Australian marsupial rodents – giant, weighing a kilo or more, with a long finely scaled white tail. With stolid logic the first Europeans called them Giant White-Tailed Rats.

Guests would appear at the bar or office in terrorized fear. They'd spotted a giant rat! Just huge! We would sympathetically nod our heads. It's in my room! It wouldn't run! It's still there! We'd get them a drink and go find Ellis the yardie. He'd don long pants, boots and gloves, and grab a big rake before entering the violated cabin. This battle gear was because the White Tails didn't back down – and they had teeth like razor-sharp chisels. An awful growling would issue from the cabin before Ellis, who had perfected this move, would corner and then flick the freaky beast out the door with the rake.

Like a gang of reverse Harry Houdinis, the White-Tails easily broke into any cabin they felt like. There was always one reason for these break-ins however; guests, though warned, had brought food into their cabins. So, you can imagine what the White-Tails thought of the kitchen.

It was supposedly animal proof but I was greeted early one morning by an appalling mess. The kitchen floor was ankle deep in debris and the shelves were swept clean. Jars were smashed, boxes torn apart and even tins had been split open! The White-Tails had popped in for a late supper.

After cleaning up, we combed the kitchen for their entry point, finally finding a hole in thick wood under the back stairs. It must have taken them a long time to gnaw through. We cut out the breached portion of plank and poured in cement, sandwiching it between two solid bits of wood. Sorted. Then a few months later those rotten bastards trashed the kitchen again. We checked the previous break-in spot and saw that they'd re-gnawed through the wood . . . and the concrete! This time we put a piece of steel mesh in, re-cemented and that finally kept them out.

Also resembling a rodent, was another problem animal – the Antechinus. These little marsupial critters would zip around hoping to sneak a meal on the fly. The Antechinus on Hinchinbrook were highly scansorial, meaning that they loved climbing, seemingly defying gravity as they ran up walls. Cakes, tarts and slices laid out on the side board for afternoon tea would attract the Antechinus, who, like fuzzy paratroopers, would drop out of the rafters with an audible plop. This noise would signal a watchful waitress to chase them away.

They were cheeky, running up the guests' legs and right onto the dining tables to see what the entree was. There were occasional screams but the guests were all very good about it. The fact that the Antechinus were 'native' and 'marsupial' made it all seem rather exotic and interesting – not dirty or unhygienic at all. Plus, we'd entertain them with the facts of their sexual life.

During mating season, the Antechinus males literally screw themselves to death, dying of the stress and exhaustion produced by fornicating with as many females as they can get their claws on. This cheery trick of Mother Nature means there's ample food for the pregnant females and the subsequent babies.

The Antechinus sexual frenzy has to be seen to be believed, as the tiny sex fiends keep running and jumping even as they repeatedly join together in congress. One night the dining room, thankfully nearly empty, was rushed by dozens of these frenzied root rats. All we could do was chase them away and hope our casual laughter would make the guests relax. One stunned American guest, brandy snifter in hand; his head whipping this way and that, repeatedly yelled, "Wow! Wow! Wow!"

Meeting the guests at the jetty as they arrived, knowing that they were absolutely gob-smacked by the wide-screen beauty around them, was a blast. We didn't actually put flower garlands around their necks and say "Welcome to paradise," but we greeted them with fresh fruit juice, ice-cold bubbly and warm smiles.

Most guests arrived by boat, but for those with the taste for it, there was a De Havilland Beaver float-plane that cruised along five hundred metres above the coast and landed right by the resort's wooden jetty.

I flew on it a couple of times and it was an absolutely splendid trip on a clear day with the immense coral structures of the Great Barrier Reef stretching away to the blue horizon.

Arriving in a float plane is hell romantic, but with speed, height and gravity in the mix there's always the chance of something going wrong. One scary day it did.

I was on dinner shift, happily getting a nice little menu together, when the gas ran out. Switching over to the new set of gas bottles was easy, but I hadn't done it before and I futzed around unable to work it out. So, I went to see Tom, who was taking siesta in his cabin.

Tom was the maintenance man, the engineer and Mr. Fix-it for the resort. In his early fifties and as fit as a bull, he could be short-tempered and was not pleased at his nap being interrupted.

"What the hell do ya want?" he said, standing in the doorway in nothing but his old y-fronts.

I grovelled and explained my inability to solve a simple problem. Tom got his shirt, shorts and flip-flops on and grumped up to the kitchen. With great irritation he showed me how to switch the gas over. I thanked him and got back to work.

I made some passionfruit mousse, popped it into the cold room. Then I piped out a tray of lime zest cookies and slid them in the oven. As I began to clean up some cute lamb chops for marinating, Mikey the apprentice and our waitresses Jane and Lisa burst into the kitchen. They were in their swimmers, breathless and in shock.

"The seaplane just crashed!" panted Mikey. "It tried to take off but then it bounced along and sank."

My stomach dropped. I knew there was a family of five on the plane including a six-year-old girl. I gaped at him for a moment as I tried to collect my thoughts.

"It sunk?" I gasped. "Did anyone get out?"

"I don't think so," said Mikey.

"OK. Jane, Lisa go and get Donnie and Ellis and tell 'em to get out there," I said. "We'll get Tom." The girls ran off and Mikey and I rushed down to Tom's cabin where I banged hard on the door.

"What the flipping heck do ya want now!" yelled Tom when he saw me and I rapidly explained. Tom's eyebrows shot up, and in nothing but his jocks he ran past me. Totally ignoring the path, he barrelled straight through the bush towards the jetty.

"Radio the emergency services now!" he yelled. Mikey followed him and I ran back to the resort. On the way I saw Donnie and Ellis sprinting towards the jetty, and when I got into the office, I heard the two resort dinghies start up and head off. Praying that Tom and the boys would get out there fast, I got on the radio and began calling the emergency services.

The manager appeared and I told her what had just happened. She turned white. I kept calling through on the resort's radio but I wasn't getting a response. Awful minutes ticked by. It was hard to believe in the possibility of death in this beautiful place.

Then the open channel on the radio crackled into life. It was an unhurried North Queensland voice.

"Yeahhh – this is the fishing trawler Ariadne Three. We're ahhhh . . . off . . . Cape Richards and yep . . . we've just pulled six people out of the sea. Their seaplane crashed. Everyone is . . . ahhhh . . . alright. No injuries."

The manager and I yelled and hugged each other with relief.

Very luckily the fishing boat had been right there when the plane bounced across some waves and flipped over. The passengers scrambled out into the water as the plane sank in two minutes. A very close call!

The trawler crew plucked the family and pilot out of the water, and aside from a cut and a few bruises they were unhurt. Tom and the lads ferried them back to the resort and the shaken adults had a stiff drink at the bar.

Now I smelt something burning in the kitchen. I opened the oven and saw that my lime zest cookies had turned to charred black discs. Thankfully they were the only casualties that day.

The boys – Steve, Mikey, Ellis, Donnie and myself – all fished. There were so many fish around the island that they'd be eating each other as we pulled them in. Sharks and big Trevallys would go the fish struggling on your line, and from above came seagulls and sea eagles. The sea boiled with action as everyone ate everyone else. For a time, there were so many mackerels that we only kept ones over a metre long. One week a plague of baby hammerhead sharks swarmed our lines, but no-one wanted to eat those stalk-eyed monsters and we chucked them back in.

One of the very best fish to eat was Flathead, also known as 'lizard' due to its reptilian looking head and green skin. Flathead was great to ceviche in lemon juice, red onions and olive oil, or to sear in morsels and serve in a light curry sauce – the emphasis on fresh roasted spices and fish stock. I never tired of catching, cooking and eating Flathead.

Another fish I loved was Rock Cod. I made a pâté with it I dubbed Rock Pâté. It had only four ingredients – gently poached rock cod, unsalted butter, fresh dill and just the right amount of rock melon. I'd serve it with toasted slices of black German-style bread.

We caught Mud Crabs too, taking turns doing the dawn dinghy run to check the pots, and we ate oysters straight off the rocks, knocking off their lids with a tomahawk and slurping the live creatures down. Yes sir – the island was lush with seafood.

We caught all the fish for the kitchen – talk about keeping food costs down – and our catch of the day gave guests gastronomic orgasms. Sometimes they caught their own fish and I'd cook it for them. Some guests were squeamish though and couldn't kill their fish, bringing them wriggling into the kitchen for me to dispatch.

I kept a hammer under the sink for this task. One day a guest came in with a live Flathead. I held it down and raised the hammer.

"What kind of fish is it?" he asked. I killed the fish with a bang on the head. "Flathead," I replied.

The best seafood I ate on the island came from Tom the maintenance man. Born and bred on the coast, he knew the whole area like the back of his big hairy hand. Tom liked his food done simply. Fish no sauce, steak medium well and always with many slices of white bread and margarine. He had an aversion to cheese. 'Bunghole,' he called it. Don't eat that stuff, he'd say, it'll bung your hole up.

One afternoon Tom popped his head into the kitchen and told me not to cook any meat or fish for the staff meal. He returned forty-five minutes later, his work clothes dripping with seawater, and in each hand was a painted crayfish. I've seen a lot of painted crays but these were truly superb – the tails alone were over a half a metre long. Tom put them on the bench and went out. I marvelled at these extreme specimens and Tom came back in with a beautiful red emperor and a coral trout.

"Knock us all up a feed with these will ya?" he drawled.

When Tom left, I silently thanked this incredible ocean bounty. Out of respect for their flavours I simply baked the fish and steamed the crays. I made up two butters – chilli/lime and dill – and a tomato, red onion and coriander salsa. At dinnertime the staff's eyes bugged out of their heads. They'd eaten lots of fresh seafood but this was something else. The crayfish were de-lic-ious, the flesh popping with sweetness and we sucked clean every claw, nook and cranny. The fish were pretty good too.

Later, I asked Tom about the painted crays.

"There's a bommie (a large free-standing coral head) that's full of 'em," he told me. "But I don't tell no bastard where. They'd all be all gone if I did."

Tom could have very easily stripped the bommie of crays and made a lot of money but he didn't. He may have been a rough old bastard but understood how the environment worked. He was a natural-born greenie, and he loved my Neapolitan tropical fruit ice-cream too.

Mikey the apprentice was a lovely young fella, all blonde hair, white teeth and as charming as hell. He took to cooking with love and care, becoming as sharp as a knife, and some years later he ran kitchens at top hotels and on private yachts. He liked a drink and we had many together. He and I, along with the barman Donnie, got into inventing cocktails.

After work we'd get the ingredients together and have a session – often with the aid of non-alcoholic mind-benders. On the staff deck with the shimmering sea lapping endlessly at the rocks beneath, we'd birth mad new drinks like the Rum and Kong, the Razorfish and the Cosmicpolitian. Full of psychedelic enthusiasm we manifested Hobbits – a subtle blend of Moet & Chandon Petite Liqueur and fresh kiwifruit juice, and perfected the Bush Serpico, concocted with white rum, spiced rum and our custom-made guava syrup.

Not all our attempts at cocktail nirvana were successful. Inspired by the drink-mixer Clamato juice – a mix of clam and tomato juice – we endeavoured to create an alcohol marinated fish cocktail. It was an unholy oily thing that made the gorge rise like squid on a full moon. The Black Sapote and Tequila margarita looked and tasted like mangrove mud, and there was nothing Zen or clever about mixing four different vodkas in the same glass. Realising that the acid was affecting our powers of objectivity, we went back to just drinking.

What was really mind-blowing though, was the perfect solitude you could experience on the island. Mikey and I would swap shifts so I could get a block of four consecutive days off. Then I'd tell everyone which day I'd be back, and with minimal kit – walk off into the big forever.

To be alone in the wilderness is wonderful. To do so for days on end is to feel a soul-deep affinity with the green and blue ball on which we live. I'm not religious but I can say with certainty that on Hinchinbrook Island

I hung out with God. She was there on sun-drenched boulders high above the sea, on moonlit beaches with a million stars overhead and swimming beside me in the crystal waters of jungle waterfalls.

And just like in the garden of Eden, the Devil came to visit. One morning, stark naked and in a state of meditative bliss, I was dreamily wandering along a glorious stretch of beach when evil arrived.

First came a huge sound, possibly the loudest noise I've ever heard and it king-hit me like a sonic fist. The sound was absolutely physical and I could feel the air all around me shuddering at the arrival of something huge and awful. I fell to the sand and looked up.

A few hundred metres above me was a terrifying presence – shiny, sharp and slick as a killing knife. The hot flames of hell roared from behind its terrifying bulk and on its ghastly swept back wings I saw . . . painted red kangaroos in blue circles.

Yep – it was a supersonic Royal Australian Air Force fighter bomber, an F-111, a hundred kilometres from its base down the coast at Townsville. I really don't think the pilot would have had enough time to see the bare-arsed freak walking along the beach – but he managed to break the sound barrier right over his head!

Then the bad news was announced – the resort was going to close down for a rebuild. In a few short months my dream job would be over.

I called some good friends and told them to come quick for a week-end holiday.

Earlier in the year, I had fallen in love with the assistant-manager Marie, who was Swiss, and it had been pure romance enjoying the island together. I told her that the two couples booking in next week-end were some of my besties. She was thrilled.

My friends turned up with some very decent MDMA for us all to enjoy. Marie became anxious, as she viewed recreational chemicals with distrust, and began worrying about how we'd be on this strange drug. I reassured her that we would be nice and mellow.

After dinner in the restaurant we adjourned to a table outside by the pool and got into the E. Soon hugs and declarations of love started breaking out, and Marie, very intrigued, now partook. She loved it and there was much laughter and cocktails.

Eventually we went down to Orchid Beach where the twinkling stars, sweet breeze and repetitive sound of the waves lulled half of our group into a meditative slumber. They lay peacefully on the soft sand drifting on waves of bliss. Marie, I and tall golden-haired Kim were full of beans though, scampering around laughing.

Then I saw flashes of white light every time our feet hit the sand near the waterline. I looked at the sea and every wave splashed with silver fire. What the . . .?

I was full of Bush Serpicos and Ecstasy but this was real – the sea was totally phosphorescent! I'd seen this phenomenon a few times before but never like this.

Whooping with sheer delight Kim, Marie and I ran around – jumping and making sparks fly from under our feet. We excitedly tried to rouse the sleepers on the sand but they sighed like babies, lost in cuddly dreaming.

We knew we had to swim in this electric magic and we stripped off, dived in and wow-ee! Our moving bodies lit up the water around us with pulsing liquid fire. Sheets of electrified quicksilver flew into the air as we dived and splashed. Every wave top glistened with diamonds and with the star-filled heavens above, it was hard to tell where the sky stopped and the sea began.

We were all in our early twenties and Marie and Kim looked absolutely divine swimming around me. They were like marine goddesses frolicking naked in a neon spangled sea, their hair lit up like molten gold as they swam through tunnels of platinum bubbles. That moment of rare beauty has lasted my whole life.

From the Agency

I was pleased. Central London is a maze of streets and lanes, but after much analysis of my street directory I was finally at the job; booked for 8 am and there at 7.50. The restaurant looked nice and I tried the front door. Closed. I went around to the kitchen door. It was closed too. I listened for kitchen work sounds. Nothing. I knocked hard on the kitchen door. Nothing. I waited for ten, twenty minutes – still nothing.

I went across the road and found a phone box to ring my employment agency. They were as confused as I was. OK they'd get onto it. Ring back in ten minutes. Then I saw a stocky fella in chef's whites go up to the restaurant's front door. There was the jingle of keys and I felt relief. As I approached, the chef started swearing. His keys were not getting him in. I greeted him and began to explain who I was. He laughed bitterly.

"No-one's working today mate! He's changed the locks! He's a #$@! -ing bastard!" I stepped back to avoid flecks of foam. This wasn't looking good.

"Ah . . . I better ring my agency," I said.

"I don't %$#@-ing care what you do!" the chef raged. "I'll show him - cheating %@#-ing scum!"

He ran down the back of the restaurant and then returned with a twenty-litre drum of used cooking oil which he hurled through the big front window. Glass flew everywhere and the drum smashed through chairs and tables disgorging its rancid contents. Inside the phone was ringing. The crazed chef glared at me in idiot triumph and hurried off.

I rang the agency again and described what I had just seen. "Oh," said the woman on the line without missing a beat. "Have you got your street directory handy? There's another job available at nine o' clock."

When the resort closed on Hinchinbrook Island, I was ready for the city again. This time I had gone to a big one. I got to share a house in Greenwich where I could come and go at will. This was perfect as I wanted to travel a bit and not be constrained by a long-term job. Using London as my base I would travel to Europe, North America, and especially Switzerland.

On my first week I arranged interviews with four inner-city cooking employment agencies. At each place I showed them my CV and convinced the interviewer that this Aussie boy was reliable, hardworking and competent. Working at an agency meant being on call to fill in at a kitchen. Possibly a crew member was sick or going on holiday, or maybe extra staff were needed. For being a fast-response cook I was guaranteed a minimum four-hour shift with a nice premium hourly rate. Each interview went well and I went on their books and awaited the call to work. I was really looking forward to working at good places where I could help out a groovy creative team in their time of need. Alas, this wasn't always so.

I soon burnt my bridges with two agencies who booked me for some absolute horror-shows; kitchens that were hygienically unsound, intellectually bereft or simply just crap. I refused to return to these sorts of jobs and, quite understandably, they stopped calling me.

The other two agencies had way better clients and work flooded in. I could work every day of the week if I wanted to. Some jobs were for a single day, others for one or two weeks. From time to time I'd get booked for a month or more and these were the jobs I really wanted.

You see, working for an agency means going in cold, not knowing the crew, menus and set-ups. There was scarcely enough time to learn it all before I was gone again. Sometimes I would cop bad attitude from a Head Chef and his stooges. I was getting paid more than they were and the pressure and hate would get piled on me. Fortunately, most kitchens were grateful as I picked up things fast and worked hard with zero fuss.

I settled into a routine. I worked, then travelled over to Europe and North America for months at a time. Upon return I reactivated myself with my agencies. All up I worked in more than fifty kitchens in London from restaurants to universities, from corporate offices to hospitals. Well, two hospitals in fact, and they could not have been more different. The first one was virtually my first booking and I knew it was a test of my willingness to work. The gig was for three weeks and when I turned up, I was shocked.

It was ginormous – an absolute behemoth of a place. It took me over twenty minutes just to find the catering section. At service, eleven electric powered hot-box vans ferried food to far-off parts of the hospital complex. The wet area was huge. Long conveyor belts moved all the crockery and cutlery as the fifteen-ladies strong dish pig crew furiously filled and emptied the dishwashers, making a colossal din.

The kitchen itself was epic – the legions of Rome could have marched through it. With cold rooms the size of temples and machines of megalithic proportions, this was a kitchen to feed an empire.

Day and night, seven days a week, thousands of meals were made in this kitchen and with section after section stretching off into the glittering stainless-steel distance – I got the feeling I could get lost in there.

The kitchen crew were an amiable lot numbering twenty-five and with the exception of me, they were either Algerian and Moroccan men or African women. Everybody had difficult names to remember so we got named by our country of origin. Cries of, "Hey Morocco where's the beef?" and "Ghana! Any butter in the back fridge?" would ring out across the cavernous kitchen. I was known as Australia.

Food was prepared in monumental quantities and then carefully portioned onto plates with insulated lids, or into long bain marie trays for the staff canteens. On my first day I met with a chef with an easy name – Maurice. I told him my name and, unsurprisingly, he addressed me as Australia.

"You can make omelettes?" inquired Maurice with a worried smile. "These gonna be for the doctors." I told him that I could make omelettes.

"OK," said Maurice. "You make one hundred and eighty omelettes. By ten thirty."

Looking at the clock I expressed surprise. With just over two hours to complete this task I didn't think it was possible.

"No problem, it's easy," demurred Maurice. "I show you."

The ingredients were prepped and ready to go. The fillings (cheese, tomato, spinach, ham etc) were on the bench next to a four-ring burner stove top. The egg mix filled three 10 litre plastic tubs. I began to feel nervous. Maurice lit the rings under four omelette pans and used a measuring jug to precisely fill each pan. With a wooden spoon he ruffled up the base of each omelette, cooked them a bit, then added the fillings. He flipped each one over, let them cook out just a bit more and then deftly slipped them onto a tray in an open warming oven. The pans got a quick wipe out before going back onto the heat. This all took less than two minutes.

"Easy huh?" beamed Maurice.

I uneasily set to work, feeling little confidence in meeting the not so far off dead-line. Maurice hovered at my shoulder, checking on my omelette prowess.

"OK, put the filling now. OK Australia? No, no keep him wet inside. Yes, like that. Good!"

After I'd made twelve omelettes Maurice gave me a cheery wave goodbye. "You doing fine. See you ten-thirty."

I had a list of how many of each kind of omelette to make and I started pouring, stirring, filling and flipping. It took my total concentration to maintain the four pans simultaneously. After a short while I darted a look at the clock. Eight fifty and I'd only made a few dozen of the omelettes. I looked around. Maurice was nowhere in sight. In fact, nobody was in sight. I was all by myself with the omelettes, or more specifically, the unmade omelettes.

I laboured on and soon got my rhythm, moving in a pattern of swift repetitions, wasting not a second. I didn't look at the clock again but took tally every twenty omelettes; when I reached the one hundred and forty mark, I checked the time. Twenty-five minutes to go! I smashed out the last few dozen and looked at the clock. I'd made it with seconds to spare.

An electric van purred up next to me, the driver hopped out and began to transfer the trays of omelettes into hot cabinets in the van. Maurice appeared with a bespectacled man in a chef's jacket, well-cut trousers and street shoes – all spotless. He ran his eyes over a tray of omelettes and grunted. It was the Head Chef.

"Chef – this is Australia," Maurice explained. "He finished the omelettes. He's a good boy."

The Chef regarded me for a moment. "OK?" he asked. I nodded. "You do this every morning." he said. I nodded again. Then he walked off and Maurice gave me his biggest smile yet. "Thank you, Australia."

So, for the next three weeks I made the omelettes so that Maurice didn't have to. He'd got heartily sick of them. Now he did something else but I never saw what it was. I hardly clapped eyes on him. After I'd madly conjured up a hundred and eighty omelettes, he'd give me another huge job to do. After lunch I'd work on yet more Herculean tasks. Alone. The kitchen was so big I rarely saw anyone else.

At lunch break the guys hung together talking in Arabic and the African ladies chatted in English or in their home tongues. I didn't feel at all ostracized but it was strange. I never saw the crew at work and I didn't talk to them on break. I'd eat my lunch and read a book.

One lunch break at the end of my second week I heard a startled grunt. I looked up to see the Head Chef peering down at me in surprise.

"You! You're still here?"

I would fax my time sheets to the two agencies, but the one at London Bridge I'd try to visit in person at least once or twice a week. The staff were mainly women and they were friendly and fun. I brought them coffees, made them laugh and I began to get better jobs.

Sometimes if I wasn't working evenings, we'd all go and have drinks. Of course, Jim Drain would come along.

Jim was the agency's junior, and the only male on the staff. He was a classic ginger-haired Irish imp and the blarney was strong with him. Though totally fluent in bullshit, the lad delivered it with such up-beat charm that everyone loved him. His irrepressible sense of optimism and dapper good looks meant he always in a sexual relationship with one of his co-workers. This potentially dangerous arrangement worked because the single agency women happily shared him around.

Jim also had a spy's knack for finding out the who, what, where and how of things. This talent was to be of great help to me.

Hanging out with the London Bridge gang got me a three-month job at the European headquarters of the Citibank Corporation – a nice long gig. The Citibank building was a temple to Mammon – a great skyscraper topped with the corporate logo. As I entered it my first day, big guys in tight suits demanded to see my security pass. I didn't have one.

"I'm from the agency," I said.

"Oh, OK – go through."

I was never asked for a pass again.

At Citibank I cooked lunch for the yuppies and number crunchers. There were three different kitchens and the lowest level kitchen, where I started, was the biggest. Here the hoi polloi of employees would eat very cheap fare. The meals were subsidised as an incentive for the workers to stay in the building over their lunch hour.

The job was a disappointment. The kitchen, a windowless basement-level factory, was uncomfortably crowded with unnecessary cooking gear. It churned out a set-in concrete menu and the kitchen staff turn-over was high, due to the very confusing, aggressive and xenophobic Head-Chef.

On lunch break he'd insist that the cooks and chefs, all white boys, sit together, using the 'us' versus 'front-of-house' dynamic as an excuse for his racism. At the tables next to us the English, African, Indian and Jamaican wait-staff, porters and dish pigs all chattered away happily.

I started mooning over one of the waitresses. She

had dark flashing eyes, a brilliant white smile and in her waitress uniform – a powder blue dress, pinafore and bonnet all trimmed in white lace – she looked very twee.

This young African woman also had the boldest tribal facial scarification on her face – lines and spirals made up of dozens of raised lumps. I thought she looked stunning and this earned me the Head Chef's undying contempt. I began to think about how I could squirm out of this job without pissing off the agency.

Then Jim Drain came to work with us. He knew bugger-all about cooking but had volunteered because no one else appeared to be available. Probably because word of the Head Chef's horrid rep had got around. Jim worked with us for weeks, learning as he went, never quite screwing up, but coming very close at times.

It was fun having Jim around, but the job really was a drag and the Head Chef just execrable. I told Jim I was going to appeal to the agency for a new job.

The very next day I was approached by the Head Chef from the restaurant two floors above. Eddie was a smooth young guy who had just lost his offsider. Would I like to work with him? I later found out that Jim Drain had already heard about the vacancy, met Eddie, seen the kitchen and had suggested me. Eddie took me up to his kitchen for a look-see and I immediately accepted.

This was a totally different set-up. The small and ergonomically designed kitchen had windows and was bright. Manned by two, it made delicatessen-style food that encompassed both decadent and healthy eating. Eddie also had the freedom to come up with daily and weekly specials and that really clinched the deal for me.

The dining room was yuppy groovy, seating fifty, and the seats turned over three- or four-times during a three-hour lunch service. Framed black and white art photos hung on the walls, the tables had good linen in pastel colours and bright new-age music wafted from hidden speakers.

The customers here were either serious eaters or health freaks. For those concerned with maintaining the temple, Eddie and I made all kinds of salads, dips, roasted vegetables, flans, veggie terrines, loaves, soups, patties and slices. We whizzed up pitchers of fresh fruit and vegetable juice, and laid on mountains of fruit salad and lakes of sorbet.

The diners who wanted the naughty rich food had lots of choice too. Whole poached fish with various mayonnaises piped on, or cold game pie, maybe venison one day, pheasant the next. We made mousses, quiches and pâtés, and laid-out big platters of cold cuts; roast beef, smoked ham, prosciutto and ox tongue. Selections of seafood – fresh oysters, smoked trout, even whelks, were there for the taking. Daily hot items – individual steak and kidney pies, mini beef Wellingtons or fish in Guinness batter rounded off the decadence.

All the sauces, relishes and chutneys were made by us in-house, and the cheese board featured an ever-changing selection, including fat slabs of flaky vintage cheddar and lovely stinkers like Stilton and Gorgonzola.

Although there was enough room in the kitchen for a third chef to work, Eddie liked having just one other person on with him. It was his own little kingdom with all the systems and routines worked out his way.

This was great because Eddie was one of the best chefs I ever worked with. He loved food and strived for perfection. I learnt so much from him. Having control over the menu meant we were always experimenting with new recipes and that was like culinary catnip to me.

Customers dug the food and frequently popped in to say hello and offer compliments. Eddie thanked them with genuine pleasure, but later he'd say, "Yuppies hey? Wouldn't know how to boil water that lot." He loved the adulation but was defiantly working class.

The other big passion in Eddie's life was the new electronic dance music and the club scene that played it. He brought in mix tapes to feed the kitchen boombox and we happily worked to the thumping rhythms of house, techno, garage and ragga. I liked this mad new music too and brought in mixes I'd taped off the airwaves. We soon became mates outside of work and at night he'd take me to the clubs; crowded rooms where crews like Shut Up and Dance, and Sonz of a Loop-de-Loop Era made you sweat and then sweat some more.

This was nineteen ninety, when electronic music was still relatively underground, so there was a sense of being part of something new and fresh, and we brought this excitement into the kitchen. It might sound like we had a little too much of Rotterdam's finest buzzing around our brains, but Eddie and I began to interface cooking with dance music.

We talked about music as though it were food. Favourite tracks were 'tasty', 'spicy' or 'chockablock with goodness.' Especially deep kick drum beats were 'chewy' or had 'a lot of stock in them.' Certain effects on keyboard lines sounded 'curried' or 'marinated' to us.

Conversely, we described food in musical terms. A successfully executed dish was rated 'four on the floor'. A complex dish had 'break-beats galore' and a good sauce or dressing was 'kicking.' A popular dish was a 'huge tune' and any new recipe was 'white label'. Our chopping boards became 'decks' and we 'dropped the needle' every time food was chopped or sliced on them.

Oh yeah, we could almost taste the break-beats, our lips smacking in pleasure at some particularly good snare drum riff cascading out of the big JVC cassette player.

But whatever was going on in our heads did not affect our ability to make great food. We never allowed the excesses of the club life we so enjoyed to interfere with our work in the kitchen.

Eddie was a guide and teacher both in and out of

work. I've since met other raver chefs, who loved the clubs as much as they loved food, but none of them were as consistently together as Eddie was.

I have a vivid memory from that kitchen. It was a boiling hot summer and we had fans going and all the windows open in a vain attempt to keep the kitchen cool. Outside, Londoners were walking around in mini-skirts and shorts, some blokes even without shirts. Eddie and I were putting together lunch with a tasty tune pumping, when the dumb waiter, our food lift from the kitchen downstairs, made its ding sound. It was signalling that a load had arrived. We looked at each other in surprise as nothing was due to come up.

The dumb waiter doors rattled and Eddie smiled deeply. He went over to the lift, flung back the doors and stepped aside. A long lean figure uncurled from the impossibly tight confines of the dumb waiter, sprung into the kitchen, shook out his dreadlocks and began dancing wildly to the music.

It was Jeremy – our superstar dish pig and good clubbing mate. Throwing mad moves, he waved a small plastic baggie at us, dancing around and pulling nutter faces. Then he boogied back to the lift, turned and threw the packet to Eddie, who caught it in mid-air. A prepaid transaction had just taken place. Jeremy slid back into the dumb waiter like he was made of rubber and Eddie closed the doors and sent him back down. He shook the plastic baggie at me and grinned. "We're sorted!"

That long hot summer got even hotter as the Irish Republican Army stepped up a major bombing campaign, with central London in the cross hairs. The terrorists went murderously ape, detonating all kinds of explosives in and around the city. The establishment Carlton Club and London Stock exchange were blasted, and an MP and a soldier died when their vehicles exploded.

Early one morning I had scarcely arrived at work when the building alarms went off. Jim Drain was still pretending to be a chef at Citibank and he and I were the first ones there. We scoffed at the ringing bells and kept on changing into our chef's checks and whites. Then the security guys came into the staff-room yelling, "Come on! Out! Out! There's a bomb gone off."

We were hustled outside to an assembly area by the street – a grimy square with a dreary fountain and concrete benches where the office workers smoked and attempted to catch some sun.

Workers from the surrounding buildings began to fill the space until everyone was packed shoulder to shoulder. Jim and I, in our chef's whites, pushed to the front to see what was going on.

It was a strange sight – central London at 7.30 in the morning with not a double-decker bus, car or person moving. Apparently, a small bomb had gone off a few hundred yards away, and sure enough, we could see some broken windows.

"Ach that's nothing," said Jim in his Irish accent. "You should see the stuff that happens in Belfast man!" I quickly shushed him as people turned with angry faces to stare at us.

We waited. News helicopters appeared. Several military vehicles arrived and two soldiers ran up to a rubbish bin and looked in. A great murmuring sprung up from the crowd. There was another bomb! It was in the bin – right where we could see it! Everyone grinned with excitement.

Then the soldiers ran back and someone with a megaphone addressed the crowd. The device in the bin was small and no-one was in any danger if it went off. However, we had to remain where we were until it had been defused or exploded in a controlled way. Another half hour passed. Then a miniature robot tank began to trundle up the street trailing its controller wire and the crowd noise went up. Ah! The robot tank! It defuses bombs!

The little machine doggedly moved towards the bin and the crowd grew silent. Tens of thousands of eyes stared. Overhead the flock of news choppers hovered, their cameras aimed at the unfolding drama. Then the tank, with fifty or sixty yards to go – stopped. A minute passed. Then a few more, before four soldiers ran out, picked up the tank and ran it back. The mission had been aborted.

There were expressions of disgust from the

crowd, wolf whistles and a bit of slow hand clap. Then two heavily armoured bomb squad fellas went up to the bin and one of them lent right in. Everyone watched breathlessly until he took his head out of the bin and gave the thumbs up. The crowd broke into cheers and loud applause.

This horrible bombing madness continued into the winter. Attacks on major junctions closed the whole railway system, including the underground, for hours. Buses became jam-packed, the roads got gridlocked and Eddie, Jim, Jeremy and I would get stranded. We'd repair to a West End bar to wait out the crush. Then, after a few hours of drinking, we'd realise that Fabio & Grooverider or Carl Cox were about to start knocking out monster tunes nearby and we'd end up making a night of it.

When Eddie took two weeks holiday, a chef from Heaven got sent down to work with me. Heaven was the nickname for the kitchen at the very top of the Citibank Tower, where the boss-men lunched. Occasionally the boys and girls up there would come down for some ingredient they were short of and they all looked sharp and sexy. Lower-level gossip reckoned they were picked as much for their looks as for their skills.

Debbie, the chef who arrived, had both attributes and was a seasoned pro from whom I learnt a lot. We got on, and even better, she was into dance music. We kept the tunes going in the kitchen and towards the end of our first week I suggested we go have a drink after work. She agreed and we became dancing buddies.

Debbie turned Eddie and I on to a great spot close by to our work at Citibank. In the Square Mile, where the corporate citadels loomed overhead, was an innocuous flight of stairs by the footpath. Down the bottom was an underground pub. It wasn't flash but the drinks were cheap and the management and staff were relaxed. Here, all the service workers of the financial district would come and unwind after a hard day's work. Cooks, dish pigs, waiters, receptionists, cleaners and security people would catch up to get happily loaded together. On Friday nights, a pair of old Technics 1200s would get set up in the corner and someone would spin bangin' tunes.

It was well wicked – a nice friendly scene; better than any trendy pricey club. There would often be E floating around, spliffs being smoked in a bus shelter up on the street and lots and lots of dancing. The hip suits from the banks cottoned on to this loved-up hot spot right under their feet and they'd come down and get on one too – dancing with, and hugging, people they would never have normally mixed with.

Then with sadness I found out that I had to finish up at this wonderful job. Word had come through from Switzerland and it was now time to go there. The gang had a send-off for me and we clubbed around London til sunrise. A few days later I caught a flight to Zurich.

Swiss Hotel

Switzerland – home of Victorinox knives, fondues, secret bank accounts, cuckoo clocks and . . . Swiss Hotels. My plan was to work in one.

Back in the day, many cooks and chefs felt that they had to work in a Swiss Hotel, as Switzerland is considered to be the birthplace of hospitality training. The legendary precision and dependable efficiency of the Swiss could teach you a lot.

Actually, the main reason I was in the land of the Alps was that I was still in love with Marie, the Swiss assistant manager I'd met while working on Hinchinbrook Island Resort. We had caught up repeatedly in London and I'd stayed with her for a few months in Switzerland, but now it was time to get serious. I'd score a job at a Swiss Hotel, learn a lot, save my money, be with Marie on my days off and eventually go traveling with her.

However, there were procedures to be followed before my plan could be set in motion. I needed a work visa, but I had to get a Swiss sponsor first. This hunt had started months earlier and now a friend of Marie's had found me a sponsor in a major tourist town. If I got the job, I'd have to live a few cantons away from Marie, but at least I'd be in the same country. An interview with a Frau Sempel had been arranged; she apparently employed a lot of non-Swiss workers and it seemed like a winner. I set off to the interview feeling pretty excited.

When I arrived, I stood in front of the hotel and man – was it impressive! The ancient six-story stone building reeked of old-world permanence. Sitting by the shore of a large lake ringed by classic alpine peaks, the hotel had a big patio of tables and chairs overlooking the promenade. Weathered old iron lattice-work surrounded the pollarded trees that grew at intervals by the lake and swans bobbed in the wind-ruffled water. It was a classic picture of old Europa and I really wanted to work there.

Frau Semple was a widow, but solidly married to the family businesses, and this hotel was the jewel in the crown. She was intricately made-up and well dressed, though the effect was more gothic than glam. We had a coffee and she laid out the deal being offered. Although not as good as I hoped, it wasn't too bad. Food and board were to be provided, which in a tourist town is great. For forty-five hours a week, occasionally a few hours more, I'd net five hundred francs.

Frau Sempel rang a bell and a chef immediately came through the door. He must have been waiting.

The man was Alex, the Swiss Head Chef, and he grilled me about my cooking history. He needed an all-rounder – a Chef Tournant – as a gun extra pair of hands to work alongside the Chef de Parties and their crews. The Chef Tournant is like the Ronin of the big kitchen and for me it might be grill one night, cold larder the next, and prep all the time. Could I do that? I sure could. Alex and Frau Sempel exchanged a knowing look and the interview was suddenly over. Thank you – they'd get back to me. I was expecting an immediate answer but polite prodding would not stir them. Thank you and good morning. I went back to Marie's and waited.

I had already arranged an interview with the Fremdenpolize (the Alien Police) in anticipation of making an application for a work visa – but I still didn't yet know if Frau Sempel was my sponsor. Over the phone I had to explain to an Alien Policeman why I was rescheduling my meeting with them.

"Why have you made the appointment if you are not going to keep it?" said the Alien Policeman.

"I'm sorry – I thought I'd have an answer by now. I am trying to get this done quickly."

"Quickly? No, it is not done quickly. There are always procedures."

"Yes, I understand but I . . ."

"You are not wanting a work visa now? We close your file?"

"No no! I need to make another appointment."

"Yes, for what date?"

"I'm sorry but I'm not sure just yet"

"I cannot make an appointment for you if you don't know when!"

A few days later I was summoned back to the hotel. This was good. In Frau Sempel's office there were some minimal greetings and then silence. It was like being called in to see the headmistress.

Frau Semple gazed at me. Finally, she sighed.

"OK. We will give you a chance. You are on probation. After a month if we like you – then we will offer you the contract. If not . . ."

Like a Bond villain she left the nasty bit unsaid.

I was chuffed. I'd made it into a Swiss hotel! I'd be seeing Marie a whole lot more and then we'd go traveling together! I felt like shaking hands or something with Frau Semple but I could see that wasn't going to happen. So, I brightly inquired as to my pay schedule – was it weekly or fortnightly?

"We will pay you after each month of work is finished," Frau Semple said firmly.

Monthly? That seemed a bit frickin austere. Frau Semple caught the tiny flicker of irritation on my face.

"If you don't want the job then you can go. Many chefs wish to work here," she said. Oops! I fired up a reassuring smile and said I was really looking forward to the job. Frau Semple nodded with grim satisfaction.

Now sponsored, I went to the first of a series of meetings with the Fremdenpolizei. The interviewer sat several feet higher than me and there was a thick glass window between us. All spoken communication was through microphones and this gave the interviewer's voice a metallic robotic ring. Or maybe that was his real voice. Forms were placed in a tray that hissed open on my side. When I took out the forms and placed my documentation in the tray, I saw it was entirely sealed. The Alien Police weren't breathing the same air as me. It was a vaguely demeaning process but it produced a work visa.

Finally, the day dawned and I arrived at the hotel and gazed up at its stately edifice. I wondered where the staff quarters were. Would I have my own room? It seemed unlikely. I'd probably have to share a room with some crusty old chef who snored and farted and compulsively masturbated. But no – it was far worse than that.

When I reported to the kitchen, Alex the Head Chef gave me an address. It was my place of residence – not the hotel. Luckily it wasn't too far and I cheerfully made my way through the picturesque cobblestone streets.

When I arrived at my accommodation, I was pleased to see it looked authentically old; a yellowing three-story stone building with a weathered facade, the roof missing a few tiles. I entered the front door and vainly tried to find the concierge or manager. Not knowing where my room was, I walked around the three floors of the building and my heart slowly sank.

It wasn't just old – the place was a wreck! On its way to dereliction, the building had got to slum stage with peeling paint, cracked walls and rusted plumbing. Grime was ingrained around light switches and door handles and walls featured unknowable stains. Ancient sour smells hung in corners and the floors were filthy.

Furniture was minimal and I could see that there was a shortage of beds as there were sleeping bags and rat-nests of pillows and bedding on the floor. Each level of the building had two kitchens and bathrooms, but the facilities in them were cheap and exhausted; beaten up bar-fridges, antiquated gas stoves, rust streaked bath tubs and dripping shower heads.

My dismay at the building's putrid state wasn't just an inability on my part to appreciate the ambiance of Old Europe.

As I soon found out, many of the facilities were illegally derelict. Toilets didn't always work and some bathrooms taps had minimal or no hot water. The heating was temperamental and a fair few lights and wall-sockets were permanently switched off. There was zero maintenance. If a light bulb blew, you'd have to buy a new one yourself. Security was non-existent. Most door locks were broken and the front door didn't close. The body corporate here was long dead and buried.

Luckily, I met a waiter who was just leaving town and I claimed his bed and some wardrobe space. As the days went by, I saw how the building was an absolute free-for all. Three hotels and a casino had rented it for their staff – hospitality workers from all over the world, there to do their Swiss hotel thing. It was a jam-packed mad-house of hot-bedding, sleeping bags and suitcases, and the turn-over was phenomenal.

What really added to this crazy railway-station atmosphere was the almost continuous movement of different shifts coming and going. Croupiers returning at dawn. Pastry chefs and bakers getting up at 3 a.m. Around midnight it grew busy with people drinking and smoking, playing games and guitars, laughing, talking, and indulging in horseplay. Unsurprisingly, I found it very hard to get a good night's sleep.

The transient nature of the place meant everyone screwed like rabbits. The lusty would commandeer a room in a bid for privacy and wedge the door shut. I frequently saw a knackered waiter or chef knocking and shouting at the door of 'their' bedroom. One night after work, in the dark, I went to flop down on the bed I assumed was mine and nearly got caught up in the exertions of a doggy-styling couple.

Everyone drank huge amounts and indulged in whatever else their wallets could handle. I smelt hash at times and saw people passing around pills. I got too busy working to really find out, but I suspected there was all manner of sin emanating from the building. Predictably the local police were frequent visitors due to all the noise and action going on. Staff would also bring trouble down on themselves through theft, drunkenness and irregular working papers. One Japanese chef, in a squabble with the cops, had his passport taken off him.

I soon learnt that the building was a scam cooked up by the hotels and the casino. Everyone was on the same deal as me – food and accommodation built into their salary. The general consensus was that without accommodation we should all get at least another hundred francs a week in our pay-packets. Multiply that by the seventy to eighty people living there, then add the local knowledge that the building had previously rented at two thousand francs a week, and it wasn't hard to see that someone was making good money out of us.

Being in a tourist town at the start of the season meant that finding alternate accommodation close to work was prohibitively expensive. I looked around but even rent on a shoe box of a room would have eaten up a majority of my weekly income.

OK, the accommodation was crap – maybe the food would make up for it. No, it didn't. Food consisted of warmed-up leftovers left out at 5 pm daily. Nations of waiters descended on the old potatoes, khaki cabbage and dried ends of roasts. By 5 past 5 it was all gone. That was it – no breakfast, no lunch; not a sausage.

At the supermarket, just breakfast supplies for a few days – tea, milk, cereal, fruit and yogurt – cost half a day's wages. It was the curse of a tourist town and I spent many off-duty hours traveling to nearby towns to buy cheaper food.

But it wasn't until I started work that I saw the full extent of the awful trap that had been sprung on me. Non-existent meals and sub-standard accommodation were bad enough, but it was the kitchen that really sunk the boot in.

Located some three metres underground the hotel and accessed by an ancient stone staircase that felt like entering the Mines of Moria, the kitchen wasn't very big. What made it even smaller was the number of tables we had to cook for. As well as the hundred and twenty seat dining room and room-service, there were also a hundred extra seats on that lovely, apparently brand new, patio outside. When the weather was good those outdoor tables briskly turned over multiple times and the kitchen might do close to a thousand covers in a day. The kitchen could handle the dining room and room service, but not the rush on the patio seats as well.

It was a hot subterranean nightmare with chefs jostling shoulder to shoulder as there wasn't enough room for everyone to really work simultaneously. If I left my space to do something, I'd often return to find someone had taken my place, with my board and knife spirited away - sometimes placed under the bench!

It was a hell of chaos – an anti-kitchen, and we didn't work in concert because we were always fighting for space. What really stuck a dog up you was Frau Semple swanning in at a peak service moment, say at 8.30 on a Friday night, to make herself a snack and chat with Alex. A valuable bit of kitchen real-estate would get hogged while she cast a languid eye around the kitchen.

Whenever Frau Semple graced us with her presence like this, the crew worked in silence; everyone with a frozen snarl/smile on their faces. Even the Sous-chef went quiet – and was that a relief!

The Sous-chef was a panzer of a man who spoke minimal English but voluble German. He was blunt and rude, cursing, cussing and moaning, and as stressed-out in that small kitchen as we were. This pressure often tipped him into outright bullying and I could see that Alex the Head Chef, also under huge pressure, was scared of him.

In my job interview I had clearly explained that I spoke perhaps six words of the local Swiss-German, all involving love or alcohol. I was assured that this was no problem as it was an international kitchen that used English as its lingua franca. However, due to this German Sous-chef's inability to speak English, Swiss-German was actually the only language used in the kitchen – and English was declared verboten. This was ridiculous because everyone else spoke it as a first or second language. Outside of the Swiss German speakers

– Alex, the German Sous-chef, a Swiss grill chef and a Frenchman – the crew comprised a Chinese Canadian, a New Zealander, a French Arab dude, a Singaporean, an English lad and me. Some of the stress would have been lessened if we'd all spoken the same lingo.

The food wasn't too complex, which was a help, mainly classic European cuisine with some semi-luxury wild dishes thrown in. Like the whole rainbow trout that swum around in an aquarium in the middle of the crowded kitchen. Pity the chef on the fish section who had to open the aquarium tank lid, catch a fish with a net, close the lid with one hand, deposit the squirming creature onto a cutting board, then dispatch it with a knife – before gutting, cleaning and pan-frying it!

The dockets of course were all in Swiss German. After a week or two I kind of understood what they meant, but understanding what was being called away during service was a total brain-buster.

So, we Anglophones started making up our own pronunciations, speaking a mutant gibberish that meant something to us. Sometimes we just had to speak English though and the German Sous would scream, "Nein! Nein English!!" To really make his point he'd use what little English he did have, and bawl, "No! No speak English!"

This awful man was the poison icing on the shit cake. Everyone disliked him and he knew it. With Alex frowning weakly in the background, the Sous-chef revved up hourly confrontations; his burly physique making threatening moves. Then he began to bump and bang into people . . . deliberately. The little kitchen got even smaller as we twisted and spun away from this troll. The air of repressed violence made that brightly-lit bunker a very dark place indeed.

The kitchen crush was dangerous. The Singaporean sprained an ankle and left. The Swiss grill chef had a nasty fall but gamely worked on with a limp. I hurt my hand whacking it against a reach-in. When the German Sous-chef cut himself, I joined in the silent malicious happiness, uncaring of the damage I was doing to my soul.

Physic rot set in. People pulled tormented faces behind the Sous-chef's back – in real anguish and not in humour. The Canadian guy got nervous skin rashes that marinated and stung. George the Kiwi grill cook was going insane, muttering and groaning to himself. He chain-smoked cigarettes and drank brandy by the bottle after work. One night he swore he'd get the Sous -chef, knock him out in the back cold room; then stick his head into a tub of bechamel sauce. I believed him.

Then Alex announced that the Sous-chef was leaving; his contract was up. This was news to us, and good news too! On his last day the Sous-chef actually mellowed out. It had dawned on him that the horrible stress was at an end. After work we were told to shower, change and join management for farewell drink. Fuck that, said Kiwi George, but Alex insisted.

We got all scrubbed up and trooped upstairs into a beautiful centuries old wooden room where little thank you speeches were given by management – in Swiss German. We nursed our one free drink and sullenly watched the Sous-chef glow red from the praise being heaped upon him. We have a special gift for you, Frau Semple said. A flunky then came forward and we watched unbelieving as he placed a cowbell on a ribbon around the Sous-chef's neck. A cowbell! The hurt on the Sous-chef's face was plain to see.

I guess he'd been expecting something Swiss like a watch or a bar of gold – but not this.

Frau Semple gave a snort of laughter and started clapping and the management heartily joined in, the lot of them smiling in a most nasty way. The poor man sat there in shock. I looked around at the kitchen crew, expecting to see some vengeful grins, but everyone looked stunned by this cruel trick.

Later that night over brandy, Kiwi George shook his head sadly.

"This place is fucked," he said. "You know how fucked it is? Those fuckers made me feel sorry for that fucker. That's really fucked."

We got a new Sous-chef who spoke English and to our immense relief English now became the language of the kitchen. That made things a little easier . . . for a few weeks. Then the summer season kicked in and we started working fifty-hour weeks, then fifty-five-and sixty-hour weeks. For the same salary. We got mighty disgruntled. It was also now clear that little kitchen could not deal with the demands of the season and there were complaints from customers about long waits.

At a staff meeting Alex told us that management was unhappy with us for not keeping up. I guess we were supposed to feel shock and horror that the gods in heaven were displeased, but everyone started talking at once – airing their grievances. Alex knew that the workspace wasn't coping, that we were all under too much stress, but he was under pressure from above. We just had to get up to speed he yelled lamely.

He also made out that the pre-season hours were us having an easy time of it, and now we must get used to the new 'normal' hours. The meeting ended in a cloud of bad energy.

That night Kiwi George packed his bags. "I'm sorry to do this to you brethren, but fuck this place."

The next morning, he was gone. It was a hard, hard service one person down but at least there was a bit more room to work.

That night after work I pondered my lot. I'd signed the contract and hung in, not wanting to blow my chance at a Swiss Hotel. Plus, I was here for Marie, but I'd not seen much of her. She'd been overseas a lot due to her job as a travel-agent and was currently in America. I wanted to talk to her but mobile phones were still in the future and I just had to wait.

I ground through another fortnight and when Marie got back, I took the train on my next day off to see her. My heart leapt as my lady met me at the station and then crashed to the ground. I could see from her face that something was very wrong.

Within a few minutes it was established that the thrill was gone and that she was not in love with me anymore. I was devastated. I loved her. We'd had great times on Hinchinbrook Island, here in Switzerland and in London town and I thought we had a future together.

We talked for an hour, and then talked some more over lunch, but she had definitely made her mind up. It was getting awkward now and I took my leave.

It was one sorry little fella who got back to the hotel. My plans were obsolete. I didn't have to be here in Switzerland anymore . . . and that meant I didn't have to be working this horrible job either. That faint beam of positivity grew brighter, and I went to see Frau Semple.

Well if I was hoping for a sympathetic ear, or a faintly Mum-like shoulder to have a cry on, I was sorely mistaken. Frau Semple listened to my tale of shattered love impassively, but when I got to the part about me giving my notice, she stood up and pointed at the door.

"You want to go?" she shouted. "We give you a chance and now you want to go? OK go. Go now!"

She wasn't being pleasant, but this was better than expected. I was prepared to give notice, but I could literally go now. I could be in Amsterdam by morning.

"But do not expect to be paid any money owing to you! You have broken the contract!"

I was nearly a week away from my next monthly pay cheque and I began to protest. Frau Semple went for me like a terrier after a rat.

"If you do not leave right now then I will bring the Fremdenpolizei here," she said with great malice. "You will be taken to the border and expelled!"

I should have pushed harder for my money but I'd had enough. Frau Semple had a parting shot for me as I left the room.

"And what sort of a man are you – letting a woman decide for you?"

Yes, what sort of a man was I, to allow my heart to be broken? I bought some brandy and got on a train. Later that evening, passing through France, I slumped in a near-empty carriage chugging on the Remy and morosely thinking about Marie.

I felt truly gutted. This was one of the worst moments of my life. I miserably swigged some more brandy and then remembered – I didn't have to go into that hellhole of a kitchen anymore! My drunken smile nearly tore my face apart.

East End Private

After a short spell licking my wounds in Amsterdam, I then reactivated myself with the London agencies and was immediately offered an open-ended contract at a private hospital in the East End. I balked at a hospital job but when I saw the brochures and menus I said yes. This was a private hospital, brand new and ultra-modern; a temple of medical science with three-star rooms and food of restaurant quality.

The five-story building was also an impregnably secure high-tech fortress. The head security honcho's office had twenty outside camera views as well as all the in-house stuff, and there were at least two security personnel on at any time of the day or night. All floors had video phones where the Ward Sisters could look me in the eye and question me about meal options and special service times.

It was very high-end and patients paid hundreds of pounds a night for a bed, three meals and basic care.

Each patient's room was made for one, with an en-suite bathroom, a separate lounge room and piped in oxygen, phone and cable TV. The room service for food and bar was like that of any large hotel. Patients could order fresh blinis with caviar, smoked salmon sandwiches and vintage champagne for their visitors. Business types sometimes held luncheon meetings in their lounge rooms.

The patients were wealthy and came from all around the world. Old tycoons and up-coming CEOs needing heart surgery. Cup final strikers and champion boxers with knees and noses to be mended. Minor royals, major politicians and religious leaders of all faiths. And people wanting to change their self-image. Things like face-lifts and nose jobs, liposuction and for the boys – genital surgery of the enlargement type.

My role was Sous-chef, working all the shifts that Marty the Head Chef didn't do. He was a Filipino family man who wanted to be home at night – so he only did breakfasts and lunches. I did most dinners and some lunches. I didn't see much of him as we only worked together one day a week.

The rest of the kitchen crew were also Filipino guys and we had a lot of fun. Charles was the young gun chef with a knock-out smile and classic *jeproks* style. Phillip, a somewhat sensitive soul, ran the cold larder and ribald comments were flung his way about what a teetotalling softy he was. Roddy was intensely married, solid at his job and softly sang Tagalog pop songs as he worked. Laughing mad Jay Jay was the apprentice and he avidly looked to Charles to show him what the discos and clubs of London had to offer. This tight crew was rounded off by the kitchen hands – Jaimie, a heavily muscled silent dude with a big laugh, and Tomas, a wizened old fella with sixty-five years of wise advice to dispense.

They had a ready-made camaraderie and I fitted right in. Charles showed me his yummy Hamonado – choice pork pieces browned off nice and crispy; then cooked in Calamansi juice. Jay Jay liked deep-frying chicken crackling for me to eat with him. Roddy told me about a popular bar-snack back home and everyone hooted with laughter at the expression on my face. Fertilized chicken eggs were hard boiled so that there would be a tiny chicken to eat, bones and all.

The patients' food wasn't as wild as that, though as high end as the prices they were paying. They could eat oysters, salmon and whole flounder, or rip into a Wagyu steak or some succulent Scottish lamb. There was a daily Asian or Indian meal, interesting salads and cold larder treats. We made everything in-house except for the bread and pastries. A designated bar cold room contained a good selection of wines, beers and spirits for the patients and their guests if they fancied a tipple.

The patients had daily breakfast/lunch/dinner menus that rotated over a fortnight. It was much like a-la-carte except everyone pre-ordered and most ate at the same time. This made service easy. I'd go through the orders tallying up sixteen of this, five of that, ten of this, from the entrees through to the desserts, and then the crew would prepare them for service.

Service was done a ward at a time, with all hands on deck. Jaimie and Tomas, and sometimes Bill the food and beverage manager, would pitch in, bringing food to the big service benches. Plates and metal plate covers were preheated and while a cadre of waitresses hovered, we dished up very quickly. Each waitress left the kitchen with the food for two or three rooms. While one floor was being plated up, we'd be cooking for the next floor. It was so quick and finely tuned that we'd have all the food out, a hundred meals plus, in forty minutes.

Not all the patients ate off the menu or at the same time and we tailored their meals to specific times and requirements. Sometimes a patient might want just toast and marmalade after waking up from surgery. I also made special meals for dietary reasons – a salad with no onions, tomatoes or dressing, or liver, poached and thinly sliced, with a few steamed greens.

One night a frustrated Ward Sister got on the video phone with me. A patient with a wired-up jaw was insisting on filet steak with pepper sauce, pointing out he was paying top dollar. Was there anything I could do? Leave it to me sister I said.

I cooked a nice piece of steak, and as Jay Jay and Phillip watched with disbelief, I atomised it in a blender until it was a steaming grey slurry flecked with brown. It looked like blended grizzly bear, but it smelt and tasted great. I poured it into a soup bowl, topped it with the sauce and a sprig of rosemary to suck on. Jay Jay clapped his hands with glee and bemoaned not having a camera to immortalise this culinary oddity. The patient loved it, and I made this same meal for him a couple more times.

I also cooked for the hospital staff and they had it good. Their well-appointed restaurant was next to the kitchen on the hospital's top floor and the good-sized dining room opened out onto a long outdoor patio. This area had a spectacular view to the Tower of London and the still being constructed monolith of Canary Wharf. In summer it was a wonderful spot to sit and eat, or just chill with a coffee.

When the staff restaurant closed at eight, the catering staff would shrink to me, sometimes Phillip or Jay Jay, and a lone waitress. For the next two hours we'd hang in there waiting. Phillip would read. I'd do some ordering and sometimes play chess with Phillip. The waitress would chat with the night nurses taking a break in the restaurant. I'd go chat with them too or wander around with a pager clipped to my belt. If nothing much happened then Phillip would knock off, leaving me in the semi-darkened kitchen.

All this waiting around was because the Private Hospital offered room service til ten at night. It was a fairly limited menu – pâtés, antipasto, salads and soup, a casserole, desserts and the fish of the day. Sometimes, but not often, there would be a little rush as families and friends turned up, but most of the time I might only do five or six covers. It was a nice way to wind down the day, and I was getting paid overtime by then too.

Soon I was feeling part of the family. Everyone was happy with me, including my bosses Steve and Bill, who wore tailored suits and groovy ties. Steve was the non-medical services manager, who handled not just food and beverages but the cleaning, laundry and other support services. He was friendly like a community policeman, stopping to briskly chat, alert to your mood and trying to get any kind of in-house gossip out of you.

Bill, the food and beverage manager was a true East Ender. With sly eyes and a tight grin, he was that perfect wide-boy mix of spot-on grooming, immaculate clothes and superbly foul mouth. Bill didn't fish for information like Steve did because he already knew everything that was happening in his manor – both inside the hospital and outside. Bill had all the intel and gossip about the East End but had only been out of London twice in his life.

What really fascinated him was the stories of my life in tropical North Queensland. Absolutely rapt, he'd question me about the snakes, sharks and crocodiles;

the freaks living in driftwood, tin and tarpaulin shacks on the beach. He lapped up my accounts of three-day long parties with magic-mushroom tripping DJs rocking home-brew sound systems. And the scrub-itch, tropical ulcers and all those nude and unshaven young women! Thrilled and disgusted in equal measure, he'd slowly shake his head in amazement and repeatedly ask, "Are you fucking with me?"

Working in big cities is a grind when there's a long commute. My fourteen-hour day included a two-hour return trip. Day after day I shared the Tube train with London commuters and their silence and stony faces made me want to scream or bare my arse or something. I knew I'd got lucky when someone at the hospital asked me to if I'd like to share an apartment located just one street away from work.

One day as I knocked off, a guy in a suit and spectacles approached me, introduced himself and suggested we go for a beer. I'd seen him around – in the operating wing one day and behind a computer in the main office the next. We'd had a brief conversation when I'd come across him replacing code cards in the satellite TV black box. He was a man of mystery.

Over drinks I found out that Nick, born and bred in Manila, had checked me out. His countrymen in the kitchen had given me the thumbs-up so he suggested I move in with him and his roommate.

I immediately agreed when I heard the deal.

The three-bedroom, centrally heated apartment with two bathrooms and two toilets, *and* all bills included, cost a grand total of forty-five pounds a week . . . split between the three of us! Wow. For all of that in the heart of the East End? It was outrageously cheap. The amazing deal was courtesy of the owner of the flat who wasn't short of a quid. He owned the whole block of eight flats *and* the grocery, bottle shop, laundry and newsagent beneath them. He was from the Philippines too, and his altruism was about helping us young fellas to study and work.

The only proviso was that once a month he'd rock up with a carton of beer, get blind drunk with us, and then sleep on the fold-out couch. That was easy – he was a nice guy and of course we loved him. As a bonus there were also three pubs within one hundred metres of the flat.

I moved in and got to know Nick. Like me, he did twelve-hour days – studying for his British MD exams while working long shifts at the hospital in several departments. He'd been a doctor in his own country, including working at Metro Manila Emergency, where Friday nights sounded like the seventh level of hell.

Nick and I soon became fast friends. He wrote music, and loved Miles Davis and Al Jarreau like I did. He'd read much classical literature and could quote passages verbatim. Sometimes he'd drunkenly jump up on a table at our local pubs and declaim Shakespeare -

startling, then entertaining the East-End drinkers.

Nick only watched CNN and the BBC and read numerous scientific and medical journals. Not only did he have a fine mind but a wicked sense of humour too.

Though he was a doctor, Nick had developed a taste back home for shooting pistols and sub-machine guns, with the Beretta Model 12 being a favourite.

"So, Nick, how do you justify this fascination with firearms when you have taken the Hippocratic oath?" I challenged him one day.

"Well, Che Guevara did it."

We got on famously after work, consuming fine brandies, blocks of good hashish and uncountable pints of beer. We got boisterous at times and this alarmed our flatmate.

Beho was a clean-cut young Malaysian guy studying electronics. A bespectacled super-nerd with no vices except Coca Cola and pot noodles, he looked upon our antics with a mixture of confused amusement and real fear. He had inherent respect for us because we were older and worldlier than him, but he sensed he could not truly be inferior when we so often acted crazy and stupid.

One night, back from the pub and fairly far gone on this and that, Nick and I protested our early morning starts by smashing Nick's alarm clock with a hammer, throwing it into the toilet bowl and then spraying it with fly spray. Poor Beho, totally unnerved by this destructive and frankly illogical behaviour, wailed fearfully from his doorway. "Please! Please stop it! I'm scared!"

Fortunately for our minds and livers Nick and I didn't share days off. I often wandered the East End streets sniffing out long gone Limehouse and prowling the Isle of Dogs. At Spitalfields Markets I heard the eternal cries of the street-hawkers and marketeers.

All around me were infamous places like the Tower of London and The Blind Beggar, and we'd often see Jack-the-Ripper tours passing by one of our local pubs. There were also a couple of spooky but marvellous Hawksmoor churches up the road. The whole area was haunted by the maddest history and I felt it.

The Private Hospital had its own history too. It had only been recently built on the site of a previous hospital – the London Jewish Hospital. This had stood for eighty or ninety years, and included kosher kitchens, nurses' quarters and a morgue.

One night I had a very strange experience there. It was after work and I was looking for Nick, who I knew was setting up operating theatres. Trotting around the empty surgery wing, opening doors and calling out, I walked into one theatre and looked around. No Nick.

When I turned to leave, I saw a face looking in through the window set in the door. It wasn't Nick – it looked like an old bloke. Then the face was gone. I hurried to the door, a few steps away, went out and felt a giddy shudder.

A lean figure was walking briskly up the hall, but

this person was impossibly far from the door! There was no way they could have walked or even run that fast. It was all wrong and when he turned to look at me, I felt a sudden urge to do wee-wee. I saw a gaunt old man whose left hand seemed twisted or injured . . . and his eyes! They bored relentlessly into me from many meters away. Then he turned and hurried off around a corner. I tried to loudly call to him, but only a squeak came out.

Thoroughly shaken I went to report the intruder. The two security lads listened, grins forming on their faces and as I got to the description, one of them cut in.

"Old fella, right? Freaky eyes and really skinny with one hand all busted up?"

"Oh, you know him," I said. "Is he a new cleaner?"

The security boys chuckled merrily. "No, he's the ghost, mate. You saw the ghost!"

The hospital had quite a few Muslim and Jewish patients, and most of them were very strict, religiously so, about their diets. We had kosher food that arrived in sealed packs like army rations and just needed heating, but the halal food was made by us. Or rather me. The Filipino lads were all fun-loving Catholics who dug pork crackling, so somehow the role of halal chef fell onto my shoulders, atheist Anglo boy from Australia that I was.

We'd get in halal certified meat and produce that

was all pre-sealed, and I worked in a special area with special knives and utensils. I had the responsibility of making sure none of the food became tainted with any non-halal products and I felt kind of honoured. It was rather magical and I took it very seriously, but when I encountered the heavy-duty religious dudes one day I cracked up.

On my way down to see a Sister, as the video phones were down again, I shared the lift with two men. They were old and looked very wise, and they had the most incredible flowing beards and their eyebrows were just. . . wow! They wore the robes, hats and accoutrements of Imams – the devout Islamic holy men. They looked like they'd stepped out of the ninth century but were no doubt visiting a patient here in the twentieth.

In my own uniform – chef's whites and checks, hat and neckerchief – I nodded politely and tried not to stare. But they stared at me – and sort of watched my chef's hat as we went down. This attention gave me an uncalled-for surge of nervous laughter, which out of respect I managed to suppress.

We went down a floor, the doors opened and in walked . . . two Jewish Rabbis! These guys were equally as impressive and old as the Imams, and they too had robes and hats on. They both had magnificent beards and their eyebrows were . . . double wow! The doors closed and we stood there in silence. The Imams looked at the Rabbis and the Rabbis looked at the Imams. Then they all looked at me. I tried to clamp down hard but my nervous laughter boiled up again. No disrespect to them or their religions, but they were just so epic and serious and had so much beard and eyebrow between them! I tried hard to behave but I couldn't help squeaking with mirth and blinking with tears. A huge apocalyptic blast of disapproval came from them. They knew I was cracking up with laughter and they did not like it one bit. I turned to the wall, stifling my hysteria but when the doors opened, I ran from the lift bellowing with laughter.

That winter the first Gulf War was declared and security at the Private Hospital got even tighter. One night there was a military armoured car outside, an incongruous sight to see parked on a leafy London street. I got the feeling that someone important had turned up.

This someone turned out to be one of the richest oil sultans in the world. He took a whole floor and stayed there for weeks with a large entourage of family and friends. He also had a team of bodyguards and they were pissed off. It seemed they weren't allowed to carry their guns on British soil. Down the hall, twenty-four hours a day, were the British government bodyguards who were allowed to carry guns on British soil. I heard all about this from my spy-of-a-boss Bill.

I got to meet the British security detail, five relaxed men in nice fitting suits; all veterans, I guessed, of Goose Green, Northern Ireland, and who knows where else. They had a room to hang up their jackets, watch telly and eat in. I'd personally deliver their dinner and try to get them to tell me about their job. They never said much and politely ignored my requests to see their guns. They would amuse themselves by peeping out the door and winking down the hall at the Sultan's un-weaponised bodyguards, who would glower back at them.

One night during the Sultan's stay I was roused from a game of chess with Philip by the kitchen phone ringing. I answered and a voice confirmed that I was the chef who had been on duty the night before. Then it said, "The Sultan of _____ will now speak to you."

Thinking it was Nick playing a prank I began to formulate a snappy reply. Then a new voice came on and I could hear ten million dollars in every syllable. It was a very polite voice.

"Good evening," the voice said. "Did you cook the steak for me last night?"

"Yes, I did."

"With the pepper sauce?" He was making sure it really was me.

"Ah no, it was a mushroom sauce; with morels."

"Yes, and very nice too," said the voice warmly. "May I have this again please?"

I liked that please. It was most gratifying to hear one of the richest men in the world acknowledging the power of the Good Cook.

He put his money where his mouth was too. When the Sultan left, he tipped the hospital staff twenty thousand pounds and I got my three hundred quid share of it.

Perks and Misdemeanours

Let's put my journey on a back burner for a minute and look at some stuff attendant to a kitchen professional's life. Stuff, unfairly or not, that has often characterised how those working in the cooking industry are perceived. Whether it's looking sharp on the job or letting their hair down after hours, chefs and cooks have carved out their own special lifestyle niche. So, let's talk about the free food, the groovy white jackets . . . and the sex and drugs.

We all know that sexual attraction in the workplace is not so uncommon, but there's a physicality about kitchens that can distill erotic thought. You see, hear and smell your workmates as they sweat, grunt, squat and twist. Thighs and bums, chests and arms are moving and stretching, wiggling, bulging and snapping into clear-cut definition.

Depending on your workmates, all this may or

may not be a pleasant thing. If it's the former, then keep those hormonal urges under the belt. Subtly appreciate how your co-worker makes you feel, but understand it's just a case of kitchen concupiscence and nothing more.

And when there comes a time when you're that little bit too tired, that little bit too drunk, and you start to get up close and personal with a waiter or a chef or, God forbid the owner – then run like hell from this moment.

'Don't get your meat where you get you bread from' is the rotten pessimistic idea that things might muck up when a professional relationship turns sexual. It's when you're both back at work the next day, sheepish and hung-over, and the work practices that flowed so naturally before are now awkward. The giving of commands, the correcting of mistakes ain't so cool anymore. It's hard to be objective and considered about someone who has ridden a runaway sex-loco with you just a few hours earlier. The balance is skewed now; the kitchen hierarchy knocked out of line. Everyone tries to be mellow and easy but a slinky, stinky spanner still slides into the works. Communication just isn't as good and crucial time gets wasted on sweet nothings.

With one exception I've never mixed work and sex. I will admit on occasion I've fished for it, all the while fooling myself it was really just a test of willpower.

One year at Frogs I worked with an apprentice in her late teens who got my heart and glands atingle.

Helen's parents had come from opposite sides of the world and the co-mingling of genes had made her curvaceous and beautiful. It wasn't just her physicality that was so attractive – she was good at her job, whip-smart, with a great sense of humour and the most appealing laugh. I was smitten.

We got on really well but I had no illusions that she might find me in any way attractive. I maintained a professional relationship with Helen until the night I suggested we go swimming in the river after work.

It was a pretty quiet service but very humid, so we were both drenched in sweat. The Barron River was a five-minute walk away and there was a good moon up. As we finished, I proposed going for a swim and was silently delighted when Helen agreed.

Down at the river it was bright with moonlight; the rain forest hummed with insects, and echoed with the peep-peep of frogs and the occasional night bird cry. The little jetty there was deserted at 10 pm and I quickly stripped off, facing away from Helen of course, and dived into the refreshingly cool water.

As I've got older, I've learnt to be a gentleman and not take advantage of a situation to perv at a nude woman. But I wasn't more than three years older than Helen, and I started chatting to her so I could keep on looking.

She stripped off her chef's clothes and boots and stood there in her bra and panties. I bobbed wide-eyed in the water, my patter faltering at the sight of this goddess. Her long hair glistened with silvery light and her divine feminine form was silhouetted against a star ravished sky.

Helen was as cool as a cucumber, talking right back at me . . . still in her underwear. Time stood still. Was she going to take everything off? Would she turn away when she did? Or would she look me in the eye as she got nude?

Then Helen stopped talking to me, gave a girlish whoop and dived into the river.

I tried not to feel disappointed. I tried hard to be an adult. All those thoughts I'd been entertaining should have just flowed off me like river water. I wish.

As we splashed around and talked, I found it impossible to forget that this wasn't just my work-mate. I was in the presence of a gorgeous water nymph who was as sexy as hell. It was most embarrassing. I knew nothing was going to happen so any obvious signs of physical excitement were most unwanted.

I swam a little way out to calm down and something close-by in the water snorted with the same volume that a medium-sized pig would make. It was a couple of metres away and it spluttered again sending up a spray of droplets into the moonlight. What is this? I swum closer and saw a dark shape in the water; its eyes gleaming at me. Now I saw lines of ribbed scales in the lunar glow. It was a crocodile.

I got a little jolt of shock but I knew it was cool. The Barron River here was three hundred and thirty metres above sea level, so this was a freshwater crocodile looking at me. Freshies are not aggressive and often very curious. Nevertheless, it was at least a metre long so I began back-pedalling. My new chum followed, and Helen, noticing something was up, quickly swam over. As I began to fill her in – the crocodile snorted water at her. Helen stared at the dark form and then shrieked with shock. She rapidly swam to the jetty and was up onto it in a flash.

"It's harmless," I called, but the sweet interlude was over.

Our professional relationship benefited from this close encounter of the crocodilian kind. Whenever it got a bit hectic at work for Helen, I'd snort like that freshie did. She'd crack up with laughter and her tension would dissipate.

Getting it on with your work-mate's partner is also not advisable. At Ringos, the Sous-chef Chris, who was put to the sword by Lyle, was a bit of a cutie. With golden locks of hair and apple pink cheeks he looked like an angel. One night my girlfriend picked me up from work and Chris's face lit up at the sight of her. You guys should come over one night and meet my lady he told us.

A few weeks later we took him up on the invite. As we had a few drinks on the lounge I could see that

Chris was eyeing my partner lecherously. I checked out his girlfriend's reaction and was surprised to see that she was doing the same thing. They both thought my girlfriend was hot. My partner was a little naive and didn't pick up on the lubricious undercurrents oozing around the room. Chris's girlfriend began to lean in close to me and I pretended not to notice the freckles on her chest. Next thing, Chris was chopping up four lines of white powder and a glossy magazine of hard-core pornography appeared on the coffee table. Chris's lady started excitedly pointing out certain positions and combinations of couples in the magazine that appealed to her. My girlfriend made up for her lack of worldliness with a very up-front manner. She loudly informed Chris's missus that she, and her man, were sleazebags, and that we were leaving.

On the way home the moral calibre of my work-mate was discussed and did I know what they had planned? It didn't take long for my girlfriend to see that group-sex and cocaine use with my Sous-chef was as unappealing to me as it was to her. Back at work Chris said nothing. It was business as usual but his cherub face had taken on some Caravaggio shadows.

My girlfriend, who was a feisty woman, had no qualms about jumping my bones at another restaurant I later worked at. Turning up in the afternoon, when I was the only person on, she'd collar me, and in the staff-shower we'd indulge in a good old stand-up knee-trembler. This all went well until the day we were interrupted by the Head Chef unexpectedly banging on the door. I grabbed a towel and emerged to the faint smell of burning. Chef had come back early to find two pies I'd made starting to scorch in the oven. Towel-clad, I stood in the doorway as he began to give me a dressing down.

Confused as to why I was taking a long shower in the afternoon, his demeanour changed when a feminine cough came from behind me. Realization dawned and as he finished up telling me off there was admiration in his eyes.

I was lucky to have a staff shower and the place mostly to myself, but for most of the time, bumping uglies at work is fraught with complications. So, when domestic circumstance, or overwhelming lust compels the randy to practice sexual intercourse in the workplace – like everything in the hospitality industry it must be done at speed. Finding a place for a quickie requires precision timing.

In one restaurant I worked at, the store-room became mysteriously locked at times and over the hum of freezers and air-con units I could make out rhythmic bumping and muffled cries. A head count revealed that two, sometimes three of the wait staff were getting jiggy in there. With great consideration for their colleagues they restrained themselves til after service and were all home and hosed in five minutes or less.

There is sometimes outrageous sexual humour in kitchens. As long as it isn't about putting anyone down or deliberately offending them, then a joke can be a good circuit breaker. With the right set of deviants, the kitchen air can turn bluer than a piece of raw steak. In such kitchens, pranks of a sexual nature, pulled by all sexes, are rife. The white flour hand print on the bum of a front of house worker's black pants is a silly giggle, and the cucumber under the apron can still raise a smile.

But I was once rather dismayed to see a chef unzip his checks to lay his own joint of meat amongst the vegetables on a garnished plate. The incredulous kitchen crew watched as this merry fellow, on some special wave-length with a waitress, carefully offer the plate to her, claiming it was for table so-and-so. Her puzzlement at the queer way he was holding the plate turned into fascinated disgust, then bawdy amusement as she saw what he was doing

"Is that an entrée size?" she crowed, then, "No, no – it's a half serve!" Her zingers got us laughing but the dish-pig used thick grill-cleaning gloves to handle the plate.

Now we don't normally associate kitchens with nudity but I've seen partially and fully naked people in the kitchen a few times. I must confess that one of those times it was me cooking in the raw.

At Frogs Restaurant, I was having a knock-off

shower out back when Rain from front of house called through the door. Could I make a spaghetti Marinara for a mutual friend, and good customer, who had joined a table late? Of course, I agreed, and for a laugh sneaked around the back garden into the empty kitchen wearing only a towel.

In the kitchen I discarded it, put on an apron and began cooking. The apron covered my front but not my behind and when Rain popped his head in to see how I was going he roared with mirth.

Of course, he had to get our friend, my plan all along, and when she saw me cooking her dinner, still pink and rosy from the shower, she screamed with delighted laughter. Soon there were a few of her friends clustered in the doorway, drinks in hand, laughing and wolf whistling.

On another occasion at Frogs the perpetrator gave me and Terry heart palpitations in the middle of a busy service. A colourful local identity had arranged a night of entertainment at Frogs, selling tickets to see an exotic dancer.

It was a hot summer night; the place was packed with locals and Terry and I were very busy. Exotic music started and the show commenced. Out in the restaurant we heard a huge, mainly masculine roar every minute or so as the dancer went through her act. This excitement culminated in sustained cheering and the stamping of feet on the restaurant's wooden floors.

Then an attractive young woman ran into the kitchen and breathlessly asked us where the cold room was. She was hot and sweaty and totally naked. Terry politely pointed to the cold room door and the nude woman disappeared inside.

Terry and I exchanged looks of surprise. We had no prior indication that the dancing was going to be this exotic. The docket rack was full and we went back to cooking, but all the while pondering the inevitable. The kitchen had no reach-in fridges so at some point we had to get ingredients from the cold room. Being gentlemen, we waited for as long as possible but the young lady remained behind the door. I needed multiple portions of marinara mix and more fish so I zipped into the cold room, where the unabashed dancer smiled at me in greeting.

It was a small cold room and she was in no way slim. I had to gingerly squeeze around her to get what was needed. She thought it was funny and made little effort in making space. Instead she wriggled a bit and giggled a lot.

This was highly irregular! Here I was in the middle of a busy service, stuck in the cold room, pressed up against a naked woman who was laughing in my face and pushing her chilled nipples into my arm. As I made the final stretch and got what was needed, she said. "I'm Josie by the way. I'm so hot."

I'd like to be able to tell you that people don't use drugs in kitchens – that all the heat and flames, hot oil, sharp knives and mad energy are a trip in itself. Or that it's just too hard and dangerous to navigate a shift while off chops. Well I can't.

Like nurses, musicians and flight crew, kitchen staff and front of house work long strange hours and they often party as hard as they work. That's fine for afterhours but there are drugged-up people negotiating the whirly-gig of a busy service. The spliff monster or gaping set of nostrils in an apron might think they are more focused, awake and productive, but medical science has shown this to be utter tosh.

Beyond their physical and mental effects, drugs can do strange things to your emotions, as can the long hours and intense pressure of service. So, getting high in the kitchen will just double down the state of one's psyche. Unsurprisingly the emotions that drug-users release in a busy kitchen are often not nice ones. The wired can scream the loudest. The loaded can spit the dummy right across the room and bounce it off the cold room door. The trippers can get really passionate just before they slip and fall. Or cut or burn themselves. Or disappear . . . owing money.

I don't recommend drug use and high-pressure cooking at the same time. I found the two incompatible as enjoyable things to do; after one deeply unpleasant experience I resolved never again to work when high.

I'd had a few tokes on a sensi fattie before work and obliterated my short-term memory. Things burnt or boiled over and I kept going into the cold room for . . . something. It was horrible. Being high ruined the fun of cooking and cooking ruined the fun of being high – at the same time!

Sometimes you have no say in it. Honestly chef. At a party in the house where I lived, some young mates wanted me to take MDMA with them. I declined. I had an early start to a busy day and the drinking and hangover would be quite enough. I eventually retired to bed and went out like a light. In the morning I awoke thirsty, and from a glass next to my bed guzzled the water I'd poured myself the night before. Within half an hour I'd showered, dressed and got into work.

As I started the morning prep, I felt a bit odd. Then a classic Ecstasy rush started coursing through me. Those little bastards had spiked my glass of water! The rush got stronger and stronger. I had been given a giant dose! It was going to be a hell busy day and if I went home, I'd really let the crew down and I couldn't do that.

I mentally gritted my teeth and began to ride the chemical waves. Time went all wibbly wobbly. My ears tingled, my prostate gland started smiling and I began prepping like a fiend.

It took nine hours or maybe thirty seconds to load the reach-in fridges for lunch service. I kind of mucked around with my boning knife and two kilos of Barramundi were suddenly filleted and portioned.

It seemed that I had reverse-engineered twenty dessert tarts, then I realised it was just the memory of making them that I was feeling. Nothing made sense but it all got done. The floor became a lot further away from my feet and I instantly invented a new way to walk. I felt intense pride at how I'd solved that problem.

The waiting staff arrived and they looked truly beautiful. I dubbed them The Forever Souls and they laughed at me just the way flowers laugh. Big hits of pleasure flooded through me and my grin felt too big for my face.

Then service started and I focused like a sniper in trifocals. The words on the order dockets stood out in the blackest black ink I'd ever seen and I could really see how the printer made such perfect edges of each and every letter. It got very busy and I became a diamond stylus stuck in the groove of the service, sweating so profusely my jacket soaked through. I used reams of paper towel to wipe my brow. It got even busier and I was spinning and moving like a manic gimbal; cooking, plating up, garnishing and ringing the bell. More orders flowed in and I felt like I was melting. Liquid lava was flowing through my veins so I called for jugs of ice-water and gratefully chugged them down. The kitchen was intensely bright and steaks on the grill seemed to turn over by themselves.

Then service tapered out, but I was still totally off my head. I looked around and there was the Head Chef, who had been working next to me the whole time, staring intently at me.

"You're really out of it," he said.

"Yes, I am," I agreed. "I don't know how I managed. How did I do all that?"

He looked none too pleased. "What the hell did you do that for?"

I told him about getting my water spiked and he shook his head in pity. He was a party monster himself and knew how hard it must have been.

"Well you did OK but I was worried." He was laughing now. "You looked really crazy but I didn't want you to go home. At least not until you screwed up big time. You wanna go home now?"

I sure did.

Sex and drugs are pretty rare at work. The most dependable perk in kitchens is, of course, food. During long shifts nourishment is certainly needed and most places allow kitchen crew to eat a hot meal. This freebie is generally a menu item that has to be used up or is present in large quantities.

Tasting food while working is fine but eating it is a no-no. Sit down, take your time eating, and then go wash your hands. Everyone has popped food into their mouths while they're working and the trick is to place it precisely into your gob so your fingers don't come in contact with your mouth.

There are perennially peckish chefs who hoover up excess food during service. Through miscalculation, we assume, too many ingredients go into a pan dish. What's left after dishing-up is scoffed down lickety-quick. An uneaten bread-roll needs up-cycling and is smeared with a gob of rich sauce. Excess fries (how can that be?) get snuffled up between rushes.

Or take a close look at someone 'checking on the quality'. Slices of lovely tuna surreptitiously consumed; oysters scarfed while alone at the sink. Chunky bits of pâté swallowed as smoothly as a python taking a sleeping mouse. Lovely caramelised ends of freshly roasted beef gone in six seconds.

Many cooks find the thought of eating at work unpalatable. Dealing with food for hours on end wrecks their appetites. Oodles of decent food is available but they can't get their mandibles around it. Besides they're too busy. There's always time for another coffee though. And a cigarette.

Finally getting hungry around midnight, the only available food is often not too healthy - cheese and toast at home or a greasy kebab at the all-night joint.

Sometimes, usually on big buffets and at cocktail parties, there is leftover food. A kindly Head Chef will give the nod, and the front-of-house staff, who pay for their meals, will flock to this takeaway windfall like a mob of happy bin-chickens. In a good kitchen the dish pig will already have been taken care of, with a selection of food put aside for them by the cooks. Of course, it goes against the grain; the whole point of the exercise, to give food away, but it's better than binning it. I got into a bit of trouble once for not throwing food away.

A major department store threw a cocktail party for a new branch opening and our catering company did the finger food. Only a quarter of the guests turned up leaving us with hundreds and hundreds of carefully made up finger food titbits. Each perfectly assembled and garnished item couldn't be reused. The client's staff and security took some and we made up a few boxes for ourselves. But there were still masses of food laid out in rows on grease-proof paper lined bread crates. No-one wanted to be the one to throw it all away.

Then I had the bright idea of stopping off at a Homeless Mission on the way back to the kitchen. We could donate the food to them. The crew agreed and we stopped at the big hostel.

Men talking and smoking out front turned to stare as I went in. Inside residents looked up from the telly and card games. A grateful manager told us to bring it all into their cold room. As we carried the food in, a few residents wandered over, their interest piqued by our chef's jackets and the trays of colourful food.

"What's all that boys?" one old fella inquired.

"OK let me see," I said. "These are Tasmanian smoked salmon rosettes on wild rice blinis. With fresh dill mayo. These are herb-encrusted roast beef and asparagus mini rolls, the mustard is seeded not hot. These are Arancini balls – rice and cheese and a touch of lemon zest. And these are . . ."

The old bloke laughed with surprise and yelled out to his mates. "Hey come and take a dekko at this! Prince bloody Charles would go these I reckon – and it's all for us!"

The homeless men absolutely loved it, the food and the irony too, but when our bosses found out where the uneaten finger food had ended up – they flipped. While acknowledging we'd done a decent and charitable thing, they loudly swore us to silence, deathly afraid that the client would hear what had happened to the food they'd spent top dollar on.

The cooking professional wears a uniform and the expectation is that it's spotlessly clean and giving off a super hygienic glow. The golden rule is - one day is one wear. Unfortunately, some grub-chefs wear the same uniform for several days. Hand wiping leaves a yellow grey sheen across the arse. Side trouser pockets develop shiny greasy openings, and because it's food the crusty culprit begins to smell quite rancid. I wouldn't eat anywhere where the kitchen crew look like this.

Some kitchens have a change room and lockers for the crew to put their street clothes in. These facilities are handy because wearing a chef's uniform in public can attract unwanted attention. I was nearly late for work once when a little old lady stopped and loudly interrogated me about a long-forgotten (but not by her) technique for larding a roast that her grandmother had taught her.

A chef needs a fresh back-up jacket and apron if they are in a customer facing position like a carvery on a buffet. At a pinch a lightly soiled jacket can be re-cycled as they are double breasted with removable plastic stud buttons. By swapping over sides, any stains in the centre of the chest are concealed. Dirty aprons can be reversed too.

Boots and clogs get pimpled with spots of blood, grease and batter – anything that drips really – and so need regular cleaning. Soles must be scraped out as food in the treads goes right off. At one remote resort a young grill chef would just chuck his uncleaned boots outside his door each night. Bush rats nibbled on them and then a pack of feral dogs turned up, ripped one boot to bits and made off with the other one to consume at their leisure. The fool had to pay through the nose in town for a new pair.

This chef shared his donga, which is slang for the demountable staff accommodation common on remote sites, with his hard-drinking barmaid girlfriend and a party-boy yardie. These kids were grots and that wasn't so unusual. While working at remote locales I saw many youngsters undomesticating themselves. Their shared dongas would be a scree of bras, jocks, condom and cigarette packets, with fishing rods, guitars and bongs squeezed into corners. Tables were covered in ashtrays and makeup and everywhere was empty alcohol bottles. Cleaning up was not a priority and these dongas grew feculent from spilt grog, old sex and dank clothes.

Living with your workmates is a lifestyle and the kitchen companionship doesn't really stop when the shift finishes. At such locales as ski lodges and island resorts, bunking with, and sharing downtime with the crew is the norm. When you're young it's a blast and lasting friendships can form, but as one gets older it's much more appealing to retire to your room with a book, cable TV and a cup of tea.

The best thing about working remote is that you usually live where you work so you don't waste hours commuting. I've travelled long round-trips to work long shifts enough times to actively seek work close to home. To be able to get to work in minutes – not hours is a very big plus.

At one time I lived in a small country town where I had an eight-minute walk from home to my job on the main street. Then I moved into a caretaker's flat in a complex right by the main street. From here it took me a minute and twenty seconds to get to work. Then I changed jobs and started working at a restaurant situated right in the complex where I lived. Walking from my front door to work now took a total of twenty-two seconds. I'd have to sleep on the kitchen floor to beat that.

Urban Vegan

When I started out, most cooks and chefs would rather be having a beer in the time it took to make something off-menu for a vegetarian to eat. With all the fantastic meat dishes on the menu it was the height of perversity to them. Nowadays chefs and cooks know that a reasonable percentage of their customers are going to be vegetarian, even vegan. Luckily for such herbivorous diners, menus nowadays are well and truly reflecting this.

When I got back to Australia, I worked for again for my mate Terry in North Queensland at two of his restaurants. I had a grand time with him for a few years and then the wander bug bit me again. The late nineties found me doing the food at a mainly vegan cafe in the heart of Brisbane's Fortitude Valley.

The café, called the Goanna, was deep in the McWhirter centre, a heritage listed edifice built in 1912. The five-story building was a warren of shops with a bustling food court occupying the basement level.

Here the Goanna occupied a lucrative little niche amongst the deep-fried chicken joints, sandwich shops, bakeries and carveries. There was nothing remotely like it around and the food was made with love and care. The cafe had a loyal following and we nearly always sold out of food by the day's end.

The Goanna's chalk-board signage explained that, with the exception of three or four dishes that contained cheese, clarified butter and honey, there were no animal products used in our food. Vegetarian food, of course, contains no meat, offal or animal fat, but it can be made with animal products – cheese, milk, butter, yogurt, eggs and honey. Vegan food however, is not made with anything produced by an animal.

I'm no vegan, or vegetarian, but I made really good food at The Goanna. I enjoyed making and eating it and was always honest about being an omnivore. Invariably a customer would eagerly ask, "So how long have you been a vegan?"

"I'm not. I enjoy a steak and a martini," I'd reply. "But I make the best vegan you'll eat in this lifetime!"

Most people, inspired by my honest pride would get some food, but now and then a customer would give me an intense look of betrayal and huff off in disgust. It was their loss.

I knew a little bit about vegetarian food and at the Goanna I learnt a whole lot more. The owner/chef Jenna had encyclopaedic knowledge and she showed me the tricks, techniques and ingredients of the vegan cook. I learnt to make cakes, cookies, slices, quiches and flans without eggs, butter or cream.

I found out about tofu and exactly what you could do with it. Silken tofu made creamy dips and substituted for eggs and cream in a quiche filling. Soft tofu was great in a lasagna, soup or a bake. Firm tofu, marinated in soy and sesame, would be grilled as a burger and served with some spicy relish on a bap.

Aside from using the tofu, and slices of grilled paneer cheese that we made, there were also burgers made with tempeh – the Indonesian soybean product with a rich fermented taste. I'd make a couple of other burger patties each day too, maybe black-eyed beans, onion jam and spinach or chick pea and fresh coriander. The customer could choose a sauce like tamarind chili or tahini lemon to complement their choice of patty.

And though they were vegan ingredients, I was taught to avoid processed food like normal wheat flour and white sugar. Soon I was shaving jaggery and sifting spelt.

Most of the menu was different each day and this made the job real fun. Soon I was cooking solo and I'd make up six salads, two pies, two pastas, quiches, two soups, bakes, stir fries, two desserts, dips, cupcakes and muffins. And maybe two curries. I'd try out new recipes while slowly rotating popular dishes across the week. The customers loved it and so did I.

Directly across from us was a McDonald's outlet and Goanna regulars enjoyed turning their backs on the Golden Arches to check out our food. There was the cold section on one side and the hot section on the other, and our daily fare was presented in abundant style.

The cafe was strictly day trade and throughout the lunch rush I'd wok up new stir fries and get the knife rocking to top up salads. More rice would get cooked and fryers would bubble and hiss with batches of bhajis and pakoras. I'd also be grilling slabs of marinated tofu, red basil paneer and tempeh for burgers, and heating up samosas and Hunza rolls in the oven.

The kitchen was separated from the service area by an ornately carved wood screen and out the front my young offsider, Denise, would make juices, smoothies and lassies, also plate up orders and work the till. She was calm and fairly reserved; a country lass just out of her teens. She had brand new tattoos and piercings and eschewed the trappings of Babylon – things like make-up and brassieres. We would thank each other at the end of work for being a good team, and we were.

The Goanna had a reputation for quality as the food was top-notch. It was also a most right-on place to eat. Our healthy soul food drew hippies, greenies, lefties and travellers, freaks, funkateers and ferals - young and old. On the week-ends when the street markets of the

Fortitude Valley mall boomed upstairs, some of the most colourful folk on the Australian east coast would come to eat at The Goanna. Many customers seemed of a spiritual bent, or maybe just bent. The edges of our shop front were plastered with posters advertising every kind of guru and visionary, all kind of classes and courses, and all the latest hip music gigs and bush doofs. I loved feeding these children of the universe.

I always looked forward to the thin, but very fit, dude I dubbed Mr. Natural. He looked somehow royal, like an incognito king from an epic ballad. He was tough enough to walk bare foot in the stinky old Valley but his gray hair and white beard were both short and neatly trimmed. Upon arrival he would look with painfully pure affection at Denise and I, eternally grateful at our continuing presence in the urban guts of it all. I'd feel his gaze, look up and call out a greeting. He'd smile wordlessly, aching with silent love for me and then, almost apologetically, his attention would be drawn back to the food.

With barely suppressed joy he'd hog the display window and methodically take in our offerings for the day. Now and then he'd glance up at me and on his face would be an expression of disbelieving happiness at some magnificent miracle of a morsel I had manifested. I'd smile and he'd smile and we'd share a soul stiffy. Then regretfully, he'd curtail our love-in and bow his head back to his task.

I reckon Mr. Natural mentally tasted everything he looked at. Finally, he would bashfully give his order to Denise and then gladly take control of his heaped-high plate. Bestowing a cascade of smiles upon us he would gracefully glide over to a table. A couple of times I'm sure I saw him floating – his feet not quite touching the food-court floor.

The real spiritual heavyweight turned up silently one afternoon after the lunch rush had subsided. Denise was taking a break, and while I did some prep, I watched the front for customers. I glanced up and saw a man checking out our food. I saw straight away that he was an honest-to-goodness Buddhist monk. He had robes, a shaved head, prayer-beads and a wise and serene Asian face. I stopped my prepping but he caught my eye and wordlessly indicated that he wanted to browse a bit longer. I acknowledged him with a little bow and went back to peeling galangal.

As I worked, I kept glancing up. The monk bent to peer through the display glass as he took in every single thing. He looked pretty damn cool – a photograph of him right now would make a brilliant ad for the place! Day-dreaming at my chopping board I imagined he was an illuminated master, possibly endowed with mystical powers. I heard a polite cough and I went to see what he'd chosen. He pointed at a bake.

"Chicken?" he said, his eyes darting to mine.

"No, no!" I nearly yelled. "No chicken in that."

I took a quick deep breath, recomposed myself and proudly pointed to our menu boards. "Please look. See there's nothing bad in our food."

He ignored the menus and his sharp eyes flicked back to the food. I waited patiently, calmly, secure in the knowledge that my food was the real deal. A gentle smile touched my face. The master was in for a treat. He uncurled a finger and I strained to see what he was going to point at. The finger came to full stretch. Ah – the spinach and sweet potato curry. Good choice.

"Pork?" he said.

"No!" I cried out. "No pork!"

I couldn't believe he wasn't getting the vibe of The Goanna and I couldn't believe I'd nearly lost it again. With some effort I re-centered myself. He was testing me – I could see that now. He nodded silently, his eyes boring into mine and I felt like he was finding me wanting. I had to do better. He quickly pointed at a samosa.

"Beef?"

I shook my head happily and felt a wonderful warm glow go up my spine. "No beef," I said. He seemed to frown and then pointed to the plain steamed rice that we always did.

"Rice please," he said. I waited for the rest of his order. We stared at each other until he said, "Small bowl."

I felt myself deflating as I served him and I went back to my galangal feeling very disappointed. My quest to give culinary satori to the master had floundered. Then a few days later I found out that some Buddhists eat meat. I now realised the hungry monk was one of them. And I thought I was disappointed!

With their own spiritual aesthetic and a taste for our food were the travelling tribes, who were also known as ferals. This mob, through whatever means necessary, travelled around Australia going to outdoor parties and festivals, generally having lots of sex, taking heaps of drugs, and enjoying and celebrating nature and its spirits.

These wild, tattooed, body-pierced party elves and pixies instinctively got the food at The Goanna for all of its economic, social and moral reasons. And it tasted great! They were a small but enthusiastic stream of business, and the reputation and location of The Goanna passed amongst them by word of mouth, like the location of a great swimming hole.

There was a punk rock regular - a big fat fella who came in almost every afternoon after lunch. He was a man mountain of pasty white skin, jet black clothes and graying stubble. It didn't matter if there was a tropical downpour in the street outside, he'd still have wraparound sunnies glued to his dial.

I never heard him talk, but back in the origin tale of The Goanna he'd lumbered up and ordered four samosas with chili-tamarind sauce. And that's how it had been ever since. Now no-one needed to speak of it again. Sometimes there might only be two hot samosas left, even none, but that was fine. He'd didn't care if they were straight out of the fridge. Looking straight ahead while Denise bagged up his eternal choice, he was never tempted by anything else. The samosas were exactly what he needed. I was sure they were his breakfast.

Although vegetarian and vegan food have pretty much entered the mainstream, back then it had a lot of baggage. For some impressionable people – how you ate was intrinsic to what you wore, what music you listened to and how you thought about and reacted to the world. This herd mentality did good food no favours. Yes, it's true – the resources of the planet are finite, animals are farmed cruelly and mainstream diets can wreak real havoc with one's long term health, but blindly following something is no path to magic.

Many a potential recruit to the vegetarian cause has been scared off by terrible cooking skills. With ignorance and carelessness, you can ruin any set of ingredients, meatless or not. Vegetarian and vegan food does not have to be bland or boring in texture, colour or taste. Being really stoned or distracted by the Milky Way and the topless boys and girls dancing is no excuse to cook crap food.

Vegetarian food has no short-cuts or easy cheats in creating rich tasting meals. Without the full-on flavour rush that a flame-grilled chicken thigh or piece of fried fish brings to the table, good vegetarian food has to get smart. It's a most subtle process creating the complexities and depth of flavour that meat just inherently has. You can't just bang soy or miso into something and hope it works.

One tropical evening, invited to dinner at the beach camp next door to mine, I watched two young women gone feral for the rest of their teens dish up a vegetarian feast. I fancied one of them and was blatant with praise. Rewarded with sly smiles, graceful moves and coy shakes of her dreadlocks, my complimentary jibber went into overdrive.

When I received my battered, enamel plate piled high with food I inhaled the aroma and gave her my number-one – Mmmmmmm!

Steaming in the fire-light was brown rice topped with tofu, nuts and leafy green vegetables. With slow sensuality I slid a bit of tofu into my mouth and . . . ah . . . ah . . . miso overkill!

It was so intense I couldn't even go Mmmmmm again.

I quickly ate some rice. No relief there as it was also cooked with miso paste. The greens were just the same and after my giant suck-up I had to eat salty mouthful after salty mouthful until it was all gone.

Though I comprehensively lied about how wonderful it was, I really did appreciate the effort they'd gone to.

Being vegan or vegetarian doesn't have to be a macho challenge either. Back then a culinary political correctness ruled in punk/hippy/leftie households and tough-as-fuck feral camps. In a grim contest to see how down to earth and no-frills food could be, every scrap of vegetable matter was eaten. Weak-as-piss concepts, like food actually tasting good, were sacrificed for the cause. I hated it. Including the skin and seeds in pumpkin soup is gross. Eating hard unripe mangoes just because some fool picked them is stupid.

These food fascists scorned flavour too. Adding a little zest or zing to a meal was considered prohibitively Western. I was told that tribal people always ate simple. Rubbish. At any time in history, anyone, anywhere in the world, always craved a bit of extra flavour. They can't always get it, but given the choice? Yes please!

This first world elitism extended to the very size into which food was cut. Big was good. None of that itty-bitty city-boy rubbish. Ah, no. Indian, Asian and Middle Eastern food is bite-sized or smaller, because it's easier to eat, especially if using chopsticks or fingers as most non-western people do.

Well thank Gaia everybody is a lot more au fait nowadays and knows that even simple rice and veggies can be done right. No-one wants their day of earth magic, skinny dipping and sensual massage ruined by

052GAWAIN BARKER

having a bland and chunky meal splodged onto their banana leaf.

The Goanna's owner, Jenna, absolutely hated bad vegetarian food. It was a pet gripe of hers as she deeply understood the magic that comes from cooking good ingredients just right. Fortunately, she also had business nous. Relying on the weekend and alternate crowd would have sent her broke. There weren't enough of them and many lived on limited budgets.

During the week the bulk of our customers were downtown workers on their lunch break. We worked hard at making each new face a regular. Diet conscious younger women liked us; the food was healthy and good for the figure. Diet conscious older women felt the same way. There were guys too, usually young, in suits and ties or in chinos and polo necks. There was also a trickle of sweaty, dusty building site tradies and we loved those boys like a preacher loves new converts.

One regular was a neat nervy chap in a crisp suit. Our food was a real adventure for him, a glimpse into a world he scarcely dared enter. He was chatty, and fished for groovy tales of the wild free life he was sure Denise and I were leading. He'd covertly peruse the posters for bush parties and techno raves. When I suggested he go and get loved-up and funky at one, he blushed and spluttered excuses. There was something most wistful in his eyes though, and Denise and I joked about possibly spiking his tempeh burger with E.

One day he turned up almost in tears. He was leaving town, this was his last day, and he was going to sure miss . . . everything. Of course, lunch was on the house but he insisted on giving Denise and I twenty dollars each as thanks for all the good times. Eventually we accepted as he was becoming emotional. As he left, I saw his face turn in the crowd and throw a look of longing back at us. My heart went out to him, but at least he had the memories – of us all getting down at the three-day dance party in his mind.

Regulars came from all over. Two French women with little English knocked back smoothies and salads every day. Filipino ladies in chatty groups and even the occasional Chinese nana made their selections. French and Brazilian guys got heaped plates and sun-tanned backpackers from everywhere sucked down juices and lassis. We had Papuans and folk from Torres Strait with big hair and even bigger smiles, and there were some old Aussie and European pensioners attracted by the quality and price.

We always looked forward to two of them, Italian guys, besties forever, who'd take ages ascertaining that their food was totally different to each other's – "So I can have a taste of his." They were fairly experimental in their choices but hung out for any bake topped with crispy cheese.

At the Goanna I learnt so much about a field of cooking of which I'd been scarcely aware of. There was enormous freedom to come up with new dishes each day, and that was key for me. If I was enthused then the customers were going to feel it. The best jobs are nearly always where I get to make the menu and daily specials.

The interaction with the customers also proved to be an unexpected pleasure and a good deal more fun than I'd imagined. There was one customer though, who was just too odd.

Banana Man was a wispy, rather inconsequential looking fellow who fluttered up to the counter one day and requested a banana sandwich on wholemeal bread, no butter. Pretty innocuous right? Not with him.

He would carefully choose his banana, always the biggest one, and was adamant that it was not sliced. It had to be smeared onto the bread by hand. As fresh-faced Debbie squished his nana onto his sanga, Banana Man would lean in to watch. Breathing heavily, his eyes bulging, he would press against the counter and vibrate with excitement. And when his hand-made prize was wrapped up, Banana Man, with a terse nod of thanks, would rush off, literally stumbling over his feet to get his 'lunch' to a more private place. With growing frequency he'd appear, mumble his request and then stare intently at poor Denise as she rubbed his banana and made it go all squishy. One day she had enough.

"Oh God he's here again," she cried. "I can't do this anymore – he's so creepy."

"No worries," I said. "I'll handle this."

Out front I greeted Banana Man.

"Banana sandwich on wholemeal, no butter?"

He looked startled by this turn of events. "Oh! Ah yes, but where's the girl?"

"On her break mate," I said and I got to work.

Open mouthed with shock he watched me pick a weeny banana, brutally tear its skin off and – thwack! – slap it down on the chopping board. With a knife a good deal bigger than his banana I chop-chop-chopped it up. Banana Man gasped in real pain and with his trainers squealing on the tiled floor, he bolted off – never to return.

On Site

I'm working a dinner for two hundred and twenty guests at a swanky function venue on the banks of the Yarra River in Melbourne. It's another cool gig with Delectable Catering and everything's been ticking along nicely. The entrees are done and in the venue's kitchen the team are gearing up to serve the mains.

I'm alone outside in a well-lit marquee in the carpark. My station comprises two portable barbecues and a big tub containing a hundred and thirty steaks, all drowsing away in an oil and herb marinade. The tub is half topped with wire racks – to drain the steaks before cooking. There will be a lot of smoke so working outside in the fresh air is the go. The barbecues are hot and in less than ten minutes I'll get the signal to start cooking all this prime eye-filet, making sure each piece is done medium-rare.

Suddenly from out of the dark carpark appears Marius, the owner of Delectable Catering. He is as polite as ever but I can see he is in a flap.

"Oh! No one came out and told you. The running order has changed and we need those steaks right now."

I tong the first steak onto my draining rack but Marius is impatient. "No, no - put them straight on. We really have no time!"

He watches as I put the dripping steaks on the barbecue - trying to shake the oil off each one. He makes movements with his hands – make haste, make haste. I do, but decide that as soon he's gone, I'll put the rest of the steaks onto the rack to drain. The first barbecue is just about full when Marius leaves. I wait a little longer and as I go to grab fistfuls of filet from the tub – big flames suddenly engulf the back part of the barbecue.

What the . . .?! I'm suddenly flambéing blue steaks! Then I see what I should have noticed earlier – the barbecue isn't totally level and the excess oil has rapidly collected at the back of the grill plate. Now it's well alight. Liquid fire drips to the ground and steaks crackle like moths in a candle. I whip these to one side and try to smother the fire with my scraper but it flares higher, sputtering out stinging drops of oil. It's getting out of hand!

I quickly turn off the gas and redouble my efforts to subdue the fire. The wooden barbecue frame is alight now and what's really scary is that the gas-bottle is firmly strapped to the whole caboodle.

Rob, the waiter designated as my steak-platter carrier, calls from the back door of the function venue.

"Can you keep down the smoke! It's getting in the dining room. The guests don't like it."

"Rob come here! I need your help!" I yell back.

When Rob comes into the marquee he laughs at the conflagration. I can see he's impressed, but more importantly he knows about cooking. I begin to instruct him as I whip the line of flambé blues off the burning barbecue and onto the non-burning one. While I speak Rob's already moving, snapping on gloves, grabbing handfuls of steaks and putting them atop the draining rack. As I trundle the flaming barbecue out into the car park I'm still talking. "Let 'em drain for a few seconds! Shake 'em too and get at least fifty on!"

On a nearby road, passing cars see me and the barbecue pyre and peep their horns, no doubt amused at the spectacle. I'm scared the gas bottle might blow and for one crazy moment I consider running the whole blazing mess into the nearby river. But this would mean coming around in full view of the function room windows and it would not reflect well on Delectable Catering.

Leaving this problem for a moment I rush back and help Rob turn the first wave of steaks, expecting to hear the thump of the gas bottle going off behind me. Rob's good for a minute, so with tongs and rolls of paper towel I rush back to my time bomb. I manically soak up the oil with great wads of paper towel on the end of the long barbecue tongs. A crazy minute passes with my hands in and out of the flames and I even use my apron as a fire blanket. The fire goes out thank God, and I dash the smouldering unit back to the marquee. Rob and I wedge up one side with my oil-soaked apron so that it drains correctly, and fire it up again. The scorched barbecue takes no time to get back up to speed and on go the oil-drained steaks.

It's an autumn night, but I'm sweating like a pig on a spit. Just eight minutes ago I was cruising!

But I get into my rhythm and soon the first wave of steaks is ready and I rest them for a few minutes before Rob ferries them into the venue. Over the next ten minutes, I cook and platter up all the eye fillets. My timing is good and Rob comes and goes, taking nicely rested steaks to the guest's tables.

Half way through all this Marius appears and checks some of the steaks. "Nice," he nods in approval. "Perfect medium-rare." Completely unaware of my epic battle with the inferno, he looks at my sweaty face and sooty hands.

"Gosh, you look a bit hot," he says with concern. "Shall I get you a cold drink?"

In the late nineties and early two thousands I worked for several catering companies – but mainly for Delectable Catering based in Melbourne. Coming from the static environs of a restaurant kitchen, where not much more than the specials board changed day-to-day, the challenges of on-site catering proved to be most exciting. On-site catering is a movable feast that leaves the comfort zone far behind. Being away from the kitchen, with its back-up food and gear, literally puts you on the spot. You're royally screwed if you forget anything or mess something up.

Catering jobs take place just about anywhere a glass can be raised and a serviette held. I've worked gigs in private homes, art galleries, purpose-built function-centres, department stores, shopping-malls, skyscraper foyers, heritage-listed mansions and corporate board-rooms – to name a few.

It wasn't all birthdays and weddings. Porsche or Mercedes might be unveiling a new car. A radio station or laser-surgery clinic would be throwing a Christmas party. Or conferences of international architects and surgeons needed to break bread after all the jaw-jaw.

Gigs could be small – a romantic dinner for two or a board room lunch for six. Or they could be big – dinner for four hundred or a cocktail party for two thousand. These different sized gigs had one thing in common – the food was just amazing.

Delectable Catering was the prodigal lovechild of its owner Marius, and was definitely at the forefront of Australian catering in that era. He wasn't a chef but he loved food. He ate at the best restaurants and a big wall in his home was a bookcase stuffed with recipe books.

Marius had an incredible eye for detail and taste-buds to match. Any critique of the food I was making was always spot-on. If the gremolata was a little too watery, he'd know that I hadn't discarded all the woody stalks from the parsley. If I had been a bit stingy with cinnamon quills in the poached quinces, he'd tell from one lick of a syrupy spoon.

I worked with a hard-core of four chefs and extra bodies were brought in for big events. Employed on a gig-by-gig basis I soon got as much work as I wanted. The kitchen crew were very knowledgeable and totally serious about cooking. They were one of the best crews I've worked with and I learnt an awful lot from them.

In our home-base kitchen, we'd prep multiple jobs, working on the day's lunches and dinners, and also starting on functions a few days away. The Head Chef sequenced the order of prep to have everything as fresh as possible.

It was a well set-up work space, but as we got busier and busier, with up to six jobs in a day on, the kitchen would appear to shrink in size.

The food traveling to the job was held in different states of preparedness. Usually each menu item would have at least eight different components, so there were dozens, maybe hundreds, of containers of food. From sixty-litre tubs of marinated meat and fish, to little containers of picked herbs, a whole bunch of stuff had to be fitted into our refrigerated vans.

Packing food for the jobs involved the ticking off of each item on the checklist. I got so good at verifying what was going out on jobs that I became the checklist guy. Sometimes co-coordinating six jobs in a day, I might deal with a thousand items in a few hours. In the years that I did this, the number of things I missed could be counted on one and a half hands.

Getting all this food to the job unharmed is at the mercy of the driver's understanding of inertia, force and gravity. Sudden hard braking can displace food to the van's floor and manic tight turns can also play havoc with its integrity and eventual presentation.

Transporting a hundred litres of iced tea in a firmly packed-in deep tub, with layers of cling-film as a seal under the lid was a good lesson in Newton's first law. We knew we had a lot of iced tea as we stop-started our way through busy after-school traffic. But when the back doors of the van were opened on-site, we saw just how much. An absolute wave of spilled ice-tea broke onto the ground and we leapt like deer to avoid this tannic tsunami. The waiters, setting up, greeted this spectacle with much hilarity. Fortunately, there was still lots of ice-tea left for the guests.

Once on-site we'd quickly set up. Often there is no kitchen or dining area on-site and for this sort of job a catering-hirer is used. They would supply the tables, chairs, glasses, linen, cutlery, ovens, gas-rings, lights, marquees and floors as needed. They'd also set it up.

Depending on the menu, we might bring our own deep-fryers and dumpling steamers. Sometimes we had to bring not just the tubs to wash up in, but the water too.

Fortunately, there were some extremely well set up function venues with proper kitchens that we used, and it was nice knowing exactly what the workspace was like. Many times, though, we'd turn wondering how difficult pulling off service would be. I've had to set-up, cook and serve food in some horrible places.

Like in office warrens with titchy staff kitchens, in narrow corridors off meeting rooms and in garages full of ski-boots, surfboards and red-hot ovens. Space is precious on-site, especially when there are twelve kinds of finger food that need to be put on dozens of platters. Of course, the function room is the best, but well set-up marquees at a private home are not bad either.

If the job is large enough, say a sit-down four-course dinner for one or two hundred, then there will be several marquees. Two or three for the dining tables, band-stand and dance-floor, and two more for the bar and kitchen. The kitchen marquee has sides so that the guests don't have to observe the kitchen crew in all their sweaty glory. This all gets set up in the client's garden and hopefully you never have to go into their house.

Cooking in the kitchen of the client's home is one of the least liked parts of the caterer's beat. Great care must be taken working in them. Catering is not cheap so many clients are wealthy. In their homes are lots of expensive things. Close to the big open-plan kitchen there might be a Sydney Nolan or an Emily Kngwarreye canvas hanging on the wall. Not the sort of thing you want to accidentally flick sauce onto or bang a portable oven into.

There might be thousands of dollars of glassware in the kitchen, antique pieces that look as though they might break just by looking at them. Don't look at them. The lovely Italian curtains and hand-done decorative paint work of the walls doesn't take well to splashes of feijoa caramel, so the utmost precision is required. Not only do you not smash, stain or break anything, you have to leave the place, and everything in it, as you found it.

This includes the very expensive bottle of vintage champagne, all on its own on a shelf in a client's garage. I discovered this while looking for space to stash some gear. It looked like bait to me and was quickly taken to the client for safekeeping.

If you're not working in a kitchen with hoods and extraction fans then some operations, like grilling or deep-frying, just have to be done outside. Even if you don't set the barbecue on fire, the smoke that a hundred and thirty cooking steaks generates will choke you, and very possibly the guests, if cooked inside. But cooking al fresco brings its own set of problems, rain of course being the worst of them. Especially when it mixes with hot oil.

A downtown art gallery hosted a dinner for forty-five in the show room and we set up out the back where the art was stored. Waiters covered art with plastic sheeting. Out in the gallery the table was set with linen, cutlery and flowers. It all looked real nice.

In our kitchen area portable ovens were fired up and tools and chopping boards were laid out on trestle tables. The entree comprised a trio of Asian morsels, including mini-Spring Rolls that I was going to deep fry. I found a power-point for the fryer, but then the plan suddenly changed. I was informed there was to be no deep-frying inside the gallery as molecules of oil in the air could potentially damage artwork.

Directed to set up on a big wooden fire escape outside, I ran a long power lead for the fryer. When I turned it on, it overloaded the circuit and kept cutting out. All I could do now was set up a portable gas ring under a pot of oil. It was do-able but only just. A deep-fryer automatically adjusts temperature, re-heating the oil after it has been cooled down with a load of food.

With a gas-ring and a pot I had to keep adjusting the flame and without a thermometer I was going to have to use lots of guess work. This is not for the novice. Too hot and everything gets much too brown before the insides are cooked. Too cool and the food goes all soggy instead of crispy. Also, a load of Spring Rolls in the pot was roughly half that of the fryer. With forty-five people getting two each, I had my work really cut out for me.

Then it all got harder. The Spring Rolls began to unfurl, spilling their crackling innards into the hot oil. A specialist spring-roll maker had used our kitchen to create them, even test fried a few, but here on-site they were failing badly. I immediately upped my skill-set in finding a solution. As soon as the Spring Rolls went in, I fished them back out, tightened up the wrappers and popped them back in. This worked but my fingers didn't like it at all.

The difficulty level now went from intermediate to extreme as it began to rain medium-hard. The big fire escape steps above me provided good cover but a gusty wind was blowing the rain in. I got wet, but even worse, the pot of hot oil began to sputter and spit in my face. The rain drops also cooled the oil and this made my tepid progress even more sluggish. I commandeered a tall drinks-waiter to hold a big umbrella over me and the pot. Working feverishly, I managed to keep up with the other items on the entree trio. With great relief I finally cooked the last batch and got back inside.

Hot oil on-site is dangerous, especially when you are tired. I came close to absolute disaster at a gig at the Deutscher-Menzies' auction house one evening. It was a cocktail party for potential buyers and I worked it with a very good chef called Megan. We had to work in a storage room and the loading-area next to it. In the storage room wrapped paintings sat on racks, and many cardboard boxes, obviously containing artwork, were on the floor. We set up our cold food station here.

On a table outside in the loading area I set-up and filled a deep fryer for tempura oysters.

The guests arrived, service began and everything went well. As the event wound down guests began to nip out the back for a cigarette and a chat, threading their way around us. Some stood in the storage and loading areas talking, and as Megan and I packed the van, bit by bit, we had to keep politely asking them to move out of way. They moved to let us pass, but didn't leave the area as we might have wished.

It had been a long day and Megan and I couldn't wait to get out of there. The deep-frying fat was still fairly hot but instead of waiting until the very end, I stupidly poured it back in the twenty-litre drum it had come in. I was pretty knackered and the oil didn't seem that hot. Then I put the drum out of the way just inside the storage room.

While quickly wiping down the trestle tables, I heard a loud popping noise behind me, followed by the sound of liquid squirting onto the tiled floor. I spun around and was horrified to see hot oil spurting from the drum, mere centimetres from the stockinged legs of a female guest! The stream was hitting a big cardboard box and soaking it. The plastic seal around the bung on the oil drum had softened from the hot oil and the bung had popped right out. Within three seconds I turned the piping hot drum over on its side so that the hole faced straight up and the flow stopped. Megan, bless her, was as quick as a hawk and grabbed a whole stack of tea towels and dashed over. Some tea towels I used to chock up the drum and the rest Megan used to stop the oil spill from spreading any further. Amazingly no-one noticed, not even the woman who nearly got burnt.

Megan silently shook her head at my error and I discretely wedged the oil drum in a big tub and slid it out to the van. I went back in and helped Megan use a whole roll of paper towel to wipe up all the oil. Finally, an auction-house staff member noticed something was up.

"Oh, did you manage to spill something?" he breezily inquired. "Well isn't it lucky the floor is tiled?"

"Yes. I'm so sorry about that," I said. "Is there a mop and bucket we can use?"

He cheerfully went and got the cleaning gear and as I mopped up every last trace of oil, I noticed the cardboard box that the initial spout of oil had hit. It was soaked through!

I nearly fainted.

I should have got to it right after stopping the oil flow! I suddenly felt sick. What had I destroyed? A stack of prints each worth ten thousand dollars? Was I going to get sacked and then sued?

My guts hopped like a bunny as I approached the nice auction-house guy.

"Um there's. . . ah. . . box there that I got oil on."

He peered at the box and I waited for the scream of horror. "Oh those. They're just a lot of old brochures. Could you chuck them in the skip when you go?"

Behind this lovely lovely man, Megan gave me a you-are-so-frickin'-lucky look.

Every style of event had its rhythms, systems and look. Buffets had lush, large and sexy presentation; long platters heaped high and fully stylin'. Everything sat up as though ready to leap onto people's plates. Dessert was big and bold – enormous round crystal bowls full of mixed berries, and trifle layered in a giant rectangular glass aquarium of a dish.

We did alternative drop gigs which featured two choices of entree, main and dessert. Each table got half and half of each choice. Diners could then swap with each other if they didn't want what was in front of them.

Then there were events with finger food. These dainty items often had up to ten components and it was like making a miniature main – but by the thousand.

There were streams of wild-rice blinis coming off the barbecue, crowned with smoked salmon and bright red beads of roe, all assembled pronto so that the blinis were still warm and fluffy in the guests' mouths. Spice-seared tuna rounds, cooked rare, served on a chilled cucumber slice and topped with tuna mayonnaise and picked chervil. Trays of oyster shooters – Coffin Bay's best, chillaxing in tomato juice and Russian vodka. We'd dish up many dozen gyoza, spicy pork pot-sticker dumplings, browned off hard on one side and glistening with the chicken stock and sesame oil they'd been cooked in.

We'd make hundreds of rice-paper rolls on-site, their fillings freshly sliced and each one finished with a chevron of Vietnamese mint. A constant stream of crisp semi-dried tomato tarts came from the ovens, each one finished with goats' cheese, gremolata and a drop or two of the best balsamic. Barbecue plates sizzled with tasty fingers of Parmesan and sourdough crumbed garfish.

Some jobs were short precision exercises; like bank heists in their execution. Many were lunches for big business in the office towers downtown. A waiter and I would head off to the city, taking a three-course lunch for six or twelve. After checking in with security, we'd rocket up thirty floors in the service lift to the corporate levels.

Here the floors had expensive carpeting, fine furnishings and bathrooms that brightly shone with marble tiles, trendy taps and sinks. In a well-appointed kitchen we'd connect with the house steward, always a very smooth operator, and after being welcomed into their world I'd get everything ready while the waiter and steward set up the corporate dining room.

Sometimes I'd have just enough time to go back down and have a smoko. Getting back up wasn't always a dead cert thing though. I'd have to get security in their basement lair to open up a service lift. One day two cars stuffed full with gangbangers came screeching into the underground car park as I was walking back in. Car one disgorged a mob of angry girls and from car two leapt a cloud of angry boys. Insults flew and slaps echoed.

Dayam! I had food in the oven and the luncheon service was a few minutes away. Security dealing with this melee would leave me stuck without the lift.

I ran to their office, knocked hard, and when they opened the door, I blocked their view and told them I really needed to use the lift. One guard went to activate it. Behind me someone started screaming and I heard tail lights being kicked in. The guard at the door looked over my shoulder and began yelling for his partner, who fortunately had opened the lift. I dashed to it, jumped in and turned to see the security boys sprinting towards the fight.

Eighty seconds later I was two hundred meters above the melee, taking entrées out of the oven.

Running out of food on-site is the worst sin in catering. I've managed to avoid such fiascos and at all jobs we had at least fifteen-per-cent extra food in case of accidents. But sometimes guest numbers blow out with a few extra guests. A hundred and thirty people instead of ninety is a real difference in numbers though.

I was forced to deal with this unpleasant scenario at a free cold buffet lunch with no formal seating .

A German luxury car company decided to tempt potential buyers with complementary lunch and wine out at a country vineyard, and a chance to test drive the new models.

My carefully composed bowls and platters went out. I began to prepare for afternoon tea to be served two hours after lunch, enough for forty guests, die-hards who would still be driving cars and hopefully buying them. Then a brace of worried waiters flitted in.

They're going through the food! We've counted a hundred and thirty – not ninety as estimated from the RSVPs! Is there enough food? Well, I made it enough.

As the serving dishes began to empty the waiters rushed them back in. I the remaining food on smaller platters; fluffed and tricked them up using any leftover ingredients and out the fresh-looking new platters and bowls went. I served all the savory components of the afternoon tea as well. Everything that possibly could went out. I waited. Then a waiter came in smiling. All good – everyone's had enough to eat he said. Come afternoon tea-time, and I knew this would happen, only twenty guests were still driving the cars and there were lots of pastries, cake and fruit for them.

One of the cool things about catering work was the amazing places and situations I'd find myself in. I did jobs at Stonington House, a fabulous Italianate style

Victorian-era mansion, which for some decades had been the Governor-General of Australia's home. The building featured two stories of arcaded loggia (huge stone verandas) and Baroque massing (heaps of cool fiddly bits). The building's interior showcased wood parquetry work of unbelievably intricate beauty. The furnishings and fittings were nearly all period. Here was history on a grand scale and after setting up I'd enjoy going for a wander around before the guests arrived. Walking through an empty building where Kings of England (George and Edward) and Lords of the British Empire (Baden Powell and Kitchener) had dined, slept and farted was a real history buzz.

Then at another gig I'd be bringing in food past dressing models at a perfume and cosmetics launch hosted by the music and entertainment stars K.D Lang and Rupaul. In the very cool retro 'Streamline Moderne' styled Mural Hall on the top floor of Myer's flagship Melbourne store, six hundred guests ate our finger food, networked and enjoyed the show. The two stars hung out a bit in the kitchen area and the sheer height of Rupaul, two metres plus in heels, made me cheekily blurt out, "Rupaul you are so big!" My co-workers were gay guys and they, and Rupaul, burst into laughter at this indiscretion.

K.D. Lang, porcelain skinned and spruce in an immaculate suit, came over and picked up a smoked salmon blini from a platter I was making up. I quickly told her to put it back down. I knew she was a strict vegetarian. We had a special platter made up for her and when she inquired where the amazing fruit on it came from, more gales of laughter were generated by the answer – Queensland.

A large cocktail party with finger food took me to the Queens Warehouse, an enormous red–brick and cast-iron column building built in 1890. The first Australian bank notes and postage stamps were printed there; now it was a classic car museum. Many superb automobiles were displayed throughout the venue and the guests could wander around them. Car buffs amongst our team sighed at some prime motors including a Porsche Spyder and a Mercedes 540k.

The enthusiasm of our car-loving chefs went into overdrive at a colossal event for fifteen hundred guests celebrating fifty years of Porsche. This took place in the elegant old Bryant and May match factory, a marvel of 19th century industrial architecture. The vast building had cast iron arches and immense polished wooden floors. This was also the location of the Porsche Centre and its high-tech workshops were as clean as operating theatres. The massed display of Teutonic automotive excellence was awesome. Amongst the sixty cars was Porsche No.1, the first prototype, shipped in from Stuttgart. There were high-performance racing cars like the three hundred and fifty km/h 935 coupe, and an eight cylinder 908 Spyder. One Porsche 911 was painted from bumper to bumper with Australian indigenous art. My rev-head colleagues swooned and drooled over all this glorious heavy metal.

Gigs could last for hours. It wasn't uncommon to spend six or seven hours on-site. Sometimes the client required a second round of food around midnight. It was simple fare to soak up the drinks.

Things like fish and chips – fresh whiting fillets crumbed in herb seasoned bread crumbs, served with crispy shoestring fries and lime mayo in paper cones. Or toasted sangas – artisan bread slices layered with buffalo mozzarella, whole basil leaves and sliced vine tomatoes, cooked on the barbecue plate in lashings of olive oil.

Finally, it would be time to load out and return to the catering kitchen. Throughout the job, stuff that wasn't needed anymore was packed away in the vans. Dirty things were often washed on-site in the kitchens or laundries of the clients and these areas had to be left spotless.

Sometimes it was too problematic to wash trays or pots on-site and they'd get stuffed into garbage bags and stashed in the catering kitchen's freezer for the dish pig to deal with in the morning.

By now it's around midnight, maybe later, and the catering cook is exhausted. At this point extra care and focus is needed in repacking the van. It's essential to check that all lids are on tight. Finding that a bottle of olive oil has spilled its guts, covering the van interior and everything in it with a greasy film ain't fun. Worst still, try getting the smell out of the van after it's been drenched with milk, cream or seafood juice. Spills like this must be cleaned up immediately, but dealing with them at 2 am after an eighteen-hour day will make your brains slide out of your skull.

Marius was an inspired, and inspiring boss, and we all loved him. He was under a lot of pressure dealing with hundreds of details and glad-handling clients who at times seemed wilfully capricious and neurotically fussy. No matter how stressful the situation became, he remained unfailingly polite and courteous, even when the corners of his mouth were turned down. During services he would come around and inquire if you were happy. On big hectic gigs he made sure we all got a glass or two of good champagne as the service wound down.

A few times he took us out to the best restaurants in Melbourne to eat and drink whatever we wanted – as long as we share-tasted with each other.

On one of these nights, at an expensively sublime restaurant with half a dozen bottles of the nicest wine under our belts, we were eating off each other's plates, passing serious comment on the food and laughing lots.

A constant stream of compliments and jokes left our waiters both amused and bemused. Eventually the maître d' came up and inquired what we all did for a living. The only reply was laughter and the now curious maître d's every guess – from advertising to television to real estate – was greeted with more laughter. Eventually someone told her we were chefs.

"God – I should have known," she said.

"We're from Delectable Catering," someone said, as though proudly proclaiming that a notorious gang of gunfighters had ridden into town. Recognition twinkled in the maitre'd's eyes and she said, "I'll tell the kitchen that some of the tribe are in tonight."

On another occasion Marius threw a party for all the Delectable staff at his house. We turned up and were blown away to find that it was fully catered! Chefs in his kitchen were making cool food and waiters attended to us with trays of drinks. This sort of treatment made us love Marius even more.

When I got booked for New Year's Eve 1999 there was an industry-wide uproar about pay rates for that night. Who would want to work on this party night of party nights? And what about the Y2K computer glitch making the year two thousand indistinguishable from the year nineteen hundred? Everything electronic would get confused, turning the streets and skies into a flaming hell on earth. You'd have to be compensated for the inevitable hardship in getting home alive. It seemed the only way to secure staff was to throw money at them. Employers faced with this sudden spike in wages either had to up their prices or just close for the night. I didn't care about this hullabaloo – I was booked and already getting paid the correct rates. The last thing I'd do would be to try and hassle Marius for more money.

Our New Year's Eve client was having sixty of their closest friends over for finger food, followed by a three-course dinner. We'd start in the catering kitchen at 7.30 am, then drive out to the gig and finish around midnight. Including the three hours travel time I was up for an eighteen-hour day.

The last day of the millennium dawned and we did the final prep and pack. The menu was lush. One of the mains was going to be barbecued Atlantic salmon fillets – partially gravlaxed. I pin-boned fifteen kilos of salmon sides and placed them in a big tub with a mix of rock-salt, sugar, freshly chopped dill and the caraway flavoured Scandi spirit Aquavit. Chopping boards with a big pot of water on top, pressed down on the fish, and effected the curing process. I let it cure for just a day, turning the fish once.

Normally it takes two days for the fish to cure right through. But what we were after was just enough penetration to give the salmon that gravlax flavour. The sides would then be portioned and barbecued at the job.

Then Marius dropped a bombshell. Our pay was being doubled, including all the day's prep and travel time too. We were just about singing as we headed off on the hundred-kilometre drive to Sorrento – right on the tip of Victoria's Mornington Peninsular.

Our destination was a large cliff-top compound overlooking the deep blue expanse of Port Phillip Bay. On arrival we checked out the dining set-up as the guests mingled on the lawn by the sea cliff's edge. I saw a bandstand with speakers and instruments . . . and some large and strange looking drums.

In the empty four-car garage we began working on a long double row of trestle tables covered with crisp white tablecloths. This was the company's only job for the night so the full hard-core of Delectable Catering's kitchen and waiting staff were all there. We'd all worked together many times and everyone was feeling a nice relaxed family vibe. It was time to make some magic.

The band began to play and finger food went out to the guests watching the sunset on the lawn. Come entree time a string quartet began to soar, and when the mains had gone out the band came back on.

We took a break outside, and sat up on the high, wide back wall of the compound. There was a splendid view – a hundred-and fifty-kilometre sweep of different town's lights around Port Phillip Bay, with the glow of Melbourne in the distance lighting the sky. From next door came the sounds of another dinner party.

Then we packed the vans with all the gear we no longer needed and got on to the dessert. A trio of Japanese drummers started playing the big drums I'd seen earlier. The deep bass tones and funky manic rhythms energised us and some impromptu dancing occurred.

Finally, the service was done and we repaired to the high back wall of the compound with bottles of champagne. It was a few minutes to midnight and we toasted each other for a job well done, and also for being the recipients of a mighty day's pay check.

We just about fell off the wall when a barrage of fireworks began whooshing up from the party next door and exploding overhead. Then a spectacle on a gigantic scale unfolded as the whole rim of Port Phillip Bay lit up with shimmering points of light. Hundreds, if not thousands, of firework displays, from right next door to Melbourne sixty kms away, were going off, each one adding to a tremendous scintillating vista. Over the distant city itself the whole sky glowed and pulsed with electric colour.

We stood up on the wall for a better view. In our chef's whites, lit up by bright bangs and falling sparks of fireworks, we toasted each other, clinking glasses and bottles. What a great gig, what a top crew and what a damn cool way to end a millennium.

Alien Worm Massacre

We'll leave my story reducing in the pan for a few minutes and look at some nasty business. Over the years there's always someone who asks me – do cooks spit into food or even worse, as revenge against customers or staff who have displeased them? Well I have never seen it. I've never even heard of it. That's extremely bad juju; the kind of karmic crime that will have demons chain-whipping your arse for your next two hundred lives.

Lots of other bad things do happen in kitchens though. Horrendous things like an apprentice turning a deep fryer into a bonfire, then attempting to throw water on it. The Head Chef punched him and the bucket to the floor. Or a cook accidentally serving a centimetre-long piece of glass in a side of Winter Vegetable Gratin. He was grabbed off the line and sacked at the back door. I've seen some very dubious moral choices too. A Head

Chef nightly stealing expensive produce from the cold room like he was shopping at the supermarket. The owner called the cops. Or two ranking managers loading cases of champagne and bottles of spirits into their car boots. They got away with it.

A little more mundane but equally as bad is when food is sent out that looks, smells or tastes wrong. It might be over-cooked, under-cooked or over-spiced. Maybe it's missing ingredients or made with dud ones, but the big fat bottom line is – do not put it up on the pass. So, here's a horror story where that didn't happen, a colossal cock-up that still makes me cringe with collateral shame.

It was a show-case lunch for fifty restaurateurs, chefs, food writers and food producers – basically a very knowledgeable crowd. The bar was raised way up and expectations were high.

I was working at a catering company and a hot young Chef used our kitchen to prep the gig. It was her baby; she had come up with the menu, and myself and Andy, another chef at the catering kitchen, helped her prep it. The next morning, the Chef, Andy and I would travel out to the luncheon venue and pull off a gasp-inducing service.

The entree was an odd choice – Brussels Sprout soup. It really shouldn't be made the day before, as Chef did, as the little brassicas are delicate and easily lose their colour and subtle taste, even turning bitter.

I was given two items to do for the luncheon – apple cider basted quail and a crisp nutty salad with a funky fruit-based vinaigrette. I prepared the quail and the glaze, made the dressing and washed and prepared what I could of my salad ingredients.

The next day, we got to the vineyard location, began to set up and . . . oh dear. The Brussels Sprout soup was the colour of baby poo. And apparently it also tasted rather bitter. I quickly busied myself checking out the oven, turning it on and putting the quail into flat trays. Then I finished prepping the salad ingredients.

As it got closer to lunch Chef began a countdown. "Half an hour til service."

Andy and I cut up loafs of artisan bread provided by a talented baker guest and then made up little bowls of balsamic vinegar, olive oil and Andy's dukkah spice mix to go with them. Andy put trays of precooked root vegetables into a smaller oven to heat up.

"Ten minutes til service," called out Chef as she put on a pot of water to cook five kilos of lovely fresh beetroot gnocchi that had been made by a guest. I gave the quails their first coat of apple cider baste and Andy put the bread, oil and dukkah on the pass. We laid out the soup bowls and I saw Chef had a pail of goat's cheese, which is one of the few edible things I hate the taste of. I checked the oven – it was nice and hot.

"A minute til service," said Chef. She brought the pot of soup over to the bowls. It looked and smelt rank.

"OK, service," called out Chef, and she and Andy began serving the soup. On top of each filled bowl she crumbled goat's cheese – I guess to mask the bitter taste of the soup. Ughhh – to me that was like putting fresh chilies in a thumbscrew.

I put the quails in the hot oven and began to put together my salads in six big bowls, carefully layering the ingredients. Every five minutes or so I quickly basted the quail with the apple cider mix, building up a perfect glaze on their skins. Salads done, I toasted a nut mix for them in a big frying pan

When the soups had all gone, Chef inspected my salads. They look good, she said. I portioned the nuts out between the six salads and checked the quail. They were coming on nice. I wanted them very faintly pink in the middle so when they got to the table, they'd be juicy perfection.

Suddenly, the soup entree started coming back. None of the bowls were empty. Many looked as full as they'd gone out. Not good. The waiting staff looked at us with embarrassment. "They said we can go straight to the mains," one of them said.

I bumped the heat up a tad on the quails and rapidly got the platters and garnishes for them ready. Chef took a side of venison out of a freezer and put it on a chopping board. This was for the beetroot gnocchi – but wait a minute, it wasn't cooked! I was thinking that Chef would wok the venison in small pieces, making it all crispy caramelized on the outside and juicy pink on the inside, before tossing it through the purple gems of potato pasta.

Seeing my startled expression, Chef explained that she had semi-frozen the venison so she could cut it into very thin slices. Then she'd toss it through the hot gnocchi and the pasta's heat would cook it. Wow – I'd never heard of that before. I went and checked the quail. It was nearly done. Chef put the gnocchi into the water and the boss of my catering company, who was also one of the guests, came in and had a hushed conversation with her. They both looked strained. I checked the quail again. Nice – they were ready to roll and I took them out to rest for a few minutes.

The conversation with my boss finally finished, Chef then poured the pot of gnocchi into a big colander to drain and started rapidly slicing the venison. The waiters had all appeared looking expectant; I went hard dressing my salads and putting them up. Andy quickly filled bowls with crispy glistening root vegetables, garnished them with sprigs of fresh herbs and put them up.

Chef, busy slicing venison, called out to me to put the gnocchi in a big steel bowl. I got the gnocchi and . . . oh dear. It had over-cooked and instead of being firm maroon morsels, the pasta had congealed into one pale purple blob. It looked like a massive bruise laying there. I took it to Chef who goggled in horror.

At the pass the waiters were getting antsy. Andy and I quickly plattered up and garnished the quail and the waiting staff whisked them away. Meanwhile Chef grimly mixed the pasta and venison together, trying hard to loosen up the mass of gnocchi. She finally gave up, divided it among the serving bowls, and put it up.

I could hardly look at it. The chilled venison had killed any heat in the pasta so the meat wasn't really cooked. The noble venison was now slimy and gray, and combined with the lifeless colour of the gnocchi, it all looked like the aftermath of an alien worm massacre.

"Food up," called Chef and I felt a deep sense of shame. Andy's face was a mask. The waiters pursed their lips, breathed deeply and blinked fearfully.

"Come on, they're ready," said Chef. Like robots the waiters picked up the bowls and took them out.

Chef went outside to get some air and Andy and I silently cleaned up. Then freaked-out looking waiters appeared inquiring if there was any more quail. Alas it had all gone out. What about roasted root vegetables? Sorry but they'd all gone out too. Anymore salad? Or bread? All gone.

Our boss came in and we all looked at each other sadly. There was nothing to say. He went outside to talk to Chef and when he returned, he looked sadder still. I never saw the Chef again, as she drove off without a word. The gnocchi came back untouched.

Dessert was an extensive selection of hot and cold

tarts, poached and preserved fruits and local cheeses. Nice normal stuff.

I'm all for innovation but Chef should have tried out her recipes first – especially if a switched-on mob of chefs and foodies was going to eat them. The poor Chef, being on-site, had no back-up food of any sort. The soup was bad enough, but if it had been my show, I would have gone out there and confessed or lied through my teeth. I would have shouted everyone free drinks, shot the President, sunk the Titanic – anything – except serve that pasta disaster.

Andy and I sadly agreed on the drive home – we should have had the guts to step in and stop those bowls of wrongness from going out.

Party All Week Long

It's busy, the crowd seething four or five deep at our counter and around the kitchen are at least twenty thousand people. I've been going seven days straight, into my tenth hour today, and now hear the sound of a fiddle. It gets louder. It's coming into the kitchen. At the counter people start looking behind me. It sounds like Dan.

I look around and threading his way around us is the maestro himself. Heavily bearded, wild-haired and barefoot, he's grinning like a loon and playing like an angel. Is the music Irish, or folk or jazz? Whatever it is – it's virtuoso stuff. With snake-like wiggles he deftly squeezes through the serving crew and goes up to the counter where he serenades the waiting crowd. Then, still playing, Dan lays down on the floor amongst our feet and we all have to jump over him as we work. Now he's playing a sound like dolphins or whales singing and new arrivals at the counter stare at us, wondering where this otherworldly noise is coming from. Welcome to Woodford Music Festival.

I've done really big gigs on private properties, in warehouses and at vineyards but Woodford Music Festival was another planet entirely. It was like on-site catering but on a much bigger magnitude of scale. We worked at the festival site for nine or ten days. There were no set service times. From 7.30 in the morning til midnight we continuously sold food. On New Year's Eve we'd go til 2 am. This absolutely taxed my stamina at times, but it was such a blast that I did it for three consecutive years.

I partnered up with a couple who had experience doing food at Woodford and at other music festivals. Pat and Kim tapped me for my cooking expertise and sense of adventure. It was a worthy partnership because they had a good menu and had perfected the systems for making it work. I was very lucky to be coming in on a winning formula.

Pat the chef was also an artist who painted and sculpted, and his menus were, for the time, creatively eclectic. Things like mussel soup, roasted vegetable and three-cheese pizza, tofu bagels, marinated mackerel steaks and sticky date pudding delighted customers. The thirsty could get quenched drinking lemon myrtle daiquiris and spicy chai tea.

This meant there was a fair bit of prep for seven days of service and Pat and Kim liked to do most of it on-site. But first we had to build the venue and kitchen.

Pat and Kim did this on a grand scale, creating a proper restaurant with lots of seating, china plates and metal cutlery. We would labour for two days before the actual festival setting it all up. A big circus-like tent for the customers and service area, and a couple of large tents for kitchen and storage were first erected. Pat had made a lovely polished wooden serving counter which we set on a sturdy frame. Out the front of the venue we made several timber chest-high counters where you could stand and eat while watching the street.

Inside, customers sat on hay bales around funky low wooden tables. The hay bales had coloured hessian covers so that hay stalks wouldn't stick up your bum. In one corner the musicians' area was established with the biggest wooden table known as the 'sessions table'. In a semi-circle around it was a hay bale couch that could seat a dozen musicians or sleep six of them. This was where the Diddly Diddly was conjured.

Shining down at night-time were strategically coloured lights and spots. The gleaming wooden service counter was flanked with sculptures and vases of fresh flowers. High up for all to see were beautifully painted menus. It was generally thought that this was one of the coolest looking venues on-site.

Pat and Kim knew the organisers well so we'd arrive a few days early. At that time Woodford had almost no permanent infrastructure – it was basically cow-paddocks and hills with a big water tank in the middle. Setting up on empty green fields with nothing but the sound of the wind and a few birds calling made it hard to imagine that a town full of music was soon to spring up around us.

Fortunately, Pat and Kim lived close by, less than an hour's drive from Woodford, so all our infrastructure could be transported in multiple truck loads. A full day of loading, driving and unloading got everything on-site.

Our cooking and refrigeration gear comprised a good stove with a six ring gas-top, a barbecue plate, a pizza oven and a hired portable cold room which was towed to the site, prechilled and full of food.

As soon as the kitchen was set up and gas bottles connected, the cooking of soup and pizza sauce would commence. Power came from a three-phase power box and we'd have to gaffer tape and hook up power-boards and leads to keep them out of the way of rain and the crowds.

At my first year at Woodford we used tarpaulins to make the floor. The ground wasn't flat of course so there was a bit of chocking up of benches and stumbling going on. It wasn't fun or safe, so the following year Pat and I made an ingenious interlocking floor of his design that provided an accurate horizontal guide for our busy feet.

Setting up the venue was a big effort and we were very fortunate in having some of Pat and Kim's friends pitch in and help each year. These boys and girls were absolute gems and the roughest diamonds of them all were The Bum-Rot Boys.

They were a close-knit mob of friends who'd shared houses, bottles, spliffs and tunes for years. Some of them worked together as house demolition men, others in crews rigging big concerts and shows. What they shared in common was a deep love of music and good times. Some of them were brilliant musicians steeped in the Irish, blues and folk traditions. Actually, they loved all music – bluegrass, reggae, country, jazz – anything that had deep roots.

When they played, the get-togethers were known as sessions. Breweries and distilleries were drained and plantations of herb were smoked as the sessions rocked inner-city houses or reeled wildly on bush properties.

The important thing about the sessions was that they were played on acoustic instruments. Of course, they would use microphones, pick-ups and amplifiers in big performance spaces, but that was for the poor wee folk at the back who couldn't hear so well.

As well as being very talented musicians and consummate party people, The Bum-Rot Boys also cared about the world. They loved the birds and creatures and the trees and plants. The supernatural world concerned them too; they felt the Celtic and Aboriginal spirits around them, and numbered tarot card-readers and psychics amongst their friends and loved ones.

These mad and gentle souls would pitch in and help us set up and we'd feed them and store their beer in our cold room.

One year we brought down a ban on beer in the cold room. A big cake was found half submerged in a sixty-litre pot of soup, with a radius of splashed soup all over the floor. The cake had been knocked down by a late-night Bum-Rot Boy tussling with a carton of beer. But the weather was very hot and humid so the beer ban lasted three whole hours.

Woodford Music Festival is one of Australia's best festivals, featuring two thousand performers and something like four hundred concerts. It's also a town for a week and on its streets the normal rhythms of town life are absent. No one is commuting, working or buying groceries. Everyone is here to enjoy themselves and it's wonderfully refreshing to be in a place totally given over to sensual pleasures. Soon it feels logical and normal to be having a good time all day and all night. All week long even. This is how Woodford first casts its spell.

The enchantment is deepened by an infectious ambience created by the festival's long roots in folk, Indigenous, hippy, green and artistic cultures. This is not just a party town made for entertainment – it's also a place to celebrate the power of creativity to heal and inspire. Now the magic envelopes you.

Then you finish your daiquiri break and boogie into a venue where a band is playing wild music that you never knew existed. As you dance with pure abandon you now see that your very presence here is a personal invocation to all that is good, great and magical. The Woodford spell is now complete.

Outside of their scheduled appearances on stage, many musicians also play in different food venues and bars. Diverse players, often mixing genres and cultures, create totally improvised jams of pure fun and often great quality. At Woodford the music never stops.

In our restaurant musicians sat around the sessions table and played and played and played and played. From mid-morning until after midnight they played. Musicians would fall asleep on the hay bale couch and then wake up, have a coffee or a beer – and start again. Everyone at the sessions table played traditional Irish jigs and reels that seemed to have no clearly defined verses or choruses. The music flowed indefinitely, with many players adding to the hypnotic lilting stream. New musicians joined in and others left but the music never faltered. We called it the Diddly Diddly and it was trance music for sure; an insistent but calming soundtrack to the days and nights of hard work.

Everyone from everywhere comes to Woodford and many are bizarre and beautiful to look at. Stalls sold bright clothes and wild jewellery, and did face painting and henna tattooing. Daily costume changes and freaky new looks were very much part of the festival's spirit. Exhibitionism was encouraged. One garbage collection man was dressed in nothing but wellington boots, tiny Day-Glo pink jocks and a matching pink cape. Nice.

The festival takes place during a tropical summer in Queensland so it was usually hot and humid – and sometimes wet. Thunder-storms would come sweeping through and we'd find out how well we had rigged the tents and power leads.

One day a nasty storm sent everyone scurrying for shelter. Our venue filled up as driving rain emptied the streets and thunderbolts cracked overhead. It got scarier as a lightning strike impacted close by. Then Pat and I saw to our horror, that water pouring off our tent roof was running down long power leads that had been blown off their hooks. The water was streaming along the leads towards the three-phase electrical box! We ran over and stared fearfully at this potentially lethal turn of events.

I didn't feel like touching it and neither did Pat, as a hundred million volts of electricity was lurking in the storm overhead. Then – bang! – a lightning strike flashed. I figured now was the moment and I flicked the master switch off. Later on, we carefully secured the leads and pulled that part of the tent roof tighter.

These sudden summer storms helped to create that amazing festival mud, and with the humidity and heat it meant lots of flies. We continuously sprayed all our tables and prep surfaces with a citronella-oil and water mix to keep them at bay – but still they came. It made prepping hard and we'd do all our fish prep in the early morning. Food had to be covered all the time as the flies were legion.

One morning, viciously hung-over, I staggered into the already sun-drenched kitchen and was greeted by something out of a Hieronymus Bosch painting. On every surface were hundreds – no millions – of flies and around me they wheeled in sniggering clouds. Parched and faint, scarcely afloat on waves of nausea, I laggardly swatted at them. My lame swipes had no real effect and the heinous horde surged and buzzed, then quickly resettled. Bewildered, I stood there swaying. I couldn't bring food out into this! In a daze I went out the back, my mind groping for the location of a citronella spray. Or a baseball bat. Then I remembered the big pedestal fans we had set up to cool the kitchen. I pulled them in close to the prep bench and blew those suckers away.

The roast veggie & three cheese pizza sold by the hundreds. We made a red wine, herb and tomato sauce for it daily; at any moment there were always two sixty litre pots of it on the gas-rings. On the barbecue plate we grilled boxes of capsicum, eggplant and mushrooms several times a day for the pizza toppings. The smell and sizzle drew people to watch, and after the sensory foreplay they'd usually grab a slice or two.

The pizza-oven was fairly old but it still kicked hard, disgorging great pizzas from ten in the morning til midnight. Pat made a brilliant pizza peel out of a long shovel handle and a piece of aluminium, and we all took turns using it to work the pizza oven.

I got dubbed Erik Bloodaxe for my dynamic pizza shovelling style. This nom de guerre referred to the spots of tomato sauce that I invariably sprayed about. A Bum-Rot Boy sighting me at the oven would yell "Hooorah! The Blood-Axe is here! Awaken Woodford awaken!"

The trusty old beast of a pizza oven had one little flaw – the door got stuck now and then. One busy night it was packed full with eight pizzas – all ready to come out. I went to open the door and bloody thing wouldn't budge! I repeatedly tugged at the hot metal handle as people patiently waited for their pizza at the counter. Hell, and damnation – the Blood-Axe was about to be massacred here! The trapped pizzas would soon go from perfect crispness to bushfire blackness.

I grabbed a big spoon and pried at the door. No good. I chucked it down, grabbed a butter knife and jemmied away. At the counter, customers now realised something was wrong and an anxious murmuring now sprang up. I resigned myself to disaster and gave the door one more wrench. It flew open; loud cheers rang out and I wielded the pizza peel as though a vanguard of Saxon warriors was upon me.

At Woodford a fair few people, including myself, consumed large amounts of alcohol. I learned to pace myself and usually saved it up for the last few hours when the rush had died and a co-worker could take over. On New Year's Eve everyone would shout me a drink and I often had ten or twelve lined up on a back bench. With no time to drink them all, most were given away to fellow workers and cool customers.

Every morning the walking hung-over would appear and start shuffling around – deciding what they might eat or drink. We had the best hang-over cure – mussel soup. From Pat's canny recipe, a tasty and restoring brew was concocted. The soup contained many things, including mussels, red wine and fresh fish, and heaps and heaps of greens like spinach and parsley. It simmered on the stove, fourteen hours a day, getting thicker and richer.

This nourishing elixir packed a healing punch for those who had overindulged and there would often be silent people sitting around our wooden tables, slowly eating mussel soup. Now and then they'd emit groans – of pleasure or pain it was hard to tell.

The soup was immensely popular, even with the non-drinkers, and the very first job of the day would be to make more. If any remained from yesterday, it was strained of mussel shells and then added to the new batch of soup. New mussels were added throughout the day, especially before lunch and dinner. The meat, as it cooked off the shells, would dissolve and load the soup with even more flavour and revitalising goodness. By the second or third day the soup was so full of iron you could have built battleships with it.

It was pretty ambitious serving meals on china plates with real cutlery, so having good dish pigs was imperative. We struck gold one year with two of The Bum-Rot Boys - Little Mick and Trev.

We had a proper wet area with sinks and taps and a floor of wooden pallets topped with rubber mats. Though it was screened off from the public with hessian sackcloth, Little Mick and Trev liked peeping through at the world and especially into the next venue to ours which featured belly-dancers. While these talented curvy ladies undulated to pounding drums, the thrilled lads danced and happily hooted in their wet area.

Trev positioned ice-buckets by the sinks so that restorative drinks – wine, beer, cider or spirits – could be accessed at will. As they smashed through the dishes - they would get smashed. They'd also take turns having a smoko break and big wafts of sinsemilla smoke would come out of the darkness. We didn't begrudge them their fun because they happily did a top job in their hessian hideout under the stars. But one night they almost flew up into those stars.

After a dinner rush I saw a few ladies ducking under the cloth to visit Little Mick and Trev. There was much laughter and they left.

An hour later a mad metallic drumming started in the wash-up area. I went over and pulled back the sacking to see the boys playing the pots with ladles and tongs. Speechless with mirth, the pupils of their eyes were like saucers. It wasn't just drinks and smokes – they were tripping off their heads! Giggling madly, they managed to explain that their visitors had laid some good acid on them. Now they were playing music.

Prepping, cooking and serving lots of food in a home-made kitchen out in cow paddocks meant taking real care in regards to hygiene. The authorities also checked that this was so. During one busy time I saw a hand emerge from the tight cram of bodies at our counter and aim a digital thermometer point blank at the food. It was the health inspector, and he routinely checked our venue and food throughout the festival.

One morning he informed us that there was a problem. At dawn he'd inspected our kitchen and all was good – except for the people asleep under the pizza oven and front counter. This was illegal, and puzzling too as we all slept in tents.

We quizzed the inspector on the intruders and it became clear. It was three Bum-Rot Boys, somewhat inebriated and too far from camp to walk home, who he'd found peacefully snoring on the kitchen floor.

In between Woodford festivals there were other gigs. One year we went to Australia's capital, Canberra, for the National Folk Festival. At the time I was working in Melbourne with Delectable Catering and I took five days off and flew up. We got to use the big kitchen at the Canberra Showgrounds and it was pure luxury. A walk-in cold room, a wet area, bright lights and a full line of ovens and stoves made prep a breeze. We trollied the food over to our stall – a much smaller affair than usual. It still looked great, as Pat and Kim had driven 1200 kms down from Queensland with the floor, counter, lights, signage and the trusty old pizza oven.

It was damn cold in Canberra, down to zero some mornings, and unlike at Woodford, the National Folk Festival wasn't so busy in the morning. There wasn't the hot orb of the sun at seven am to wake up a camp ground full of seven thousand people, so we got to sleep in til eight or nine.

Here at the annual gathering of all things folk, the Diddly Diddly was strong. When all the official shows finished each night, musicians gathered around fires and summoned up the Celtic spirit music to swirl around for hours on end. Because of the later morning starts, I spent every chilly night drinking mulled wine and whisky with the jamming musicians.

On the last day we went straight from cooking into pulling down our stall and packing our gear. We were on a tight schedule and took no break. Even as the last things were loaded up, I was having a drink. Finally done, and without pausing to have a shower, I got stuck into the final session around the fire. As it got dark the remaining musicians and festival folk got stuck into a last hurrah. Many beer and whisky toasts were made and big pots of hot mulled wine were consumed. Even though I had an early morning flight to take me back to work - I got stuck into some serious carousing.

Next thing I knew was that I was laying on hay and dirt next to the dead fire with my breath steaming in bright sunlight. It was dawn, bitterly cold, and the showgrounds around me were deserted.

The last time I looked there had been a roaring party going. I'd been with the Ulladulla Kid, knocking back mug after mug of hot mulled wine. I looked at my watch and freaked. My plane was leaving in twenty-five minutes!

I leapt up and mulled wine sloshed in my head. I found my bag and drunkenly staggered to the nearest phone box. I called a cab and desperately inquired, "Do you think I can get from the showgrounds to the airport in twenty minutes?"

"I hope so love," was the reply.

The cab arrived and I promised the driver a big tip if we got there in time. He got it.

I ran from check-in to the plane and fell into my seat. Next to me a commuter in a business suit flinched in horror. I was covered in dust and ash; hay was stuck in my hair and on my clothes. I smelt of grog and wood smoke and hadn't had a shower in over twenty-four hours. Not just folky and rustic – I stunk.

Although I did a variety of other gigs with Pat and Kim - Woodford was the main event. We did well there due to Pat's clever menu and all our hard work. Covering costs and making a profit was important but the experience of the festival itself was priceless. To be able to work, and play, in such a phantasmagorical place – well that was a crazy trip in itself. It was like Brigadoon on acid and its sights and sounds are forever etched on my brain.

The length of the event was both a blessing and a curse. After the first two days I'd get in the rhythm, with all the kitchen bumps ironed out and the first few hangovers under my belt. Now the full dreamscape of Woodford would unfold. The sense of being a particle in a huge organism became all encompassing. I'd feel like I'd arrived, that I was home and that I'd always been there.

Kohl-eyed gypsy angels, big-hatted troubadours, fuzzy bush-punks looked normal. Jingling spangled harlequins, dandified partyists, hippy goddesses, jungle pirates and sensible folk in good hats, corduroys and wellies cruising the streets all felt like friends and neighbours. Mega-pixies, dream-captains and those who paired a kaftan with a tiara, or a top hat with a sarong were my brothers and sisters. Riotous costumes and wild make-up became the most natural things to see. You often couldn't tell the roving street performers from the punters until they started performing.

I often felt like I wanted to meet everyone and some nights I had a damn good try. It was complete social overload, but just par for the course at Woodford. Strangers became friends in a few hours and there were bosom buddies who only saw each other at the festival each year.

All around me while I worked was an incredible sonic kaleidoscope of music being played; all mixing in into each other in weird and wonderful ways. Guitars wailed and didgeridoos hummed; the voices of acapella groups sweetly soared and Latin rhythms skipped and bounced. Massed poly-rhythmic drumming came from the Chai Tent and the fairy mist of the Diddly Diddly drifted through my days, nights and fitful dreams.

Sixteen-hour days left me wired, and then there was someone to talk to or music to hear when I finished. Some nights yielded only three or four hours sleep and this, coupled with lots of drinking and the inevitable joint or two, produced a continuous hallucinatory buzz. The days blurred in a rolling continuum of prepping, cooking and partying.

There was no future and no past – only the now of Woodford Festival, a wonderful magical mystery tour seemingly without end.

Coming down from Woodford could be hard and we sometimes got the flu after the festival finished. The combination of battering immune systems with hard work and play and being among tens of thousands of people could be a knock-out. Pat and Kim would dose themselves with huge quantities of vitamins throughout the festival. I tried to drink mainly fruit daiquiris.

The last day was tough – and wonderful too. My body and mind would be near collapse, but I'd be fully Woodford by then, soaked through with fabulous music and serendipitous connections. What a wonderful time I'd had – so many beautiful people, so many bands, so much music, dancing and laughter. One year, two of our customers summed it up perfectly.

It was 1 am on New Year's Day, and an Australian Indigenous man was sitting next to me on a hay-bale. He was happily drunk and naked, except for a small multi-coloured loin cloth and a profusion of new henna tattoos.

Five days ago, he came into our venue dressed like the working stiff from Sydney that he was – in loafers, pressed slacks, nice shirt and wearing a good watch. But five days is sweet eternity at Woodford. Drinking one of our lemon myrtle daiquiris, he cackled with delight at discovering the Woodford state of mind.

"If only I could bottle the way I'm feeling now!" he cried. "I want this every weekend!"

"Exactly!" said the freckled, red-haired woman sitting next to him. She was also sloshed, wearing a feather dress, a mad Dr. Seuss style hat and a sloppy smile on her beautifully painted face. "You just have to keep this feeling up all year!"

That sure sounds great – but you'd have to be made of stainless steel to do it!

If You Can't Stand the Heat . . .

The kitchen swum before my eyes. I knew it was going to be hot – but not this hot.

"Half a litre of water every hour. Truly bro, I've seen 'em faint in here," Tez, the Maori Head Chef, sympathetically advised me. It was my first shift at a resort in Australia's blazing hot Northern Territory and I was feeling very dizzy. Maybe I couldn't do this.

"Take a little break," said Tez. "We don't want to kill you on your first day."

By my second week I had got acclimatized and though it was still hard – it was do-able. Over the three seasons I worked at the resort I found that the extreme heat would sometimes be the least of my problems.

I came to work during the tourist season, when it was apparently cooler and the resort accommodated every kind of visitor, each one attracted by the wild and rugged beauty of the country.

International and domestic travellers of a certain age and economic demographic toured in coaches and four-wheel drive buses equipped with drivers and guides. These guests enjoyed air-conditioned rooms, drank mango daiquiris by the swimming pool and dined in the refreshingly cool a-la-carte restaurant. The more intrepid internationals arrived in four-wheel drives and sported expensive cameras and hiking gear. They too would seek the chill air, fine dining and clean sheets of the resort.

Roughing it were the global back-packers and gap year kids, traveling in beaten-up old vans and cars. These gypsies had encampments in the resort caravan park where they cooked, got drunk and tried to root each other. Everyone was impossibly sun-tanned and many worked as housekeepers, bartenders and waiters. We always had some of them working with us. It was perfect for the owners because when the super-heated build up to the wet season started and the tourists all evaporated – the extra staff would also vanish.

The caravan park filled up with Australians too; families from the southern states escaping winter, and many Grey Nomads (retirees who drove around the continent seeking adventure before dementia). There were also hard-working couples following work in the fruit and tourist seasons. These tooled-up campers had clever custom rigs and I met a few who travelled with herb gardens and stills for making spirits.

I got my own cabin with an attached bathroom and laundry. My deal also included all flights and coach fares and a nice premium hourly rate. For all this I was to work long hours, and most importantly – be on call for more.

This was because it was hard keeping staff. The isolation, lifestyle and working conditions were not for everyone. People missed family and friends. There was nothing to do after work and sharing sleeping quarters with drunks and weirdos was hard if you're weren't a drunk or weirdo yourself. And it was hot.

Suddenly it would get too much and there'd be a rush for the exit, often with a few days' notice given, usually just after pay day. Then I'd step in, working many extra hours until a replacement could be found.

The first season went great as everyone was Bottom End Gruntmeisters of the first order. As well as Tez, the affable Head Chef, there was Ketut, from Bali and he was top notch. He'd been in big brigades as a Chef de Partie, Sous-chef and Head Chef, mainly in five-star restaurants in his country, the Philippines and on cruise ships. Ketut was a shrewd dude and did not suffer fools, shirkers or pretenders in the kitchen. You had to prove through hard work and skill that you were worthy of his respect. It took a little while but he warmed to me.

For four hours during service, five nights a week, we had Dougie, a decent local chef with a day job. He was a good man under pressure, working with zero fuss.

The apprentice was young for his age and so was semi-capable, but our ex-boxer kitchen porter Pauli was strong and cheerful. He'd happily pitch in with prep and help us during busy services. Tez's wife helped us too - smashing through prep and making luscious desserts.

There was one al-la-carte service, dinner, at the hundred and sixty seat resort restaurant. During the day guests headed out to see the natural marvels in the area – like Nitmuluk, a truly awesome system of gorges and waterfalls up the road.

We also served a big buffet breakfast to fortify the guests for their day of adventure. As well as the always busy dinner service there was sometimes a dinner function in the eighty-seat banquet room, or a large pool-side buffet. It was hard work but pretty easy too. My living and working conditions were good, so I was most happy to sign up for next year's season.

Eight months later I returned and hit the ground running. Tez, his missus and Pauli were gone and the current Head Chef was leaving under a cloud after clashing with Ketut and the owners. Ketut was also in battle with the owners who wanted him as Head Chef but on his current salary. The other full-time chef, Mark, was waiting for a job on the Gold Coast to come through any week now. So, would I run the kitchen? The owners had a pay rise ready and I accepted.

The departing Head Chef was an elusive bugger and I finally got to speak to him about something that was crucial out here – ordering. Instead of giving me a decent heads up the vengeful bastard gave me wrong information. Petty stuff like the size of the eggs and steaks, and much more seriously – delivery schedules. His bogus briefing was designed to make me run out of stuff or over order. He'd also run stock up and down in crazy ways.

The fruit and veg cold room was too full and I could smell the vegetative rot when I opened the door. Everything inside was unrotated to the crapper. Bags of cucumbers dissolving into ploppy goo. Lettuces melting and excreting foul juice. Punnets of strawberries and kiwifruit grown old and grey bearded. Hidden in a corner was a leafy garden of sprouted sweet potato. A three-way chefs and owner fight had resulted in a mess of wasted food.

It was the total opposite in the walk-in freezer. It was near empty and, because we were remote, there was a ten-day delay between ordering and delivery. I rang the suppliers, using more of the dud information, and managed to make the same big meat and frozen goods order twice. A nine grand order became an eighteen grand one. After the shock of its arrival I queasily spoke to the owners but they were unperturbed and told me not to sweat it. I was lucky – not every business can absorb an extra nine grand cost in a month.

Just like in any kitchen, but especially here, I had to check that the orders arriving were actually there. The delivery invoice is just a piece of paper and a few minutes cross-checking that the food ordered has really arrived is imperative. So is checking the quality. I didn't want some rogue of a supplier thousands of kilometres away off-loading second-rate merchandise onto me.

I got the hang of it fast, even the human Rubik's Cube of rostering staff, but it was really Ketut's kitchen. He'd been there for three years and knew everything. I liked my new rate of pay but I went to the owners and suggested they pay Ketut a Head Chef's salary. I was politely told to mind my own business.

The love of the previous year was totally gone. Ketut was pissed-off and uncommunicative and now worked hours that were set in stone. Local boy Dougie was still there and still only available for four hours a night during service. The local apprentices didn't always remember to come in to work and the one-eyed kitchen hand was a nasty bitch of a man. Twelve-hour days in thirty-five-degree heat made me a bit damp, but dealing with the staff began to fray my edges.

The other chef Mark kept up with a busy service and prepped reasonably quick, but he was a horrid man who revelled in spouting filthy racist, sexist dribble for shock effect. I told him to shut up and so he racked his brains for even more offensive things to say. Ketut ignored his poo-poo mouth and I followed suit. Mark pretended to give up on us, but now and then he'd drop an awful clanger designed to make us gag.

He was gross in appearance too, his boots greasy and pock-marked with dried food, and his chef's jacket resembled an action painting that smelt. A diet of chips and chops, full bowls of gravy, ice cream and two-litre bottles of fizzy drink covered him in pimples and made him obese. The heat slaughtered him, turning his jowls shiny with sweat and making him reek. Many nights he'd totter away early after bullying an apprentice or dish-pig to clean up his section. Any comment from me would get the same cheerful reply. "I'm out of here real soon. Maybe next week – so do I care?"

It was a relief when he finally left. We all felt a lot cleaner too.

Mark's replacement started well but when love came to town, he fell apart quicker than a nut schnitzel. Pete was pretty quick, but cooking was just a job to him; one that kept him from hitting the resort bar. Here after his shift, he nightly toiled, trying to whisk a waitress, female guest or local lass back to his donga for some Swedish yoga – Australian style.

A new waitress, Matilde, turned up, young, fit and French, and Pete fell hard. So did Matilde and soon they were inseparable and making post-season plans – travel to Thailand and France; marriage even.

New love is wonderful but Pete started coming in haggard and spent from all the rumpy-pumpy. He was unfocused: running out of prep during service. I had words with him and he grew surly. He was stubborn but not as stubborn as Matilde. They began to repeatedly clash, indulging in midnight screaming matches and smashing things.

One morning Pete, with a bandaged right hand, told me he was unable to work for the next few days. He'd punched the wall in his donga. I racked up the hours doing his prep and the owners had to pay Ketut extra to come and do the dinner services. A few weeks later Pete didn't turn up for a shift. He went to Darwin to bring back a runaway Matilde instead. The next shift I told Pete not to piss us around again or else, but it was a hollow threat as he knew we needed him. A few days later he rocked up with a black eye – courtesy of fit young Matilde.

This lovesick saga staggered to its final round and young Ryan, our supernaturally cheerful assistant manager broke the news to me.

"Pete's left," he grinned unhappily. "Matilde gave her notice a week ago, all hush hush, and she went last night while Pete was at work. He's gone after her. We've started looking for a replacement. You'll be OK until then won't you?"

"We'll have to be," I groaned. "But give Dougie a pay rise now!"

I now did double shifts and the build-up to the wet season enveloped me in its fiendish heat. The ground heated up and every cold-water tap at the resort ran warm. I had to get buckets of ice from the ice machine to have a cold shower after work.

The owners wanted no input from me in getting new staff. They were a family, all working at the resort, and though polite, they had their ways of doing things thank you very much.

So Ketut and I awaited the new chef, hoping for a cheerful gun all-rounder. But like a tray of champagne flutes crashing to the floor, our hopes were thoroughly and utterly dashed.

The new chef, Marilyn, was rake thin and had the same scary eyes and mad stare as Rasputin. On her first service I was stunned to see her separate the first two orders from the rest – and work exclusively on them.

"Ahhh, what are you doing?" This question got me a glower of menace. "I can only do two orders at a time," she said.

"You have to work on more tables than that!"

"Well I can't!" she snapped, looking ready to physically fight me. I digested all this, then slapped on a smile.

"OK, let's start with two orders and then I'll show you how you can do more. It's really easy."

Marilyn, her jaw tightly set in mistrust, watched as I demonstrated how much jolly fun it was creating two tables of entrees at a time, while simultaneously setting up the next three tables.

"Nah. I can't do that," she said after a while.

I soothed away my anger and pushed back my disappointment. She obviously had very limited al-la-carte experience and her fear of failure was fuelling her aggression. So, to learn the menu and gain confidence, I got her making just the same three entrees on the menu each time they were ordered. This worked but I couldn't keep running between two sections.

At knock-off I was nice and positive to her about her efforts but inside I was fairly riven with dismay. A dud chef *and* an angry stress head! I felt sorry for her but Ketut wanted her gone.

Management pleaded with Ketut and I to give her a chance and over the next week I ran my arse off trying to get her up to speed. I was a patient Mr. Smiley but her worry and resentment grew, and she focused this bad energy on me. Everything became a problem. I talked too fast and if I used slightly different words from last time, then I was confusing her. Deliberately.

When I used a different garnish on oysters she freaked out as though she'd caught me cooking a turd. I suggested she have a go at making her own garnishes for each dish.

"What!" she said. "I have to do that as well?"

"Yeah. You wanna have a bit of fun too."

"You call this fun!"

After eight days I pleasantly explained that it was now time for her to do what was expected of her – and what she was being paid for. But when she pulled two orders aside and began working on them, I asked her very nicely to speed the fuck up. I didn't use that word of course, but as if on cue Marilyn started shouting that I was a slave driver who enjoyed harassing her.

I remained coolly oblivious to this outburst and the next morning I went with resolute empathy to her donga for a talk. Yes, I agreed – it is difficult working remote, and sure, we all felt isolated and insecure at times. I asked her to really have a go and to trust that she would do well. I was sympathetic and gentle and she apologised for her tantrum and resolved to get on with the job. This was what I wanted to hear and I started the day's shift pleased that progress had been made.

But when service started, Marilyn pulled aside two orders and worked on them. I managed to ignore a spike of anger and dug deep for some love. But all I felt were my fingernails scraping on the bottom. Loudly, but without emotion, I asked to do what she was being paid to do.

From that moment on I was the Devil himself (I wish). Jittery with anxiety, eyes bulging in permanent rage, Marilyn made every shift unbearably tense and I began to feel physically wary around her. Other staff avoided her and Ketut, utterly disgusted at this excuse for a chef, refused to acknowledge her at all. This only added to her paranoia. When she began to angrily talk to herself, I sensed some kind of mental breakdown. I informed the owners who started their lamentations, but I insisted they start advertising now. I didn't think she would last much longer.

I was right. A few days later she gave the owners a generous two days' notice. Her abysmal treatment by the Head Chef was the reason for leaving. Ketut and I were getting kind of mean now and we agreed that we would not put up with any ka-ka from the next chef. And we sure as hell didn't.

The new chef, Laura, was a tiny blonde woman who made the blokes in the kitchen sigh. They silently resolved to protect and support her but she needed no help. Laura was right on it, intensely professional and with real experience too. Within a couple of weeks, she could do any section. She relished a busy service and made great specials. Nothing was too hard and she was happy to work extra hours and give me some days off.

Laura was keen to learn the ordering too and loved nothing better than tidying the hell out of the cold rooms. This slight young woman had Bottom End Grunt in spades. Sometimes she even told me to go home early!

The sound of breaking hearts was loud when her handsome boyfriend arrived at the resort to work bar, but the love for her never stopped. Everyone was all smiles around her and the happy gleam came back into Ketut's eyes. We were blessed indeed by Laura's energy and skill, and having a decent core of crew again meant that I could deal with everyday problems with a little less stress.

Problems like the walk-in cold room dying late on a Friday afternoon. The one and only local fridge technician greeted my urgent request for help with a chuckle of pity. He was off on a weekend fishing trip. I pleaded and promised him extra payment wouldn't change his mind.

"Nah. I can't do it mate – I'm going fishing," he said. "*Fishing* you understand? I'll see ya Monday."

Now everything in the dead cold room had to be transferred to the fruit and veg cold room. This meant taking it all through insect-screen doors, fifteen-metres down an outside path, through more screen doors and down a hallway. Prep became a nightmare of endless to-ing and fro-ing, and delving through the densely packed cold room. The weekend seemed to last a week and come Monday, a very chilly silence greeted the fridge-tech's tin-eared attempt at conversation.

Every day the sky was blue and cloudless and at work I felt like I was being cooked in an oven. We drank litres of electrolyte replacement daily. A thermometer by the grill section showed 52°C.

Frogs and tree snakes would appear in my toilet bowl seeking water. I had to gently pull these reluctant reptiles out from under the rim, the frogs gripping on for dear life, the snakes twisting and writhing.

The build-up to the wet now held the land in its

fiery embrace. Dry thunderstorms set the night sky alight and crackling with electric crawlers for hours on end. One morning it rained for about two minutes, the first precipitation I'd ever seen there, and the local staff ran outside laughing with pleasure.

I was teetotalling and declined invitations to the nightly staff piss-ups that sometimes ended up in the town of Katherine. It could get rough there at night with brawls and occasionally someone bashed to death.

Some French guys working at the resort hit town one night, and the next day I saw one of the boys with half his face scraped off. Drunk and denied entry to a bar, this fool decided to fight the doorman. Man, I wouldn't want to even look at a Katherine bouncer! This wannabe Jean Claude van Damme got picked up bodily and thrown face forward into the road. A couple of times. Then he was arrested and locked up til he was sober.

Though he looked like a pizza, the young fella was surprisingly happy. He excitedly passed around the police banning order he'd received. Every licensed premises in Katherine was now off-limits to him. "Look at this!" he cried proudly. "Every pub! Every bar! What a souvenir of Australia I have!"

On my third and final season at the resort, Ketut and Dougie were still there but a new Head Chef had recently arrived. Ketut grimly shook his head when I asked about him.

"Not experienced. Lazy. Drinking all the time," he said. My heart sank. "Angry man?" I asked.

"Yes – but to himself. Too scared of me."

The new Head Chef, Jason, was at least ten years younger than Ketut and I, so the senior/junior dynamic was out of kilter. He knew that Ketut and I had worked two seasons together and it worried him.

To put him at ease, I joked that, thank God, I didn't have the responsibility of being Head Chef this year. Instead of a laugh I got his deeply anxious eyes staring at me. I was a bit surprised by this but assured him I had his back whenever he needed it. He thanked me but the smell of desperation on him was strong.

On my first shift I saw why. He was crap.

After a nice easy start to the service he couldn't keep up and proceeded to panic for three long hours. Working grill, he dropped several serves of lamb shanks on the floor. He used up the last serve of baked fish on a tray before getting a fresh tray into the oven. He set up sauced mains on plates and then realised he had no vegetables ready to accompany them. Tables got their meals in dribs and drabs. He mixed up steaks, and valuable time was spent frantically going through the spiked dockets while frowning waiting staff fretted at the pass.

Worst of all, Jason threw tantrums, screaming

and shouting as he made mistakes. He hurled a ladle across the floor, punched the counter a few times and emitted loud groans as though his leg was being pulled off. It was a terrible display, but the one-eyed alcoholic dish-pig loved it; he'd turn from the sink and grin happily at each outburst.

Jason also had to call away the orders at the pass. Dougie and I knew just how long mains from the grill section took to cook and we instinctively got our mains ready only to find that Jason was many tables behind. So, we slowed down and waited for him. Having many orders up that I couldn't yet cook was a very unpleasant paradox. As service crawled to an expiring snail's pace, I went to help Jason.

With a relaxed smile I quickly read the orders, and started calling away a table that I knew Dougie and I had the mains ready for. But Jason wanted no one else but him calling orders away and became red-faced and highly emotional at my perceived intrusion.

Remembering my earlier promise to back him up, I stepped away from the docket rack and helped him to fumble through the service. I kept an eye on all the steaks on the grill and racks of lamb in the oven so they wouldn't overcook. I sauced up fish and put veggies on plates. All while I dashed repeatedly between the cold larder and the grill. When the awful service ground to a halt, Jason quickly holed up in the office nook to do some ordering. Dougie rolled his eyes at me.

Oh man, our 'Head Chef' must have bullshitted his way into the job. He wasn't even up to running a section, let alone calling away the tables. And he knew it. Every day he was putting his incompetence on show and this was hi-octane fuel for his temper tantrums.

As the weeks went by, any sympathy I might have had for Jason dried up like a forgotten French-fry under a chest freezer. I tried to put him at ease but he was a queer fish. During prep he was unctuous and chummy; full of false cheer, but come service and he'd turn into a sweating, cursing liability. But what really drained my empathy tank was that he was a lazy bastard too.

When I had Head Chef duties, I never took two whole hours doing the ordering, or spent ten hours on the monthly stock-take. And I certainly never took mid-afternoon breaks that stretched into an hour or more. He was taking the piss big time.

It was incumbent upon us to come up with at least two specials each day. Whenever I could, I'd make things I could freeze down – sauces, soups, sweet dough – for those busy days when I needed a quick special.

Then I found that Jason was using this prep of mine for his specials. When I fronted him, he said he was so busy doing all the Head Chef stuff, like the ordering, that he'd didn't have time to come up with a special or two. Without using any profanity, I told him to make his own fucking specials.

Jason's non-leadership and panic during service was causing so much grief that Ketut and I came up with a plan. Jason, almost bowing and scraping before us, readily agreed to it. Between us, Ketut and I would do four of his five services working grill and calling away the orders. He could do larder or pans and have just one day a week of terror to contend with.

It wasn't so much about being compassionate but more about having services that were not the culinary equivalent of Custer's Last Stand. It worked and Jason's doomed screaming was now restricted to one night a week. But his laziness was terminal. Instead of getting uptight, Ketut and I both made three or four specials each day, things that made good money. The owners were very happy – the old team were kicking goals and as this status quo coalesced, Jason became sidelined. I figured that the rest of the season would go by fairly peacefully now. I was dead wrong.

One morning Jason brightly informed us that his girlfriend Amanda was arriving to work at the resort. Even more exciting, his best mate Damo would be joining us in the kitchen as a first-year apprentice. Ketut stared at Jason like Charles Bronson and I silently groaned. This didn't sound good.

Sure enough, Damo was a stocky little prick with a wannabe jailbird's disposition and bad tattoos. On his first shift we all said hello and got back into it. But he got bored quickly and swaggered around attempting to start aggressively friendly conversations with everyone. Ketut ignored him and he came over and leaned on my bench like a standover man and laid a self-aggrandizing spiel on me. He didn't get much of a response, zero in fact, and he inflated his 5-litre beer keg of a chest and gave me a well-practised tough-guy look.

"You don't like me, do you?" he drawled.

"Mate, I've just met you," I said. "How could I form an opinion either way?"

But I had, and no doubt Jason had put in a bad word for Ketut and I as well.

Oh yeah, Jason and Damo were champion work-dodgers, strutting around the kitchen and yodelling to each other like magpies. I didn't get angry, much, but I couldn't shake a vague and impending sense of doom. My Nostradamic intimations were confirmed within a couple weeks.

Jason's gang, along with a few dumb waiters, went into town to drink one night. Totally loaded, they lurched back home, walking along the highway which was lined with four-sided steel power poles. For a laugh, daredevil Damo climbed five metres up a pole and leapt off. He landed heavily but seemed OK, yet over the next few days he was subdued at work.

One night, just after Jason had left the kitchen, Damo approached me in a worried and deferential way

"Mate, please tell me what you think of this." He pulled his chef's jacket up his back and I felt real nausea.

It hadn't broken through the skin – yet, but one of his vertebrae was sticking out like a fat nipple!

His drunken jump from the power-pole had done serious damage to him. He was feeling a tingling numbness in his fingers and toes too, but Jason had assured him it would heal on its own. I told Damo it definitely wouldn't and firmly advised him to ring for an ambulance right now. Looking very scared he said he'd go to the hospital tomorrow.

Dumbfounded at Damo's ignorance and Jason's lack of care I went and told the owners in the morning. The sight of the spine nipple shocked them too and upon Damo's presentation at the hospital, the doctors went into full emergency mode. He was strapped into a stretcher and immediately helicoptered 270 kms to Darwin, where surgery just saved him from becoming a paraplegic.

A guilt-stricken Jason retreated into his shell, and Ketut and I had even less reason to respect him.

A week later Damo returned, unable to work. Apparently with nowhere else to go, he secretly bunked in with Jason and Amanda in their cabin, recuperating with cartons of beer and Foxtel. Proper sustenance was covertly provided by Jason, who nightly ferried kitchen leftovers to the fallen warrior.

Our only communication with the Head Chef now was us calling tables away. It was sorry scene alright. There was no love lost as Jason really believed that Ketut and I were stuck-up bastards who had not only done his good mate out of his job, but had totally undermined him as Head Chef.

Early one morning, on my twelfth consecutive day of fifteen-hour shifts, I was feeling a bit ordinary. Even with my cabin's air-con going full bore - a decent night's rest had been eluding me for days. It was too bloody hot to sleep and I was tired. Actually, I felt fried.

The breakfast buffet was over and I struggled to think about the day's prep. With a function of seventy booked for tonight it was set to be a busy day.

Then the insect screen door banged and one of the owners came in looking most concerned.

"I just saw Jason, Amanda and Damo, who I thought had left, driving out the entrance," he said. We hurried over to their cabin and indeed, the Jason Gang had just ridden out of Dodge. There was nothing in the cabin except for lots of empty beer bottles. The owner was shocked but I felt relief. We all had to work hard that day but the mood in the kitchen made up for it.

With what seemed like perfect serendipity the owners immediately found a Head Chef who could start at the end of the week. He'd just finished up running the busy kitchen at a big sports and social club in town.

That afternoon, Ketut and I and the owners met him. I was appalled. He was one of the scariest chefs I've ever seen – a feral leprechaun with bloodshot eyes, badly shaven and reeking of last night's go on the booze.

As he fidgeted and talked a mile a minute, I saw that some of his knuckles were broken and popped from hitting things. He assured us he'd run a very tight ship, a *very* tight ship. He'd be bloody hard on us but we'd all have lots of beers together after work and forget about what had gone down in the kitchen. At one point I heard him grinding his teeth.

The owners nodded and smiled and Ketut stared at the floor in abject misery. I had a very bad feeling about this man and so did Ketut. Ryan the assistant manager came into the kitchen later, and we shared our fears with him. The next morning Ryan appeared in the kitchen grinning wickedly.

"I checked out the new Head Chef," he said. "He left the Sports Club just before they could sack him. Apparently, a sum of money went missing. And he's a drunk too, who starts fights."

"Have you told the owners?" I said.

"I'm going there now."

This was great news and Ketut and I cheerfully prepped until Ryan came back in with a downcast face.

"Sorry guys but they still want to employ him. There's no actual proof he's a thief and he won't be working with any cash here. We can't stop him from drinking but they'll tell him there's no fighting allowed."

With our reprieve smacked down, we worked the week in glumness. But, the day before our nemesis' arrival, Ryan came into the kitchen with a radiant smile.

"The new Head Chef's not coming now. He was up in Darwin and got into a brawl. Someone broke his leg and I think he's on assault charges too."

Never had so much pain caused so much joy, and the management, as worn down as we were, finally did the right thing and paid Ketut to become Head Chef.

Things got even better when Lasiyah, a serious Indonesian third-year apprentice came on board. It was now really hot but she kept her cool while learning the ropes, and quickly made the cold larder her very own domain. Our local apprentices, both boys, got energized by Lasiyah's work ethic, and by her being a girl and all, and they stepped right up. Ketut and I now figured that we could make it through the rest of the busy period. We did, but during that season I had eighteen days off in six months.

Finally, my contract was up. My hard work and sobriety led one of the owners, Tony, to tempt me with unlimited free drinks on my last night. Some front of house girls and boys liked me and they were keen to give me a send-off too. To everyone's delight I agreed.

At sunset we started with cocktails and then settled into vodka and rum. Many of the group had early starts and so we finished up at midnight, well drunk, slurring goodbyes and hugging like panda bears.

Tony then suggested he and I go and see the local rev-heads racing customised V8 cars on the derelict airstrip next to the resort. With a bottle of vodka for company we walked over and rode shotgun with the young dudes as they all-out gunned their high-powered machines at close to two hundred km/h along the vast stretch of cracked tarmac. Flying through the night I whooped and yelled and had so much fun that I couldn't remember how I got home.

In the morning I awoke and my brain painfully un-crinkled like a squashed-up ball of cellophane. With a mega hang-over I shuffled into the kitchen to say goodbye and a frowning Ketut wagged a finger at me. Waiting staff joined in the admonishment, complaining about being called in early or on their day off. I gingerly inquired what I had done and was told that no less than three staff from last night's drinks were unable to work today.

"You dangerous," said Ketut. "It's good you only drink once a year or you kill everybody!"

The Damage

It's a hell of a machine. Gleaming under the lights, the meat slicer has a razor-sharp circular blade and its edge is a blur of kinetic stainless-steel spinning at two hundred rpm. This high-end piece of equipment is a powerful prep-buster, easily turning sides of preserved meat and blocks of cheese into slices of any thickness.

Craigie Boy, a second-year apprentice is working with this heavy-duty appliance. We're all heads-down and bums-up, trying to get the prep done before a booked-out service starts, when Craigie Boy lets out one almighty shout. As I turn to see what the hell he's done, I already know.

His hand is pressed against his chest; his white jacket turning crimson as red speckles appear on the tiled floor around him. I run over, turn off the slicer and ask the obvious, "Did you cut yourself?"

He nods in shock and I can tell he doesn't want to look at his hand. Neither do I. But he takes a quick peek, goes grey with shock and slumps against me. I brace him, thinking he's going to faint.

"My thumb," he moans. "It's split open!" I take a look now, grimace at what I see and yell for front of house to ring an ambulance. It's a real shocker. Against all common sense he's given himself two thumbs on the one hand.

He doesn't fall down and the Head Chef appears. I quickly fill him in while Craigie Boy moans with pain. He looks guilty too, and with good reason. He's given himself a bad fluke wound – the kind you should never get.

I call out to the dish pig, "Job for you here! Hot water. Mop. Sanitizer!" I grab more paper towel, hold it to catch the streaming blood and Chef and I gently steer Craigie Boy out the back door. Out on the street we wait for the ambulance to arrive. Passers-by look with alarm at Craigie Boy's red soaked jacket and he quickly stops moaning. I slap him heartily on the back. "You cunning bastard," I say. "You got out of tonight's service!"

Why don't we take a break from my tale? Go on - duck out back for a cigarette, or eat a creme brulee that's nearly too old to serve. Let's take a few minutes and enter a world of pain.

You will get hurt working in a kitchen, that's in no doubt, and the odds of getting hurt get better as it gets busier. In the rush of service, corners are cut – sometimes literally. I saw a poor chef rupture a vein in his groin by running full tilt into the edge of a stainless-steel bench. His testicles rapidly swelled up with blood. Ow. I saw a cook spin around into a colleague's knife. Luckily it sunk into the meat of his upper thigh – not his femoral artery or guts. Yow.

It's best not to move faster than your ability to stop in a second, and only build momentum that can be instantly dissipated within ten centimetres. It's ninja jazz ballet in clogs and boots.

Kitchen pros become wizards at floating through time and space, slipping and flowing around each other like quicksilver. They rarely, if ever, touch. In many kitchens everyone says "Behind!" to whoever they are passing right behind. It might sound anal but with sharp knives and burning hot things potentially part of a collision – it's well worth doing.

A badly set-up kitchen is often an obstacle course leading to calamity. Repeatedly moving through a line of busy chefs' work-spaces, in order to replenish prep, or to use cooking equipment, multiplies the odds of an accident.

Small kitchens – like the torture chamber in the Swiss Hotel – are equally as bad. Orders fall behind, tempers fray, the food quality suffers and invariably there comes a cry of pain. As an agency chef I worked in some miniature horror shows.

Every square meter of land is worth a fortune at Melbourne's Southbank restaurant precinct and I got sent to a kitchen there that was a real little stinker. Six people worked in a space meant for three. Oven doors opened out onto shins and ankles. The hand-washing sink stuck out like a ceramic elbow. Reach-in fridges malfunctioned because they were flush to ovens going full-bore. The kitchen crew slipped and pushed around each other like gin-soaked street trash in an old etching.

Guess where the cold room was? Upstairs on the next floor! As I emptied the reach-ins I had to grab a four-wheeler trolley, dash up the hallway, go to the lift, press the button, wait for the lift, get in, go up to the next floor and go to our cold room to get what I needed. Then I had to repeat the whole process to go back down again . . . while I had things on gas rings and in ovens cooking. And this rigmarole might happen three or four times in a service.

It got worse. The three restaurants next door had their kitchen crew doing the same thing. Their kitchens, like ours, were also the size of Dachshund kennels, so their cold rooms were upstairs too. The competition for the one and only lift was fierce.

Then a bright spark used a trolley to keep the lift doors open while they accessed their cold room. Chefs had to run up the stairs and some wrestling over the trolley ensued. Then a bit of serious bashing occurred and the police got called and they also cluttered up the lift entrance. And no-one cleaned up the smears of chef blood on the cold-room door either. I lasted a week in that bedlam.

Of course, the classic way to injure yourself in the kitchen is with a knife. They possess an odd duality - as tools of creativity and also as lethal weapons – and are a link between the Lucky Hunter and the Good Cook. Kitchen knives, unlike hunting or combat knives, have a single-edge blade. At one end is the tip and at the other end is the heel. Knives have different sizes and shapes specific to the job they perform. Cook's knives are triangular with a big heel – just perfect for the up-and-down motion of chopping. Boning knives are long and pointed – all tip and no heel. There's a multitude of knives and they can all cut you.

A cut brings pain, and frustrating interruption to prep or service, but what really hurts is the loss of face. It's the obvious, junior thing to do. A freshly cut cook stifles a curse, flits to the first aid kit, surreptitiously puts a plaster on the wound and hopes everyone is working too hard to notice. Any comment on this is greeted with busy silence.

Like poor old Craigie Boy, some people have bad reactions when they find out what they're made of. A wonderful manager-waitress sliced the tip of her finger off cutting lemons on my chopping board. The little cap of flesh fell onto the board and her shocked face drained of colour. She didn't feel pain yet but I knew she was going to faint. I snatched up her fingertip, popped it into my mouth and started chewing. "I've always liked you," I said.

In horrified surprise she completely forgot to faint. I wasn't really eating her fingertip – I'd hidden the little scrap of flesh in my hand. Colour rushed back into her face and I applied paper towel to her finger. She began to splutter in disgust and I held up the fingertip for her to see, then flipped it into the bin. "I do like you," I said. "But not that much."

The unkindest cut is to slash an existing cut. It's almost healed and ow! – the blade finds it. Or you cut a healing burn, because the other most popular way to hurt yourself in the kitchen is to get burnt. Everyone gets burnt, it's just the severity that matters. The sound can be attention grabbing too. Hearing your flesh sizzle on hot metal is always a surprise.

Check out the undersides of a cook's forearms for the heat tattoos that oven racks leave. Reaching at speed into super-hot ovens and negotiating the searing shelves is not always easy. Faint scars on my forearms remain from burns inflicted years ago.

Fortunately, no scar remains from the stupidest burn I ever suffered. Hey cooks – you remember those chef's pants with the Velcro fastenings at the waist and drawstring ties at the front? Trendy pyjama-looking nonsense that I fell for when I was young and dumb. Dumber still was that I had rocked up to my shift sans jocks.

Working grill, I stretched out over the smoking hot flat-plate to grab some serves of fish from the head-high salamander. Right then those stupid pants un-Velcroed themselves and fell open. For a split second I experienced eye-watering pain. Absolutely ambushed, I sprang back and was very lucky that nobody saw my sausage getting a red-hot basting on its tip. A quick check-up in the men's room revealed a blister that Aloe Vera and abstinence soon fixed. I ditched those chef's pants pronto and forever after made underpants an essential part of my kitchen kit.

This unforced sizzling of my wiener was nothing compared to my baddest burn. Hot ovens, pans and utensils can burn you good, but the pain makes you instantly jump away or let go. With oil and fat burns there is nothing to drop or leap back from. The oil sticks to your flesh.

I got it bad while lifting down cooked bacon from the top shelf of a head-high oven. The big tray was covered in sizzling middle rashers and I tilted it slightly. Bubbling hot bacon fat ran down my right arm. I screamed, Lordy I did, and dashed to the sink and ran cold water onto my arm while tears of excruciating pain squirted out of my eyes. A nasty second degree burn now stretched from wrist to elbow. Bottom End Grunt or not – I had to leave work and go and get treatment.

The big bag of fluid hanging ten centimetres off my arm was lanced, slowly drained and the loose skin very carefully put back into place on my forearm. The burn was smothered in antiseptic salve and bandaged up not too tight. Some days later I removed the bandage and a mass of flaky dead skin fell away to reveal pink new skin beneath.

Burning and scorching are simple agonies. The sheer atmospheric heat generated in kitchens is a much more cunning excruciation. Long shifts with ovens and grills going full bore tax the body from the skin to the kidneys. The thermal ambiance ratchets up over service and many a time I have finished a shift with my whites and checks saturated and absolutely steaming. In this world of streaming sweat, diaphoretic cooks need to employ antiperspirants as the stinky chef is an olfactory ogre in the kitchen, second only to the flatulent chef as someone you'd least want to spend a shift with.

Some lucky kitchens are air-conditioned – but many rely on ceiling fans. I've utilised portable electric fans, stuck in corners and perched on shelves. Wet tea towels, freezer-cooled and worn around the neck can provide relief. Snatched moments in walk-in cold rooms are bliss. I've even put my head in a stand-up freezer to relieve my overheated cranium. Anything that works is good.

Other kitchen ruinations are even subtler. Over time the simple act of breathing becomes hazardous. The kitchen air, saturated with aerosoled fat and an invisible mist of greasy steam, can cause respiratory problems. Combine this with a pack or two a day cigarette habit and lungs become swamps.

Extractor fans in overhead hoods remove most gaseous effluent, but even as they help, they harm. Every cook must endure loud impact noises – chopping boards getting hammered, the metal-to-metal banging of pots and pans on cook tops – but the insidious drone of the overhead hood fans is mentally debilitating and saps concentration and energy. Constant kitchen noise is unbelievably tiring. Exposure to more than eighty-five decibels of noise over an eight-hour shift will start damaging the ears. Many kitchens exceed that level, and in the wet area the dish pigs really get it in the ear, with noise levels over one hundred decibels. With my ears still ringing an hour after knocking off I've often wondered if permanent hearing damage has been suffered. Or was it the years standing near the bass-bins in clubs? Oh yeah, as a bonus risk, chronic long-term noise also increases the risk of heart attacks.

Maladies of the skin can force a cook from the kitchen. Dermatitis caused by sustained wet work, the food being handled or by the detergents and cleaning products used in the kitchen, crawl up hands and arms. Beyond these allergies, having one's hands constantly wet means cuts and nicks don't get time to heal. One time I worked for three months with only eight days off. By the seventy-eighth day I swear I saw a bone peeking out of a hole on my fingertip.

The most dreaded epidermal phenomenon of all is chef's arse. This fiendish complaint is not fatal, but its caress is unadulterated agony. Services are filled with anguish and pain, and all you can think of is knocking off work and just being still.

Chef's arse is when one's buttocks, the lowest inside curve of the cheeks to be exact, rub against each other while marinating in sweat. The constant chafing movement makes two extremely painful weals rise up and rub, rub, rub against each other.

It's a real bummer. It's hell on two legs. Things like Vaseline and baby powder don't cut the mustard and relief can only be gained by applying, before one's shift, special creams to the chafeable areas. It's hard to know when to use these balms because one day chef's arse is there, and the next day it's not, and the kitchen is as hot and sweaty as it ever was. It has nothing to do with your personal hygiene. You might maintain the squeakiest, cleanest baby-show fresh bottom in the world and chef's arse will gitcha.

Eventually, like a long serving pick-up truck, the kitchen professional's working parts just get worn out. Decades of long shifts standing on hard floors cause irreparable physical deterioration – things like varicose veins, knee joint damage and lumbar back pain. Old campaigners develop carpal tunnel syndrome from the constant tension of holding and using tongs and knives. Hernias pop out as a result of lugging heavy pots or forever power-squatting at the reach-in fridges and low oven doors. The graceful glide across the tiled kitchen floor now becomes a ragged shuffle; cheery whistling is replaced by groans of decrepitude.

The salt in the wound is the low and stagnant cooking industry rates of pay. I'm eternally peeved that the creators of crap culture get paid much more than some wonderful cook does. I could easily swap many movies, books and songs for some nicely smoked eel – or even a decent sandwich.

Sometimes chefs and cooks die before their time. Beyond the raw kinetic hurt they suffer in kitchens; immune systems corrode and minds unravel. The dark side of Bottom End Grunt takes hold and unknown kitchen soldiers and star chefs alike perish. I worked with a chef who hung himself and another who died from a heroin overdose.

Kitchen work is not for sissies and I defy any cook doing it until they're seventy, no matter what any fat politician says. Anyone who's got good in the kitchen has put up with pain and discomfort. Respect not just their culinary skills, but also their physical and mental tenacity. It is sad that an industry that creates so much pleasure can cause so much pain.

Here's Something I Prepared Earlier

As far as I know, I've only ever appeared on television once in my life and I didn't even know it at the time. Seeing that I was as grumpy as hell when it happened – it was probably a good thing I didn't know.

Back when I was working for Delectable Catering in Melbourne, a friend said, "I saw you on TV last night and you looked pissed off."

"Really?" I was puzzled. "What was I doing?"

"You were cooking. And looking pissed off."

I still didn't get it.

"It was at some food show with Reg Livermore interviewing Jamie Oliver," my mate explained. "You were prowling around in the background with the worst angry face on. What was going on?"

Now I remembered.

I'm backstage at the hottest gig in town. There's the noise of ten thousand people around me. It's busy, it's hot and bright lights beat down on the crucible that I'm at the centre of. There's an excited buzz in the air as media types, security and entourages flutter on the periphery of my workspace.

I'm going hard, with things in the oven, things on the burners and I've got lots of produce to process. I'm not really hearing the voices, a few meters away, of hundreds of paying fans filing in to take their seats. I've been going for hours and I am in the zone – full of grace and subtle steel. Totally in the groove, I turn in my workspace to find two dickheads, one holding a boom microphone and the other wheeling a video camera right in front of my oven door.

My composure disappears. These clowns are in my way! They cannot be here! I quickly and politely impart this essential knowledge to the pop-up film crew. They totally ignore me, not even looking at me.

"Hey fellas. Fellas – you can't be here!" My voice rises. "You're in my way!"

They ignore me even more. I'm starting to lose it and look around and see Reg Livermore and Jamie Oliver grinning at me. It's like they're saying, "Welcome to show biz buddy." It flashes on me that I'd overheard earlier that an interview with Jamie Oliver was going to happen. Sure – but not in front of my oven!

I quickly body-block the film crew fools and begin pushing the camera away on its wheeled tripod. That gets their attention. They try to push back but I now have my dander up. I shirt-front the cameraman, get a solid grip on the tripod and rush the camera out of my space and around the other side of the bench. I point down the bench to where I've made a little display and storage area of herbs in vases, fruit in bowls and tall bottles of olive oil and vinegar.

"Right!" I say in a voice that brooks no dissent. "You guys set up here, stick Jamie and Reg down there and stay out of my space. OK?"

I let go of their expensive camera and the boys, looking relieved, take my direction. I hurry back to my work; yet another problem sorted at the amazing circus that is The Good Food Show. All good. Cool again.

Except what my friend saw on TV told another story. I thought I had got back to smiling, but there in the background of a most congenial interview was one grouchy looking cook.

I had got a phone call from my joker of a chef mate Gerry, who sometimes got me doing gigs at his catering company. Would I like the chance to work with Jamie Oliver? Rick Stein? Jaques Reymond, Gabriel Gaté and Elizabeth Chong? It was a pretty dull gag by Gerry's standards, so I asked him what the real job was.

He wasn't joking. Gerry had been contracted to put together a small crew to prep for the celebrity chefs at The Good Food Show. Well I couldn't say no and for eighteen mad days over three years I prepped for a whole mob of famous faces. It proved to be a rare treat seeing the worlds of cooking and entertainment coming together in perfect fusion.

The show started out in the UK, and in Australia they'd hire big convention centre halls in Sydney and Melbourne, and over a Saturday, Sunday and Monday put on the show. The main part of the show was an expo with booths selling a range of foodstuffs and cooking gear. Knives, pans, wine and cheese; chocolate, spices, blenders and whisks. Anything to do with food, its preparation and cooking was represented by Australia's finest.

Stall-holders would demonstrate the tools that they were selling and there were blenders whizzing and knives a-chop-chopping – so avid punters could get a taste of what they could do in their own kitchens. All this kinetic action lead to the second part of The Good Food Show – the chefs showing you how it's done.

There was a demonstration kitchen featuring top Aussie chefs – hardcore fellas like Luke Mangan and Shannon Bennett, backed by their own teams. This kitchen stage seated two hundred and anyone could just sit down and have a gander. These demonstrations were often full, with the overflow standing. I wished I could have watched these wizards, but I got too busy working at the other demonstration kitchen.

It was solid kudos for me when I told the gang at

Delectable Catering why I wouldn't be available for a couple of weekends in a months' time.

As the gig got closer Gerry went into high gear, organising the kitchen and produce, and liaising with the Good Food Show crew, the celebs, sponsors and suppliers. Just like with an on-site catering gig, every little detail needed sorting before the event began. I rang him a few of times to see how it was going. Gerry was a born organiser and trouble-shooter and he was loving it.

In the last weeks before showtime the simmering hype around the event began to really boil over. Snappy television spots and big print ads in the state and national press touted the event and it was talked up on radio and TV. When billboards and banners began to appear around Melbourne and at the Convention centre itself, I realised how big this was going to be.

D-day arrived and I convened with Gerry at Jeff's Shed – the Convention Centre at Melbourne's South Bank – where two of the immense halls had been booked. We went down one end of the space where two adjoining kitchens had been put together entirely from scratch. The walls, power and gas lines, plumbing, sinks, ovens and burners of both kitchens had been set up a day before.

The first kitchen was glammed up, looking like it came from the pages of an interior design magazine. Though it was fully functional it was essentially a stage for the cooking demonstrations. The shiny white and stainless-steel fittings twinkled under careful lighting. There were vases of fresh flowers daily and whoever was doing a demonstration onstage had their cook book on display.

Theatrical lighting was rigged up overhead, with spotlights aimed down onto the large counter where the burners and chopping boards were. A lighting desk up the back controlled all this. There were a couple of static video cameras and a roving steady-cam person for closer work, so that every little chop and whisk of the cooking action could be seen on a big screen above the stage. Speakers at the stage sides amplified every word and sizzle. On either side of the kitchen were wings, covered by black curtains, that led backstage.

Around this kitchen stage was a purpose built four hundred seat auditorium, cut off from the hustle and bustle of The Good Food Show by thick curtain walls. At the auditorium entrance was a box-office that sold tickets for each one of the shows and there were frequently long lines of eager cooking fans.

I'd seen cooking demonstrations before but this was something else – this was rock'n'roll.

Behind the kitchen stage was another kitchen – the place where something was prepared earlier. This was a brightly lit bare bones of a beast where I'd be prepping. The space was corralled in by demountable walls separating us from the crowds at the show, and only accessible with a pass checked by a security guard.

A partitioned-off corner served as the Green Room. In this VIP haven were couches, flowers, a fridge full of cool drinks and a big TV screen that showed the cooking on the kitchen stage. Celebs waiting to do their show, or those who had just finished, could catch the action of their peers on this screen.

In the kitchen area of this backstage space we pushed trestle tables around and slapped down rubber floor mats to create our different work spaces. Power boards and leads got gaffer-taped out of the way. The wet area with sinks and a dishwasher lined one side, and behind the kitchen wall silage lines snaked away to the edge of the hall. The squeak and pop of bubble-wrap and Styrofoam filled the air as we unpacked brand new tools and equipment – all supplied by sponsors.

As we got everything in place the produce began to arrive. Like the equipment, it was all being given free by businesses keen to be recognized by the celebrity chefs and their audiences. It was absolute primo food, the very best the country could offer, and even though the recipes called for small amounts, the suppliers brought a whole lot extra. All this was carefully packed into a humming portable cold room.

Aside from Gerry and I, we had a couple of kitchen hands and Rose, a bubbly eighteen-year-old apprentice. Gerry had lots of non-prep organizing and trouble-shooting to do, so, with Rose's help, I did most of the prep. There were seven half hour shows each day with a half-hour break in between shows to clean and set up for the next chef.

The headliner that first year was Jamie Oliver. His debut TV series, The Naked Chef, was huge and his star was rising. We found that out at his very first show.

The excitement levels were high and the crowd was really buzzing as his theme song, Toploader's cover of Dancing in the Moonlight, came jingling through the speakers. Huge cheering greeted him and he got on with his funny and crowd-pleasing demonstration. Soon ladies began hopping out of their seats to get in close and take photos. Jamie Oliver had his own security man and the Convention Centre had provided another, and the two lads politely ushered the over-eager snappers back to their seats. Then as Jamie finished his show, a hoard of women rushed the stage to talk to their idol. He deftly zipped into the backstage kitchen, went into the Green Room, and closed the door.

I had to co-ordinate cleaning the kitchen stage and setting it up for the next demo, but as I attempted to go out front to do this, a flood of excited women swept into me. It was like the Beatles had just finished playing and I was pushed aside as they spilled into the prep kitchen. Caught in the bottleneck at the wing, in a gyrating gyre of hips, boobs and hair, I could see potential mayhem in the kitchen. Trestle tables shook and bowls and plates of ingredients looked ready to spill. It was estrogenic chaos and the two security guys couldn't cope. They ran around after individual women, reluctant to lay hands on them, while the kitchen filled up with the overwrought crowd. Eventually, with no Jamie in sight, they all left.

Come his next show there were now five security guards, and like in some epic tale of Sparta they locked arms to hold back an even bigger rush. One security bloke looked absolutely shocked, his eyes bugging in disbelief at the mass of inflamed womanhood heaving against him.

It would have been funny except it cut down on the time I had to set up for the next show. To deal with this, Rose, the kitchen hands and I got a routine going. While the security boys dealt with the initial surge and backstage runaways, we'd clear people off the stage. I played nice at first but polite requests to move along were ignored. Rude requests were ignored. Directions through the public address system also fell on deaf ears.

I'm sorry to say that I got mean. I pushed like I was in a rugby scrum and I even singed the occasional arm with pans still hot from the show. I'd be yelling "Hot pans! Hot pans!" though, and that, combined with a scream, really helped to clear a path. Using the big plastic tubs that we carried dirty pots and pans away with, our kitchen crew would form a wedge and assault the stage, taking ground metre by metre. From up in their mixing-desk eyrie, the light and sound crew, watched in awe and amusement as we cleaved the mob asunder. It felt like being at The Gates of Valhalla at times.

Jamie Oliver had his own prep chef – a slim, calm lady called Ginny. I set her up with her own area and if I could help her, I did, finding another power point or pot for her. She needed no culinary assistance as she was a stone-cold pro.

"What did you do before working with Jamie?" I asked her.

"You know Two Fat Ladies? Well I did all the prep for their TV shows and their tours," she replied. Wow.

So, I ended up having nothing to do with Jamie Oliver at all, but I did use the only time I spoke to him to zing the boys back at Delectable Catering.

I'd nipped out to the back-stage gents for a whizz and there was The Naked Chef using the urinal. We exchanged hellos and got on with it.

When I got back to work at Delectable Catering the following week someone teasingly said, "Was Jamie naked?"

All the chefs were gay men and I went there.

"No, but I did see his willy."

Snorts of incredulous laughter and curious looks greeted my ridiculous statement. The Head Chef looked pained. He disliked any sort of crudity in the kitchen.

"No, it's true," I pushed on. "I stood next to him at the trough one day."

I kept working and the silence built. The Head Chef could see what was coming and began to speak, but the youngest, cheekiest chef couldn't help himself.

"So, what was it like then?"

I pounced. "Not as big as mine."

Everyone screamed with laughter except for our long-suffering Head Chef, who closed his eyes and slowly shook his head.

My written brief for each person's show included all the recipes and lists of ingredients, tools and cooking equipment. However, these briefs did not have any instructions as to how much prep to actually do. Some of my charges wanted most of the prep done so they could take time to explain something or tell a tale or two. Others were concerned with showing the prep processes themselves. Generally, they would turn up an hour or two before their show and I would find out exactly what they wanted. Now fully informed, I could then reproduce the prep over their subsequent shows.

Rick Stein gave me a scare as he wasn't there an hour or two before his first show. He was one of the headliners, with a hot TV show and book, and Gerry and the organisers were fretting. But not as much as me! I had covered all bases for his first show and glass bowls of ingredients, organised by recipe, covered a bench. I had all his fish and seafood ready – cleaned, filleted and portioned. I also had whole specimens for him to show or fillet as well.

Everything was ready, but the man wasn't there. I worked on other prep as the clock ticked away. Gerry made some inquiries. On his way, I was told. Then it was half an hour to go and then fifteen minutes. Anxiety levels peaked around me and I put myself in the hands of the cooking gods.

As it hit ten minutes to show-time, Mr. Stein steamed in and was hurried over to me. I guessed he was on a mad schedule so I turned up the calmness dial. I concisely matched each set of ingredients with each of the recipes, while Mr. Stein listened most intently. He checked everything and then smiled – it was all good.

He also nodded in approval at the whole fish and uncleaned seafood I had laid on for him.

"Oh that's great," he said. "So are you OK for me to come in like this from now on – just before the show?"

I serenely agreed, hiding the relief I felt. My full-spectrum prep had passed muster.

Rick Stein tells a good story; he obviously enjoys spinning a yarn while rustling up a feed. He made it look easy, but trying to fit several tales and dishes into a half-hour cooking demonstration is not easy. One year we ran into some timing problems.

Mr. Stein had a grilled fish recipe and instructed me to have the grill on low so he wouldn't have to fiddle about lighting it. He'd turn it up just before using it.

Unfortunately, while entertaining the audience with a story about his dog Chalky, he put the fish on the grill without turning it up. The fish never really sealed, stuck to the grill and then broke into pieces when he plated it up.

I suggested being by the stage for the next shows so I could hop up and manipulate the heat as needed. Mr. Stein declined, knowing I was busy with prep, and instead instructed me to have the grill up higher.

At his next show, while the audience laughed at his diverting stories, the plate got hotter and hotter. When he finally put the fish on, it went up in a cloud of smoke and the fire alarms in the giant hall went off.

I was prepping out back with Ainsley Harriott and didn't twig that the alarms had been triggered by the kitchen theatre. We looked at each other.

"What do we do?" said Ainsley. Beyond the glass kitchen door was an empty car park and I gestured to it.

"You can go out there if you're scared," I cheekily said. "It's a false alarm, nothing to do with us."

Then someone ran in and yelled it was to do with us – specifically me. Ainsley laughed as I rushed out. On stage I quickly dealt with the piscean incendiary. Mr Stein was very good about it, but over the rest of his shows he kept a keen fisherman's eye on that grill.

The incident had legs. The next day Mr. Stein was on national TV and they set up a demonstration grill for him to cook something on. As he put the first thing on it a prank smoke bomb was set off under the grill. Poor Mr. Stein then had to laugh along with the jovial host and studio audience.

I didn't get to talk about food or cooking with Rick Stein. Rocking up ten minutes before his show, he'd check the prep, thank me, do his demonstrations and then zoom off. I know I did good because he asked me to do his prep for the following two years. I did find out one thing though – he loved Flathead.

Ainsley Harriott enjoyed a chat up though. A born entertainer, he came across as larger than life, but his trademark smile was real. I found Ainsley rather Shakespearean, his constant repartee punctuated by merry laughter and bawdy jokes. He even slapped me on the arse one time! In the kitchen however, where he did much of his own prep, he became quiet and focused and I saw how genuine his love for cooking was. At the end of his shows he was generous in thanking me.

I also did the prep for the then food-editor of the venerable British newspaper The Times – Jill Dupleix, and she was just . . . lovely.

Jill was a gem, effortlessly sophisticated, relaxed and polite. Being primarily a writer, she may have been nervous as hell on stage for all I knew, but she exuded utter sangfroid. Her onstage manner was precise but warm, knowledgeable without pomposity. And did I say she was wonderful? I think my puppy dog expression got picked up on by her husband Terry; he seemed to be eyeing me with suspicion. Or possibly he was just checking out how I was going with the prep.

I did right by Jill, helping her in an admiring daze. At her last show she thanked me from the stage, telling the audience she'd like to take me to London as her prep chef. I stared bashfully at the floor. Her goodbye back-stage included giving me a hug! I nearly swooned and stammered my goodbyes. Then I saw her husband looking hard at me, his eyes meeting mine with real significance. His head appeared to be shaking up and down with anger and I quickly got busy.

When I calmed down later on, I realised he had just been nodding at me in thanks – acknowledging my efforts in supporting his missus.

At the first Good Food Show the bulk of the prep was on my shoulders and that made me the fastest moving, most cooking-orientated person there. I was doing the long hours, actually sweating at an oven and poring over prep lists. I was making it all happen, and with the exception of giving that TV crew the bum's rush, I was calm and politeness itself.

I got nods of acknowledgment – recognition of my status as a central cog in the whole kitchen machine. On rare occasions I'd go into the Green Room, grab a cold drink and flop onto the couch for a few minutes and watch someone turning my prep into a meal on the CCTV screen. People sympathetically inquired how I was feeling and told me what a great job I was doing. They knew Bottom End Grunt when they saw it.

The more shows I did the less stressful it became and I grew familiar with the entertainment industry vibe swirling around me. As well as the celebrity chefs, there were managers, press agents, photographers and journalists. And all manner of food groupie with a book to sign and compliments to bestow.

The man in the beret, Ian Parmenter, probably understood the rock'n'roll ethos of the Good Food Show better than anyone, due to his remarkable career in television and music. Though his very short (five minutes long) and ultra-cute cooking show, Consuming Passions, was an international hit, it was just the tip of the iceberg lettuce with Ian.

He was an award-winning producer and director with credits including concerts with Ray Charles and Dionne Warwick. He'd worked with Kiss and David Bowie on Countdown and created the legendary live TV music show – Rock Arena. When I first met Ian, I had a question. He waited for the inevitable cooking query.

"What act on Rock Arena really blew you away?"

He liked that. (I recall it was The Birthday Party that lifted his cranium). I also knew about his own blues band and he liked that too. We got on well and he requested me as his prep-man for the next two years.

Ian brought dead-pan comedy to his shows. He had a hair dryer, clothes iron and ironing board onstage for a gag meal demonstration. Due to constant travel, he'd learned to make a meal in his hotel room. The hair dryer warmed up a bread roll and a piece of fish in wax paper would get cooked with the iron on the ironing board.

I got into Ian's absurdist spirit. The folk at the Furi knife stall let me borrow their metre and a half long advertising knife for his shows. When Ian produced the walloping great blade to cut up a cherry tomato it got a big laugh.

One of the coolest of the cool was Elizabeth Chong, a pioneer of Chinese cuisine in Australia. Her long running (fifty-six years!) cooking school, her many cook-books, TV shows and appearances, had educated and entertained millions. She was hands on with her prep; I helped, watched and learnt. She knew heaps and I wouldn't wanted to have been wrong around her.

In the Green Room one day, she was watching the live feed from the stage. The person demonstrating was cooking a whole chicken in a throw-away pastry case to keep all the moistness in. The person said that he'd come up with the technique. A big pfftttttt came from Elizabeth Chong. "No, you didn't! That's Beggars Chicken - a recipe that is a thousand years old!"

She saved my bacon out at Homebush in Sydney. Ainsley Harriott had a duck breast entrée as one of his demos and I'd mistakenly allowed him to use up all the duck on his first show. He shot me a sharp look when I asked him where the rest of the duck was.

"You've got enough for the next shows, right?"

"Yeah Ainsley – all good," I lied.

Bugger. Ainsley was on again in three hours and I needed duck breasts pronto. I considered dispatching a kitchen hand in a taxi to go find some. Or maybe there were ducks around Homebush that he could hunt and kill.

Elizabeth Chong had overheard all this and of course she knew someone in the kitchen at the Novotel Hotel right there in Olympic Park. Like the legend she is, she quickly organised duck breasts for me. I thanked her profusely, raced outside across the plaza into the hotel foyer, and sure enough there was a white-jacketed comrade-in-arms with a fat package of duck.

I also had a bit of a muck-up with the true culinary heavyweight on the bill. Multi-award-winning chef Jacques Reymond got annoyed when I, urgently needing the gas ring, pulled a reduction he was making off the burner . . . and forgot to put it back. I copped a bit of a growling but he quickly forgave me when he saw the forethought I had applied to one of his recipes.

It called for poaching a chicken in an Asian master stock before re-cooking it in pieces. I made the stock, poached one chook and left it whole. I poached another and cut it up ready for re-cooking, and also had a raw one trussed up ready for him to place in the stock. I got an appreciative pat on the back for that.

Jaques Reymond is old school and hell cool. His career has spanned decades, including Michelin Stars and his beautiful restaurant that consistently dazzled diners and critics alike. It was an honour to help him.

The food suppliers were always overzealous and at the Good Food Show's end, the cold room would still contain a stack of food. Really good food too – like fresh tuna, wild game, amazing cheeses, succulent oysters and trays of berries. That first show I tried to give food away but the Good Food Show staff were busy and the techies were packing up. The security had hours to go and the kitchen crew were over food. With the green light from Gerry and management, I loaded up large Styrofoam boxes with these superb victuals, iced them down and went back to breaking down the kitchen.

When I finally finished, I rang for a taxi and loaded its boot and back seat with my booty. That first show was in Melbourne where I lived. I had two mates, one a chef, the other a waiter, who shared a place and I went over there. I knew they had the night off and would be quaffing Red Stripe beer and listening to imported ska and reggae 45s. Amazement and delight greeted my arrival and we ate and drank long into the night.

This became my modus operandi at the Good Food Shows thereafter. In Sydney, I'd take food back to the friends I was staying with. There was always a lot. One morning I ate oysters for breakfast with a musician mate. We had three dozen. Each.

I've worked in theatre and live music – on stage and behind the scenes, and I could clearly see how the Kitchen Stage had achieved a fusion of cooking and performance. Delivering a show was just like a service. I worked hard, but being in the spotlight cooking four to six dishes and being entertaining is doubly hard. I take my hat off to everyone who cooked at the Good Food Shows for pulling off two difficult things at the same time.

Cooking Tea

Kuranda, the tropical village in North Queensland where I'd started out cooking at Frogs, had a close-knit community that practised social enterprise. When the musicians and thespians needed a space for concerts and performance – they made one, building a venue that has hosted international, national and local In the twenty-first century this amphitheatre boasts all the infrastructure of an outside performance space that caters for three thousand.

But back in the day the venue was very rough and ready. In a clearing in the rainforest, a big slope of wide grass tiers faced an open wooden stage with a canvas roof. All around the venue were stands of palm trees and gardens filled with canna lilies and hibiscus.

With a big full moon rising up behind the band playing onstage and a few thousand people dancing uninhibitedly under the stars – it was pure magic.

Local musicians would play gigs and community groups would hold fundraisers. One year in the mid-eighties I was asked to do the food at a concert raising money for local musicians to buy equipment. It was a voluntary job and I was most happy to work for free, as supporting the community, and musicians, is a most worthy cause.

Marco, the event's organiser, was a charming rascal. Handsome, funny and charismatic, he was a face on the alternative scene and grew marijuana for a living. He'd taunt the police for their inability to catch him green-handed, sometimes using a trail bike to escape a raid. The girls said, "He should have a licence to use those eyes." The boys said, "Jump out the window when he gets busted or the cops will shoot you too."

There wasn't much of a budget so I came up with a small menu of two-and three-dollar meals. Tickets were only available at the door on the night so I had no idea of possible numbers. I made a guesstimate of two hundred meals.

I bought all the dry stores a week out, and on the morning of the day itself I got all the fresh food. Marco told me he had helpers coming and I sure was going to need them.

The bar and kitchen were in a rough timber and tin-roofed shed and the only cooking facilities were an oven, a row of gas-rings and a barbecue plate. I had checked the gas bottles a few days before, but it was the amount of food I was worried about. There were a lot of cars and vans in town and the music-loving Indigenous community would be supporting the local headliners.

I began cooking lentils, peeling garlic and ginger, and frying onions. My helpers turned up, a relaxed and barefoot crew comprising two young feral women and a long haired old hippy dude. I designated tasks and they peeled potatoes and onions, washed salad greens and rice. I made dressings, sauces and salsas and tried not to stress.

As my menu took shape I mentally portioned plates of curry and bowls of salad but it just didn't seem I had enough. I had made pakoras but there were only fifty of them. The potato and Ceylon spinach curry tasted great but there were only thirty serves. The fruit salad had a nice lime, mint and honey dressing, but there wasn't much of it.

I wasn't getting paid but I still didn't want to run out of food. People were up for a grand night raising money for a good cause and I wanted my contribution to be just right.

Then three sun-tanned lads came in, each with a Styrofoam box. It was a freshly caught contribution to the cause. In each box were two big mackerels. I thanked them and cut the up fish and marinated it. Two women appeared and plonked down a big tray of rice puddings they'd made, also for us to sell. A furry fella rocked up with a big box of kang kong and other greens.

Marco's coconut telegraph had sprung into life and my anxiety blew away as more people turned up with food. Fifteen water melons, some soursops and a sack of mandarins bulked up the fruit salad. Six Jap pumpkins got roasted into caramelised slices, and a big bag of the sweetest cherry tomatoes meant that we could sprinkle some on every bowl of salad. Ten kilos of sweet potatoes got baked, each root first tossed in orange zest, oil and salt. Slabs of coconut fudge arrived. A hessian sack full of taro became deep fried chips. A trailer of coconuts got emptied onto the ground and a couple of cane-knife wielding jungle boys cut them open all night for people to eat and drink.

By five o'clock the first batch of rice was ready and we started serving. One of the fishermen cooked the marinated mackerel steaks on the barbecue and a wise hippy lady ran the till.

The first band fired up and our kitchen gang put our heads down and over the next few hours served up some great food. Compliments came thick and fast and I got hugged and kissed by soft-faced ladies and whiskery blokes. Then Marco came in, thanked me loudly and got everyone to give me a big cheer. I felt very chuffed. And also very pleased that everything to do with the food had turned out good

The bands played great, the crowd danced wildly and the police turned up, some in plain-clothes. Many people were smoking joints and several got busted.

In response, Marco grabbed the microphone and gave a speech about what bullies the police were and how the green stuff came from God. The crowd roared in approval, but this was the deep north of Queensland in the nineteen eighties and the red-faced boys in blue rushed forward intent on nabbing Marco. The whole place went into uproar and our cheeky mate exited the stage and in full view scaled the back fence. At the top he turned to give his pursuers the finger, then leapt down into the dark rainforest and disappeared.

Outside of this rock'n'roll rebellion, and three or four smokers hauled off to the clink, things turned out pretty well. Five hundred payers came through the gates and the food raised well over a grand. I had worked for sixteen hours straight, but I felt very good being part of a larger thing.

This sense of community is the glue that holds us all together in this sometimes-fractured world. The community of the village, the neighbourhood or the block can provide real security and meaning. At home the true microcosm for this happy social state is the kitchen or dinner table. This is where family and friends can reconnect and renew all the strengths, qualities, and love inherent in the group.

In this tropical village I lived with my partner, and we loved getting our friends around to catch up and eat. I'd never say we were having a dinner party though; that sounded way too fancy and might scare some of them off. I'd tell everyone to come over for tea.

When I first came to Australia, I often heard talk of people going out for tea. Or someone wondering what to cook for tea. Cooking tea? What they really meant was cooking dinner. Cooking tea is an old working-class term from England and I liked it. It had a cosy homely feel to it. It was informal and unpretentious. It spoke of cooking for loved ones, of making magic in a relaxed and unhurried way.

At our home, my partner and I grew a small but abundant garden. There was bok choy, lettuce, tomato, capsicum, eggplant, spring onion and three kinds of spinach. On bamboo and wire frames grew crunchy green snake-beans and cherry tomatoes, and in big ceramic pots grew a variety of herbs. Our meals always included things from the garden.

When we invited our friends around for tea there were usually about six or seven of us. But on one special occasion, a double birthday party for me and a mate, we packed the house with fourteen.

First up on the menu was finger food. From the garden I picked spinach, blanched it and squeezed out the liquid. This was for a Spanakopita-style mix, made with toasted pine nuts, feta, Grana Padano and freshly grated nutmeg. Just before cooking this I'd fold in whipped egg whites, dollop the mix into mini-muffin trays and then bake them into fluffy mouthfuls. The accompanying dipping sauce was simple – a creamy mix of balsamic vinegar, roast capsicum and oven dried Roma tomatoes.

I peeled a kilo of juicy fresh banana prawns and tossed them in cracked black pepper and lemon zest. I made a thick reduction of cream and fresh dill, and when it was cool, put a nice blob of it on prawn sized rectangles of puff pastry. I topped each of these with a prawn and folded two corners over so the crustacean looked like it was tucked up in bed with its tail hanging out. I planned to cook these at the same time as the Spanakopita souffles.

My partner made some of her old school chicken liver and brandy pâté, and to go with this I sliced up a couple of batards and toasted them nice and crisp.

With the starters all sorted I knocked up a herb mayonnaise in which I'd toss oven-caramelised potato, sweet potato and purple yam for a big carbs salad. The garden would provide the crunchy green salad and I'd top it with a good handful of sunflower seeds – toasted and then Tamari-finished just before serving. There was always a bottle of house dressing in the fridge door so that was taken care of.

The main event included lamb kebabs, each cube of meat rolled in my own ras-el-hanout spice mix. The same mix went onto squares of capsicum, zucchini, red onion and Haloumi cheese, which I also turned into kebabs. A big bowl of yoghurt and finely chopped mint partnered both lots of skewers.

Little steaks were cut from a few kilos of choice Tablelands eye filet and marinated in a mix of tamarind paste, fish sauce, apple cider vinegar, Dijon mustard and oil.

I used my pickled chillies to make a tomato and chilli relish to go with the steaks. Scotch Bonnets and Habaneros grown in the garden had been sliced in half and deseeded, put on a plate and covered with salt. Twenty-four hours later all the hot oils and acids had leached out and I had washed the chillies and pickled them for a few weeks. They were still bloody hot but not bitter or harsh.

A whole snapper was to be baked in the oven, Fiji style, with coconut milk, thin slices of red onion and sweet home-grown cherry tomatoes.

For dessert my partner whipped up a big crunchy meringue with a gooey hazelnut centre. I made whisky and marmalade ice cream and got the fixings together to macerate a kilo of local strawberries. For this I used sugar and pineapple sage, its tiny red flowers adding a burst of mint.

An hour before the gang showed up, I was ready to roll – showered, clean and dressed up funky. My partner and her daughter had set the long dinner table and were making cocktails. It wasn't long until I was enjoying my first Cosmopolitan.

Now it was time for a party with a slap-up tea!

When everyone had arrived and been hugged, I whipped the egg whites into the Spanakopita mix and got the mini morsels baking. The pate and toasts were put out and I began feeding the oven with the prawns, abed in their tiny puff pastry blankets. Within ten minutes food was being passed around, and within thirty minutes it had all been eaten. I put the fish in the oven, fired up the barbecue and socialised for a bit.

A cork popped from a bottle of Pelorus, exquisite bubbles from New Zealand, and an icy flute of it was most refreshing. The fish was coming along nicely so I took the steak and kebabs downstairs to the barbecue.

It was set up where there was a light − directly below the veranda full of loudly talking friends. I loaded the grill plate with food and the usual barbecue smoke rose into the air . . . and slowly crept up on the throng of merry makers above. Intent on cooking, it took me a while to hear the shouting and I stepped out from under the veranda to acknowledge my admirers.

But I couldn't see them! A huge pall of barbecue smoke had engulfed the party. Now I understood all the shouting. The veranda was set up for eating, so I had to move.

With only one light source downstairs I quickly improvised a solution. A lead with a light bulb on its end was hung from the kitchen window. I wheeled the laden barbecue out under it, and the bulb was lowered to a metre or so above my head. Now I could get back to cooking.

Soon enough the platters were heaped high with food and ferried upstairs. I toasted off the sunflower seeds, gave them a sizzling splash of Tamari sauce and tossed them through the salad. Then I served up the fish on a platter and sat down at the long table. Tea was on!

Later as I sat amongst my friends, I felt replete not just in body, but also in soul. This was the best thing ever – eating with the tribe. This was the real essence of sociability, the true heart of civilisation.

Here the simple animal bliss of stuffing your face had been splendidly transcended by the company of loved ones – and some pretty good food. Cooking food and appreciating it with others is what really makes us human. For a few hours we could bless our existence, by making an occasion out of imbibing the very stuff that maintains it.

The stereo got turned up and a few bods began to boogie. Out on the veranda some of the old crew were sharing a jazz cigarette, and chocolates and liqueurs were being opened.

With some industry I had created magic. I could have made macaroni cheese; everyone would still have come, but I didn't. I wanted to give them pleasure along with the calories.

I've worked in a lot of kitchens over nearly three decades. I'm not really sure how many, but two hundred sounds about right. While satisfying my curiosity – I've always strived for magic. It's not always easy to find in the industry of cooking but it's crucial to search for it. Magic is absolutely what makes it worthwhile, and at times bearable.

Good food for me is synonymous with love and that's always a main ingredient in any recipe. When I share that love, at home or at work, then it's about as good as it gets. In the madness of a busy commercial kitchen, laying that love on your co-workers while you are all stressed, tired and in pain, is about as hard as it gets.

I get real pleasure from cooking. It doesn't have to be as complex as the double birthday party menu but it's got to have love in it. That vital ingredient can never run out. It's always there in the pantry or fridge.

And it's always at the back of my mind when I start thinking – what shall I cook for tea?

Acknowledgements

A mighty thank you to **Gonzo** for his editorial diligence, wise encouragement and sense of style, and also to **Renn Barker** for his most perceptive suggestions and consistent positivity.

Most of all, big love and deep gratitude to **Jan** for all her support, love and patience.